"Isaiah is a book of such large scale that it can be hard to come to grips with it. Walter Brueggemann and Brent Strawn offer here a great gift: a compilation of pathways into its grandeur by way of key moments. One could hardly ask for two guides with more knowledge and wisdom about the Bible, and it's a particular blessing to hear Brueggemann's voice now that we have lost him."
—Christopher B. Hays, D. Wilson Moore Professor of Old Testament and Ancient Near Eastern Studies, Fuller Theological Seminary

"When I think Brueggemann, I hear, 'The gospel is fiction when judged by the empire. The empire is fiction when judged by the gospel.' Breathtaking truth. Crisp, clear, poetic, prophetic, more than most of us can imagine. Dangerous, like the gospel itself. This book does not disappoint. Brueggemann and Strawn's prose brings Isaiah's fierce prophecies to life in this time and for all times. You want to preach truth to power? You want to teach your lay leaders how to be prophets for the reign of God? Run to this book, with tools for you and your community."
—Jacqui Lewis, Senior Minister and Public Theologian, Middle Church

"Few books of the Hebrew Bible have had a greater influence on Christianity (already evident in the New Testament) than the book of Isaiah. What a privilege, therefore, to have two of our finest Old Testament scholars leading a study of key texts from this powerful, prophetic work. Here we benefit from a fascinating collaboration between Brent Strawn and (in one of his last projects) Walter Brueggemann. In fact, it would be hard to think of two finer navigators for a voyage through the book of Isaiah. In sum, this study guide isn't merely helpful, it matters."
—Daniel L. Smith-Christopher, Professor of Old Testament Studies, Loyola Marymount University, Los Angeles

Unwavering Faithfulness

Pivotal Moments in the Old Testament

Brent A. Strawn, *Series Editor*

Other books in this series:

Delivered out of Empire: Pivotal Moments in the Book of Exodus, Part One

Delivered into Covenant: Pivotal Moments in the Book of Exodus, Part Two

Returning from the Abyss: Pivotal Moments in the Book of Jeremiah

Other recent books by Walter Brueggemann

Prayer books:

Waiting in Gratitude: Prayers of Joy

Following into Risky Obedience: Prayers along the Journey

Acting in the Wake: Prayers for Justice

Group studies:

Materiality as Resistance: Five Elements for Moral Action in the Real World

From Judgment to Hope: A Study on the Prophets

Interrupting Silence: God's Command to Speak Out

Sabbath as Resistance: Saying No to the Culture of Now

Individual studies/devotionals:

Journey to the Common Good, Updated Edition

Gift and Task: A Year of Daily Readings and Reflections

Unwavering Faithfulness

Pivotal Moments in the Book of Isaiah

Walter Brueggemann and Brent A. Strawn

© 2025 Walter Brueggemann and Brent A. Strawn
Series foreword and discussion questions © 2025 Westminster John Knox Press

First edition
Published by Westminster John Knox Press
Louisville, Kentucky

25 26 27 28 29 30 31 32 33 34—10 9 8 7 6 5 4 3 2 1

All rights reserved. No part of this book may be reproduced or transmitted in any form or by any means, electronic or mechanical, including photocopying, recording, or by any information storage or retrieval system, without permission in writing from the publisher. For information, address Geneva Press, 100 Witherspoon Street, Louisville, Kentucky 40202-1396. Or contact us online at www.wjkbooks.com.

Unless otherwise indicated, Scripture quotations are from the New Revised Standard Version of the Bible, copyright © 1989 by the Division of Christian Education of the National Council of the Churches of Christ in the U.S.A., and are used by permission. Scripture quotations marked CEB are from the Common English Bible, © 2011 Common English Bible, and are used by permission. Scripture quotations marked NIV are from the Holy Bible, New International Version. Copyright © 1973, 1978, 1984, 2011 by Biblica, Inc. Used by permission. All rights reserved worldwide. Scripture quotations marked NJPS are from *The TANAKH: The New JPS Translation according to the Traditional Hebrew Text.* Copyright 1985 by the Jewish Publication Society. Used by permission.

"Wait for the Lord," song from Taizé, copyright © Ateliers et Presses de Taizé, 71250 Taizé, France, based on Psalm 27:14. Used by permission.

Book design by Sharon Adams
Cover design by Nita Ybarra
Cover art: Private Collection © Radiant Light/Bridgeman Images

Library of Congress Cataloging-in-Publication Data

Names: Brueggemann, Walter author | Strawn, Brent A. author
Title: Unwavering faithfulness : pivotal moments in the book of Isaiah / Walter Brueggemann and Brent A. Strawn.
Description: First edition. | Louisville, Kentucky : Westminster John Knox Press, [2025] | Series: Pivotal moments in the Old Testament | Includes bibliographical references. | Summary: "Leads readers through the prophetic book of Isaiah, moving between looming predictions of punishment against Israel for breaking covenant with God and exultation in the ultimate hope of Israel's restoration"-- Provided by publisher.
Identifiers: LCCN 2025035810 (print) | LCCN 2025035811 (ebook) | ISBN 9780664267292 paperback | ISBN 9781646984398 ebook
Subjects: LCSH: Bible. Isaiah--Criticism, interpretation, etc.
Classification: LCC BS1515.52 .B777 2025 (print) | LCC BS1515.52 (ebook)
LC record available at https://lccn.loc.gov/2025035810
LC ebook record available at https://lccn.loc.gov/2025035811

Most Westminster John Knox Press books are available at special quantity discounts when purchased in bulk by corporations, organizations, and special-interest groups. For more information, please e-mail SpecialSales@wjkbooks.com.

*For Tia and Holly,
for putting up with the full sixty-six chapters (and then some!)*

Contents

Series Foreword: Pivots in Scripture by Brent A. Strawn	ix
Preface	xvii
Suggested Sessions for Study Groups	xxiii
1. The Vision of Isaiah (Isaiah 1:1)	1
2. Afterward... (Isaiah 1:26b)	7
3. Promise Post-Judgment (Isaiah 2:4)	13
4. Four Contradictions versus the One Lord (Isaiah 2:17)	19
5. Bad Grapes (Isaiah 5:7)	25
6. Isaiah's Second Vision (Isaiah 6:3)	33
7. The Holy Seed-Stump (Isaiah 6:13b)	39
8. Standing Firm (Isaiah 7:9)	47
9. "God-with-Us" and the "Virgin" (Isaiah 7:14)	53
10. A Child Has Been Born for Us! (Isaiah 9:6)	61
11. The Rod of God's Anger (Isaiah 10:15)	67
12. The Shoot from Jesse's Stump (Isaiah 11:1)	73
13. The Lord's Plan (Isaiah 14:27)	79
14. "Egypt, My People; Assyria, the Work of My Hands"? (Isaiah 19:24–25)	87
15. Apocalyptic Pollution (Isaiah 24:5)	93
16. Your Dead Shall Live (Isaiah 26:19)	99

17. The Strange Work of God (Isaiah 28:21)	105
18. Salvation by Returning and Rest Alone (Isaiah 30:15)	111
19. Exodus 2.0 (Isaiah 35:10)	117
20. The Lord Said to Me: Destroy (Isaiah 36:10)	125
21. Hope (in/for) the Lord! (Isaiah 40:31)	133
22. I Am He! (Isaiah 43:10–11)	141
23. Cyrus, God's Messiah (Isaiah 45:1)	149
24. Short-Term Superpower(s) (Isaiah 47:6)	157
25. A Man of Sorrows, Acquainted with Grief (Isaiah 53:4–6)	165
26. Wrath for a Second—Love Everlasting (Isaiah 54:7–8)	173
27. A House of Prayer for All People (Isaiah 56:7)	183
28. Wealth Brought and Transformed (Isaiah 60:6)	191
29. Parent and Potter (Isaiah 64:8–9)	201
30. God's Newness (Isaiah 65:18–19)	211
Notes	223

Series Foreword

Pivots in Scripture

Not long after arriving in Atlanta for my first tenure-track job, still very green in my field and profession, I somehow found the courage to invite Walter Brueggemann, who taught a few miles away at Columbia Theological Seminary, to lecture in my Introduction to Old Testament course. To my great delight he accepted, despite the fact that the class met at eight o'clock in the morning and Atlanta traffic is legendary. (Those who know Walter better than I did at that time know what I discovered only later: that such generosity is standard operating procedure for him.) I either offered, or perhaps he suggested, that the topic of his guest lecture should be Jeremiah. And so it was that a few weeks after the invitation was extended and received, my students and I were treated to eighty minutes of brilliant insight into Jeremiah from one of the masters of that biblical book, not to mention the larger Book to which Jeremiah belongs.[1]

Even now, more than twenty years later, I remember a number of things about that lecture—clear testimony to the quality of the content and the one who gave it. In all honesty, I must admit that several of the things I remember have made their way into my own subsequent lectures on Jeremiah. In this way, Walter's presence could still (and *still can*) be felt in my later classes, despite the fact that I couldn't ask him to guest lecture every year (alas!). One moment from that initial lecture stands out with special clarity: Walter's exposition of a specific text from Jeremiah 30. I suspect I knew this particular text before, maybe even read about it in something Walter had written, but as I recall things now it was that early morning lecture at Emory

University in 2002 that drilled it into my long-term memory banks. The text in question was Jeremiah 30:12–17:[2]

> [12] For thus says the LORD:
> Your hurt is incurable,
>   your wound is grievous.
> [13] There is no one to uphold your cause,
>   no medicine for your wound,
>   no healing for you.
> [14] All your lovers have forgotten you;
>   they care nothing for you;
> for I have dealt you the blow of an enemy,
>   the punishment of a merciless foe,
> because your guilt is great,
>   because your sins are so numerous.
> [15] Why do you cry out over your hurt?
>   Your pain is incurable.
> Because your guilt is great,
>   because your sins are so numerous,
>   I have done these things to you.
> [16] Therefore all who devour you shall be devoured,
>   and all your foes, every one of them, shall go into captivity;
> those who plunder you shall be plundered,
>   and all who prey on you I will make a prey.
> [17] For I will restore health to you,
>   and your wounds I will heal,
>   says the LORD,
> because they have called you an outcast:
>   "It is Zion; no one cares for her!"

The passage is striking for a number of reasons, but what Walter highlighted was the remarkable shift—or better, *pivot*—that takes place in the space between verses 15 and 16. Prior to this point, God's speech to Israel emphasizes the incurable nature of its wound: "no healing for you" (v. 13)! Israel's wound is, on the one hand,

> the blow of an *enemy*,
>   the punishment of a *merciless foe*. (v. 14)

On the other hand, the blow is also and more fundamentally *God's own doing*:

for *I have dealt* you the blow (v. 14)
I have done these things to you. (v. 15)

Like the original audience, contemporary readers are left no time to ponder this double-agency since immediately after the second ascription of this wound to the Lord's hand, the text pivots both suddenly and drastically. From verse 16 on, we read that those whom the Lord used to punish Israel will now themselves be punished; we also learn that what had before been a terminal illness turns out to be treatable after all (v. 17a). The reason for this dramatic shift is given only in verse 17b: God will cure the incurable wound because God will not stand by while Israel's enemies call it "an outcast," claiming that "no one cares for Zion."

Now in truth, what God says to Israel/Zion in verse 13 sounds very much like "no one cares for you," but as Walter memorably put it in his lecture, while it is one thing to talk about your own mother, it is another thing altogether when *someone else* talks about your mother! God, it would seem, claims privilege to say certain things about Zion that others are simply not allowed to say. If and when they ever do utter such sentiments, God is mobilized to defend and to heal. Zion, it turns out, is no outcast, after all; there is, after all, One who still cares for her.

The space between verses 15 and 16 is a *pivot*, explained most fully in verse 17. This, then, is a turning point that changes everything in this passage—a passage that can be seen, more broadly and in turn, as a pivotal moment in the larger book of Jeremiah, coming, as it does, early in a section that shifts decidedly toward consolation and restoration.

And Jeremiah 30:12–17 is not alone in the Old Testament. Another remarkable pivot takes place in the space between the two lines of Psalm 22:21:

Save me from the mouth of the lion!
From the horns of the wild oxen you have rescued me.

In the first line, there is an urgent plea for immediate help: "Save!"; in the second, testimony to past deliverance: "You *have rescued* me." Something drastic, something pivotal has taken place here, in between two parallel lines of Hebrew poetry. Before this pivot, the psalmist knew only of *God-forsakenness* (v. 1). But after it, the psalmist is full only of *God-praise* (vv. 22–24) that extends to the most remarkable and unexpected corners of the world and underworld (vv. 25–31).[3]

Spiritual writer and humanities professor Marilyn Chandler McEntyre has written recently of "pausing where Scripture gives one pause."[4] She comments on memorable biblical phrases like "teach me your paths," "hidden with Christ," and "do not harden your hearts." Phrases like these, she writes,

> have lives of their own. Neither sentences nor single words, they are little compositions that suggest and evoke and invite.... They are often what we remember: "Fourscore and seven years ago" recalls a whole era, triggers a constellation of feelings, and evokes an image of Lincoln.... In the classic film *A Bridge Too Far*, one soldier, rowing for his life away from an impending explosion, repeats again and again a fragment of the only prayer he remembers: "Hail Mary, full of grace ... Hail Mary, full of grace ... Hail Mary, full of grace ..."—and somehow we believe that such a prayer at such a time suffices.[5]

So it is that key phrases are "powerful instruments of awakening and recollection for all of us."[6] McEntyre goes on to note that the spiritual practice of meditative reading known as *lectio divina* encourages readers to pay attention to specific words or phrases:

> Learning to notice what we notice as we move slowly from words to meaning, pausing where we sense a slight beckoning, allowing associations to emerge around the phrase that stopped us is an act of faith that the Spirit will meet us there. There is, we may assume, a gift to be received wherever we are stopped and summoned.[7]

Pivotal moments in the Old Testament like the ones in Jeremiah 30 and Psalm 22 aren't exactly the same thing as the practice of pausing commended by McEntyre, but the two seem closely related nevertheless. Pivotal texts are precisely the ones that arrest us, demand our attention, change everything:

- Suddenly, *healing*—Jeremiah 30:16–17
- Suddenly, *deliverance*—Psalm 22:21b

Of course, the pivots found in Scripture are not always so benign. One may think, alternatively, of these:

- Suddenly, *trouble*—as in 2 Samuel 11:5, Bathsheba's report (only two words in Hebrew) to David: "I'm pregnant."
- Suddenly, *judgment*—as in 2 Samuel 12:7, Nathan's statement (also only two words in Hebrew) to David: "You're that man!"

Now one could, especially in a more skeptical mode, wonder just how many pivotal moments, how many *suddenly*s like these, might actually exist in Scripture. But before we assume that the list is quite finite—more of a curiosity than a persistent call to attention—and take our leave to attend to some piece of distracting drivel on our electronic devices, we should stop and remember the Gospel of Mark, which makes a living on *suddenly*s. Jesus is always doing something or having something done to him *suddenly* or *immediately* (*euthus*), and the same is often true for those gathered around him.[8]

What Mark shows us is that, in the end, *suddenly* can aptly describe an entire Gospel, an entire life lived toward God—indeed, a life lived most perfectly toward God. The same may be true for the gospel of God writ large, across both testaments of the Christian Bible. And so, along with the practice of pausing where Scripture gives us pause (McEntyre), the practice of pivoting where Scripture itself pivots has the same effect: it turns us toward something new, something deeper, something *transformative*. These texts are places where the Bible, and we who read it, may pivot toward another world—another *divine* world—that can change our own world for the better, forever. In contrast to McEntyre's pauses, which anticipate that the Spirit will reach out to us through the text, these pivotal moments in Scripture are not acts of faith but *places* of faith, established sites where the Spirit has *already* met the faithful. They are gifts *already* given, though they seem largely still waiting on us to receive them. The goal of the present volume, and this series dedicated to pivotal moments in the Old Testament, is to mediate those gifts.

With the present work on Isaiah, the Pivotal Moments series comes to a close. It is hoped that the kind of approach modeled in its volumes may be practiced by others in the other nooks and crannies of Scripture with its countless pivots. Professor Brueggemann has admirably set us an example to emulate in his two-volume contribution on Exodus, which inaugurated the series, and then in his subsequent volume on Jeremiah.[9] I consider it one of the great honors of my life that Walter invited me to complete this last volume on Isaiah alongside him. While we have not identified which of us composed which entry—not least to protect the lesser of the two authors (yours truly)—I am confident that readers will be able to quickly make such discriminations, identifying which entry, for instance, is "authentic Brueggemann" and which "merely (secondary) Strawn"! I am equally certain that Walter's invitation to join him in this work on Isaiah is just the latest installment in a countless series of kindnesses that began way back when, in an early morning class about the book of Jeremiah one spring in Atlanta. And so I can end the foreword to the present volume as I have the previous ones in the series: We (here meaning *me*) are fortunate to have Professor Brueggemann lead the way . . . — . . . and, now, to conclude the way with this final volume in the Pivotal Moments in the Old Testament series. Once again, I consider it a high point in my career that Walter entrusted the completion of *Unwavering Faithfulness: Pivotal Moments in the Book of Isaiah* to me, and together we hope our volume helps readers encounter this great—dare one say pivotal?—prophetic book in meaningful, even transformative ways.

※※※※※※

Walter Brueggemann passed away early on Thursday, June 5, 2025. Though he was unable to respond, I spoke to him by phone only two days prior, eagerly reporting that I was reading the copyedits of this joint volume that very week. Far more importantly, I used those last precious moments to try to convey how thankful I was for him and for our friendship—how much I loved, admired, and respected him. And of course, I still feel that way, as so do millions of others who have encountered his words over his long, illustrious, and prophetic career. Walter's voice will continue to resound, if only we have ears to hear, in his many publications, including this one and a few others that must now appear posthumously. The paragraphs above recounts one instance of Walter's generosity—that guest lecture way back when—but his innumerable gifts to me begin with his book *The Prophetic Imagination*, which I read as a college freshman. Coauthoring the present volume is thus just the latest installment in a history of blessing he bestowed on me. I know those blessings will continue, as I continue to return to his numerous writings. I hope *Unwavering Faithfulness*, along with Walter's many other publications that testify to his way and work among us, will be a blessing to you as well.

Brent A. Strawn, *Series Editor*

Preface

*T*he book of Isaiah is exceedingly complex; it is also especially important in Christianity and thus to Christian readers. The complexity of Isaiah is due to the fact that it is a poetic articulation of the history of the city of Jerusalem that was many centuries in the making. That history stretches from the time when Jerusalem was a "faithful city . . . full of justice" to being described as full of "murderers" (1:21), through its profound dislocation in exile (see 40:1), and to its restoration as "a joy" (65:18). According to most biblical scholars, this long and complex poetic work—some might go so far as to call it a musical *oratorio*—was generated by a series of poets, most of whom we do not know by name, but all of whom (eventually) flew under the flag of "Isaiah."[1] For centuries, it has been a common critical judgment that at least some of the material now found in chapters 1–39 of the book may be traced back to the work of a prophet named Isaiah, Amoz's son, who was active in the eighth century BCE (see 1:1). But it is obvious that chapters 36–39 are largely appropriated from 2 Kings 18–20, and it is equally clear that the oracles against the nations found in Isaiah 13–23 are highly stylized and belong to a recurring genre found elsewhere in the prophetic books. These factors, among others, complicate any easy assignment of all of chapters 1–39, the so-called First or Proto Isaiah, to the eighth-century prophet by that name.[2]

It is commonly agreed, further, that the middle portion of the book (chaps. 40–55) reflects the moment when (or slightly before the moment when) the displaced exiles in Babylon were permitted by the Persians to return home to Judah. Finally, it is also typically held that the last chapters of the book (56–66) reflect the resolve and struggle for Jerusalem's restoration after its demise at the hand of the Babylonian Empire—a restoration financed in part by the Persian Empire. These two parts are commonly called "Second" or "Deutero" and "Third" or "Trito" Isaiah, respectively.

There is, in brief, a rich diversity of poetic voices in the book of Isaiah that corresponds to (and emerges from) an equally rich diversity of historical circumstances. Despite that fact—or better, these facts—it is nevertheless possible to identify a coherent perspective for this entire many-splendored book. That perspective is the conviction that Jerusalem is both *beloved of God* in generous ways and *accountable to God* in uncompromising ways. However many "Isaiahs" there may have once been, there is in the end *only one biblical Isaiah*.

The biblical Isaiah has been particularly important for Christians because the narrative accounts of the life of Jesus offered in the four Gospels make frequent appeal to the book in order to situate Jesus amid the hopes of ancient Israel. A glance at the Scripture index of Richard Hays's landmark work *Echoes of Scripture in the Gospels* is suggestive of the numerous ways the Gospel writers appealed to the book of Isaiah.[3] The links between the text of Isaiah and its use in the Gospel accounts are once again—as Hays makes abundantly clear—complex and variegated. It is clear, in any case, that Isaiah was indispensable in shaping the imagination of the early church concerning the person and work of Jesus, so much so that one early church writer, St. Jerome, called Isaiah both "evangelist and apostle," making the book of Isaiah "The Fifth Gospel."[4]

There is not space in the present brief treatment of Isaiah to even begin to capture the richness of this book within itself or within its reception and use in Christian faith and practice. What we *can* accomplish here is to offer a series of expositions in the hopes that when readers are finished, they will have newfound appreciation not only for the complexity of Isaiah but also for its beauty, wonder, and importance for faith. We have selected specific texts that we believe will guide the reader through the book—passages that we deem, moreover, for one reason or another, to be *pivotal* (see the series foreword). Our expositions are intentionally brief and designed for study in local congregations and small groups. It is our hope that these expositions give access to the main claims of the texts under discussion. Following the form of other volumes in this same series, each exposition is oriented around a specific verse, but with due attention paid to the immediate context of that verse and to the wider context provided by the larger book of Isaiah. When it has seemed clear to us to do so, we have not refrained from suggesting traces and points of connection to contemporary biblical faith. Contrary to outward appearance or commonplace assumption, serious textual study of the Bible is neither easy nor obvious, especially at the start. But as one leans into it with patience and alert attention, one is quickly and easily drawn into the imaginative drama traced out by the poets. When that is done well and rightly, one is never the same again. We have found that true throughout our careers and with many biblical texts, not least in this joint work on one of the true treasures of Scripture.

In our offer of these expositions, we are greatly indebted to a host of Isaiah scholars. The format of this series limits extended engagement with them and their work, but it is important to recognize that the essays presented here are done with and only possible because of the help offered by a great cloud of witnesses.[5] In addition to biblical scholars, we have also kept in mind other key members of the interpretive community—most especially the faithful clergy and churchgoers for whom this book is primarily intended. In the end, we hope that our joint exposition will serve the purpose of any and all study of Scripture, which we deem to be a, if not the, primary source for Christian nurture and empowerment for wise, courageous, and faithful living in these days.

One further point that might prove helpful: The book of Isaiah, like every other prophetic book, comes to us in a form that, despite the general contours sketched above (chaps. 1–39, 40–55, 56–66), is not always clear—especially within chapters or smaller units. It is customary in scholarship to believe that some, maybe much, of the present form of prophetic books is *by design*. Even if we can't be sure that such design was intended by author(s) or editor(s), various insights about order can be recognized—perhaps better, created!—by readers after the fact. But *readerly construction of order* is not the same as *author/editor–intended design*. Indeed, many scholars of the prophets would posit that, at least in some cases, the biblical books were put together with *no* discernible order (at least for stretches). This no doubt is what makes prophetic books so hard to read: it is not always clear why one part leads into another, and there is no guarantee that the parts appear in any thematic let alone chronological sequence. As a result, best practice is to focus on identifiable units within the prophets, often called *oracles* by scholars or, more simply and frequently in the pages that follow, *poems*.[6]

It must be admitted that determining where a poem begins and/or ends is not always easy. As a result, most readers will likely depend heavily on established translations of the Bible in English, which often use stanza breaks or headings of various sorts reflecting decisions about such matters. For present purposes, we wish simply to underscore that the oracle or poem is the basic unit of prophetic speech. In the chapters that follow, we sometimes discuss more than one poem—especially to provide further context or setting—but the focus is often and resolutely on one particular unit. In a lengthy book like Isaiah (or the Bible for that matter), there is always more than just one particular unit. But we are convinced that readers of Scripture would do well to focus as much as possible, even if only for the duration of the chapters that follow, on the unit at hand. It is important to listen to the singular witness of each poem. Each has something to say and contribute and should not be confirmed, critiqued, or chastened too quickly by other poems, let alone other books of the Bible. The chapters that follow show that we have no problem making large connections within Isaiah, as well as across other books of the Old Testament and New Testament. Such larger connections are part, at least, of what it means to construct a biblical theology or think about the Bible as a whole. It is nevertheless clear that some of what we say is only sayable because we have done our best to remain—again, at least for a moment—under the spell of the particular poem at hand. We invite readers to do the same, lingering with us in the wild witness of these poems, without domesticating them too quickly by other things we know (or, even worse, by things we *think* we know).[7]

A final word of thanks is offered to the good people of Westminster John Knox Press, especially Julie Mullins, for assistance, care with production, and patience. We are also grateful to Tia Brueggemann, Isabel Packevicz, and Caleb Punt for their help with the preparation and editing of the manuscript. Finally, the dedication of the book to our two wives is *beyond* deserved.

Walter Brueggemann
Traverse City, Michigan

Brent A. Strawn
Durham, North Carolina
Second Week of Advent 2024

Suggested Sessions for Study Groups

Week 1	=	Chapters 1–2
Week 2	=	Chapters 3–4
Week 3	=	Chapters 5–7
Week 4	=	Chapters 8–10*
Week 5	=	Chapters 11–12
Week 6	=	Chapters 13–14
Week 7	=	Chapters 15–16
Week 8	=	Chapters 17–19**
Week 9	=	Chapters 20–22***
Week 10	=	Chapters 23–25****
Week 11	=	Chapters 26–27
Week 12	=	Chapters 28–30

*Chap. 25 might be profitably read alongside chap. 9.
**Alternatively, instead of chap. 19, chap. 20 could be read this week.
***Instead of chap. 20, which could be read the previous week, chap. 19 could be included here.
****Chap. 9 might be combined with chap. 25 (see week 4)

Chapter 1

The Vision of Isaiah (Isaiah 1:1)

The vision of Isaiah son of Amoz, which he saw concerning Judah and Jerusalem in the days of Uzziah, Jotham, Ahaz, and Hezekiah, kings of Judah.

> **Scripture Passages for Reference**
>
> Isaiah 1:1
> Isaiah 6:1–13
> 2 Kings 15:1–7, 32–38
> 2 Kings 16:1–20
> 2 Kings 18:3–6

This opening verse of Isaiah is an editorial introduction to the book and to the *geopolitical* and *historical* location of the prophet. Geographically, the prophet Isaiah is situated in the city of Jerusalem, a royal city dominated by royal ideology that was regularly reinforced and legitimated by temple liturgy. The book of Isaiah thus amounts to nothing less than a prophetic, imaginative construal of the city of Jerusalem, favored by divine privilege and promise, as it faced the vagaries of the historical process characterized by economic and military reality. The actual history of Jerusalem is not difficult to trace for the time of Isaiah. The prophetic, imaginative portrayal in the book of Isaiah, however, is something quite different, as we will see.

2   Unwavering Faithfulness

Given this geopolitical location, it was inescapable that the prophet must deal with royal reality. Indeed, we are able to see that the prophet Isaiah was an intimate of kings and had ready access to royal power. This introductory note identifies four Davidic kings from the time of Isaiah. The first, *Uzziah* (also called Azariah), had a long and prosperous reign (783–742 BCE; 2 Kings 15:1–7). He is mentioned only once in the book of Isaiah, in his famous "call narrative" (Isaiah 6:1–13). Uzziah is named only as a chronological marker for the prophet, so he does not really figure in the book. The second king named in our verse is *Jotham*, son of Uzziah (742–735 BCE; 2 Kings 15:32–38). His was an inconsequential reign; he is not mentioned in the book of Isaiah beyond this editorial notation. He is included only for the purpose of dynastic sequence. The third king to note in our introductory verse is *Ahaz*, son of Jotham (735–715 BCE; 2 Kings 16:1–20). According to the narrative, Ahaz's rule was dominated by foreign policy crises. He had to deal with the immediate threat of the minor states of Northern Israel and Aram (Syria). In the face of what turned out to be a minor threat, Ahaz, in his great fear and anxiety, appealed to the superpower Assyria (located in present-day Iraq) for aid against his lesser enemies. This appeal to the superpower was a measure of Ahaz's fear and, according to the biblical perspective, a measure of his failure to trust the promises of YHWH. As a result of this foolish appeal, Ahaz was drawn into the sphere of aggression by the Assyrian king, Tiglath-pileser III. In his attempt to suck up to the power of Assyria, Ahaz replicated an Assyrian altar and undertook the worship of gods other than YHWH. Such an effort of accommodation to Assyria was, of course, ineffective. In the long run the effort failed. Ahaz was forced to dismantle his elaborate altar and send the valuable objects to Tiglath-pileser in tribute (see 2 Chronicles 28:21). In the book of Isaiah we have a report of a major confrontation between King Ahaz and Isaiah. According to the prophet, appeal to Assyria was an act of loss of faith in YHWH. For Isaiah, the defining issue for the king is his inability to trust the promise of YHWH to defend the city and the people of God.

The fourth king in our introductory verse, *Hezekiah* (715–687 BCE), is the other king with whom Isaiah interacts extensively. Unlike his father Ahaz, Hezekiah is reckoned to be one of the two most faithful kings in the long Davidic dynasty (2 Kings 18:1–20:21):

The Vision of Isaiah (Isaiah 1:1)

> He did what was right in the sight of the LORD just as his ancestor David had done. He removed the high places, broke down the pillars, and cut down the sacred pole. He broke in pieces the bronze serpent that Moses had made, for until those days the people of Israel had made offerings to it; it was called Nehushtan. He trusted in the LORD the God of Israel; so that there was no one like him among all the kings of Judah after him, or among those who were before him. For he held fast to the LORD; he did not depart from following him but kept the commandments that the LORD had commanded Moses. (18:3–6)

Unlike his father, Hezekiah is portrayed as a model practitioner of faith who trusted YHWH even in dire circumstances. Specifically, he was confronted, as was his father, with the threat of Assyrian aggression, but he trusted in YHWH, and so, as a result, the text asserts, the city of Jerusalem was saved by the protection of YHWH (19:35–36). In the midst of the threat from Assyria, the prophet urges the kings to place trust in YHWH; Hezekiah dares to do so! Thus in this encounter the issue is once again faith or unfaith, as it was with Ahaz. This "faith," however, has nothing to do with abstract theological proposition. It has to do, rather, with the practical matter of refusing to make decisions in fear, as though YHWH were not active in the life of the world. Thus in the horizon of Isaiah, the two kings, Ahaz and Hezekiah, father and son, come to embody models of faith and unfaith. Isaiah is identified as the one who calls kings (and the people of God) to trust in YHWH in the midst of great danger.

It turns out, however, that the editorial introduction of our verse is incomplete. It is incomplete because the book of Isaiah extends as a prophetic witness in long centuries after the person of Isaiah. It turns out, moreover, that the vexed historical experience of Israel continued long after the Davidic timeline was exhausted and had come to an end.

Thus we may imagine that the editorial timeline offered in our verse might be continued with a list of foreign kings not of the Davidic line. Such kings are cited in the book of Isaiah and become a convenient way to understand the historical sequence of the book. Specifically we might construct a timeline continuing our verse: ". . . in the days of Tiglath-pileser, Sennacherib, Merodach-baladan, and Cyrus." Such an extended royal timeline will help us locate the extended work of the book of Isaiah.

4   Unwavering Faithfulness

Tiglath-pileser III, the great Assyrian king (745–727 BCE), is not mentioned in the book of Isaiah. Nonetheless, he constituted a great threat to Jerusalem (2 Kings 16:7–10; 2 Chronicles 28:20). A second Assyrian king, *Sennacherib* (704–681 BCE), implemented the threat posed by Tiglath-pileser and figures prominently in the Isaiah tradition. It was he who mounted a most formidable threat against the city of Jerusalem, wherein the city was saved only by the return of Sennacherib to his own country, an event credited in the tradition to "the angel of the LORD" (Isaiah 37:36).

We have only one mention of the Babylonian king, *Merodach-baladan*, who became a "friend" of King Hezekiah (Isaiah 39:1). In the time of Hezekiah, Assyria was the dominant superpower in the north of the Fertile Crescent. At that time Babylon was a modest state with great ambition. For that reason, the Babylonian king sought an ally in Jerusalem, surely to gather strength against Assyria. We can imagine that Hezekiah was drawn to seek an alliance with Babylon as a way to resist Assyria. We hear no more of that alliance in the eighth century, except to notice that the prophet Isaiah judged Hezekiah to be overly eager for such an alliance at the risk of national security. Babylon will figure more centrally in the later part of the book of Isaiah.

The fourth king in our imagined royal timeline is *Cyrus* of Persia (550–530 BCE). It was he who led to the demise of the Babylonian Empire in 540 BCE that gave breathing space to the deported Judeans in Babylon. For practical reasons of policy, Cyrus was amenable to the hopes and needs of Judean deportees, permitting them to return home to Jerusalem (see 2 Chronicles 36:22–23). Given that generous policy toward Jewish exiles, the latter part of the book of Isaiah was to regard Cyrus as a deliverer sent by YHWH to save God's people.

Thus in sum we have a very broad sweep of Near Eastern history that is the horizon of the book of Isaiah. That sweep includes four Jerusalem kings, plus four more from the expanded timeline: two from Assyria, one from Babylon, and one from Persia. All of these kings figure, in specific contexts, in the destiny of Israel. For that reason, all of them are rendered, in prophetic imagination, according to the purposes of YHWH.

In our verse the very first word of the book of Isaiah is "vision." The book of Isaiah is a prophetic act of imagination wherein the prophet "sees" and articulates what a more mundane royal history could not. What the prophet "sees" is the transcendent rule of YHWH over all the nations, a rule that poses, in every generation, the deep issue of *faith or unfaith*, the question of the ways in which the rule of the holy God is at work in, with, and under historical reality.

An awareness of historical specificities is essential. Beyond these specificities, however, the book of Isaiah continues to raise the decisive question of *faith or unfaith*. It turns out that amid the daily vagaries of history, this God has "got the whole world in his hands"! Imagine: in God's hands are the Jerusalem kings as well as Tiglath-pileser and Sennacherib of Assyria, Merodach-baladan of Babylon, and Cyrus of Persia! Safe hands indeed!

Questions for Discussion

1. How is faith or unfaith still a key question for today?
2. Is prophetic vision different from other kinds of vision? How so?
3. What do you find significant about ancient Near Eastern kings being included in the vision of Isaiah?

Chapter 2

Afterward . . . (Isaiah 1:26b)

Afterward you shall be called the city of righteousness, the faithful city.

> **Scripture Passages for Reference**
>
> Isaiah 1:2–26
> Isaiah 55:12
> Hosea 2:4–5

The first word of our lines, "afterward," is a welcome and abrupt surprise. The word *afterward* evokes the wondering "After *what*?" To answer this question, we must read back behind our lines to the beginning of this poetic unit (1:21–26). We may read even further back from our focus verse, 1:26 (specifically its second half), to verses 2–20. In these earlier verses, the prophet offers a characteristic prophetic indictment of Jerusalem—namely, that the city has behaved like Sodom and Gomorrah in complete contradiction to the purpose of YHWH (v. 10). The upshot of the harsh indictment is that, in characteristic prophetic fashion, Isaiah "sees" that the disobedient city has suffered and will suffer grievous wounds (vv. 6–9). The prophet concludes, moreover, that the usual redress of worship and piety will be of no avail (vv. 11–15). With an intense urgency the prophet issues imperatives of reparation (vv. 16–17), but these possibilities for amendment of life hold little hope for the city. Thus verses 2–20 culminate with a devastating anticipation:

> If you refuse and rebel,
>   you shall be devoured by the sword;
>   for the mouth of the LORD has spoken.
>
> v. 20

The will of YHWH cannot be outflanked by willful recalcitrance. The "sword" in verse 20 is an anticipation of foreign invasion, for Judah lived among many threatening neighboring states.

Drawing closer to our lines of "afterward," we may consider the more immediate poem of verses 21–26. There are two ways in which we might reflect on this sequence of verses. First, we might consider that these verses line out the *historical experience* of Judah and Jerusalem. Read historically, verses 21–23 present a summary of prophetic indictment of the covenantal failure of Jerusalem. There was a time, according to verse 21, when Jerusalem was full of justice and righteousness, permeated with neighborly well-being and covenantal fidelity. That ideal moment, however, is immediately interrupted by the searing verdict, "prostitute." In the tradition of Hosea (see Hosea 2:4–5), the covenant with YHWH can be imagined in a marital metaphor; Israel has forsaken true love for YHWH and has "slept around" with other gods. The specificity of such promiscuity is evident in disordered social life. That disorder is reflected in violence (murder) and a mismanaged economy. Social life is skewed because the leadership (princes of the royal family!) traffic with thieves, economic predators, corner-cutting bankers, exploitative landlords, and all manner of oppressive operatives. Everything and everyone is up for sale to the highest bidder. The economy is skewed toward ruthless power. The inevitable result of such disorder is that those "left behind"—widows and orphans who lack a male advocate in a patriarchal society—are bereft of viability. From a prophetic perspective, that is the scene in Jerusalem, a city far removed from the covenantal requirements of Mt. Sinai.

That harsh rendering of the city is followed in verse 24 by the characteristic "therefore" of the prophets. Such wayward policy and conduct do not go unnoticed in a world where YHWH governs. The "therefore" identifies YHWH, the sovereign, the one who occupies

Afterward ... (Isaiah 1:26b) 9

prophetic imagination, who is committed to neighborly urban economics. Verse 24 heaps up titles for YHWH so that we do not miss the claim that Israel's history is fully occupied by the Lord of history. This divine occupation yields an "ah," which means, "Alas! Big trouble is coming!" The big trouble that is coming is because the Lord of the covenant does not take lightly the violation of the covenant that intends neighborly economics. YHWH is presented through the image of a "smelter," who by hot fire will sort out the waste of the people of Israel in order to preserve the few elements of value. The poem anticipates a reduction of the population of the city to those who have not participated in the economic violence of the leadership. The smelting process will be painful and costly, and many will not survive. The image serves the anticipation of coming divine judgment of the city. Indeed, the entire king-temple order will be swept away, and the city will be returned to premonarchal simplicity managed by "judges" who have none of the accouterments of power and pride that are so precious to the royals (v. 26a).

It is in the wake of this harsh denunciation and this costly judgment that we get the "afterward" of our verse. When we trace out the sequence historically, we can see that (a) the indictment pertains to *the royal history* of the city that stretched from David (ca. 1000 BCE) to the exile (587 BCE); (b) the season of wrath pertains to the *deportation of exile* (587–520 BCE); and (c) the "afterward" refers to *the return of the faithful remnant* of deportees, a remnant included in the movement of Ezra and Nehemiah in the fifth century BCE. It is anticipated that the returnees (without monarchs) will return to a city that is "righteous" and "faithful." Its righteousness will be a practice of neighborly well-being in which all share social resources. Its faithfulness will be a practical acknowledgment of the rule of YHWH in the city. Thus verses 21–23 bespeak royal Jerusalem, verses 24–26a reference deported Judea, and verse 26a anticipates a returned faithful remnant.

A second way to read our verse is *literarily*. Thus the early Isaiah of *chapters 1–39* reflects the time of the historical prophet. It turns out that Jerusalem under monarchy, especially under Ahaz and Hezekiah, is a failure in terms of covenantal fidelity (vv. 21–23). Verses 24–26a match up with the middle section of *chapters 40–55*, often termed "Second Isaiah." That hope-filled poetry is addressed to the

Babylonian exiles. And while hope-filled, it nonetheless concerns those who now suffer, in the horizon of the prophet, from the disobedience of the royal centuries. The "afterward" in our lines also prefigures the third part of Isaiah, *chapters 56–66,* in which the faithful remnant of returned Jews sought to reorder the city. That faithful remnant, without kingship, understood authentic worship to be neighborly care (58:6–7), and that worship in the restored temple was intended "for all peoples" (56:7). Thus the restored community made an effort to embody in its order and practice the markings of righteousness and faithfulness.

In sum:

> read *historically*—
> vv. 21–23: royal history
> vv. 24–26a: deported Israel
> v. 26b: restored Israel as remnant
>
> read *literarily*—
> vv. 21–23: First Isaiah (1–39)
> vv. 24–26a: Second Isaiah (40–55)
> v. 26b: Third Isaiah (56–66)

While this pattern may help us make clearer sense of the literary structure and movement of Isaiah, and may help us better understand the complex history reflected in the book, we should not miss the main point of this passage. That point is that YHWH, the Lord of history—the one deeply offended by fickle, prostituting Israel—nonetheless wills a good future for Jerusalem beyond its disobedience. That anticipated "afterward" came to *historical fruition* in the emergent Judaism under Ezra. That afterward came to *literary expression* in Isaiah 56–66 after the grand procession of return to the land of promise:

> For you shall go out in joy,
>   and be led back in peace;
> the mountains and the hills before you
>   shall burst into song,
>   and all the trees of the field shall clap their hands.
>   55:12

Notice that the "afterward" here anticipated cannot be derived from what has gone before. It cannot be extrapolated from the exilic community. Nor can it be extrapolated from the earlier chapters in the book of Isaiah. The afterward comes only from the determined will of YHWH to create a future for Israel that, by itself, had no claim on any future. Israel of itself has no reason to expect a better future. It is all a fresh initiative from YHWH. It turns out that for all the recalcitrance of Israel and all the disappointment of YHWH, the future is still in YHWH's hands. YHWH wills a newness; that is the thrust of the book of Isaiah. That newness is beyond human capacity to create or even any human capacity to imagine. As we read this verse 26, we should notice that after the first two lines the poetry makes a big leap to "afterward." "Afterward" as an element of gospel faith is always achieved by a big leap from what has gone before. It is a leap made possible only through the powerful fidelity of the Lord who wills and gives newness in the midst of sordid failed history.

Questions for Discussion

1. How is Isaiah's "afterward" present in the rest of the book?
2. Do you agree with the literary and historical readings of Isaiah 1:21–26? Why or why not?
3. How do you see the future as being in God's hands?

Chapter 3

Promise Post-Judgment (Isaiah 2:4)

He shall judge between the nations,
and shall arbitrate for many peoples;
they shall beat their swords into plowshares,
and their spears into pruning hooks;
nation shall not lift up sword against nation,
neither shall they learn war any more.

> **Scripture Passages for Reference**
>
> Isaiah 2:2–4
> Isaiah 39:5–7; 65:25
> Micah 4:1–5
> 2 Kings 19:6–7, 15–19
> Jeremiah 31:31–34

The first interesting matter to notice concerning this familiar divine promise in Isaiah 2:2–4 is that it is placed immediately after the speech of judgment (and the "afterward") in chapter 1. We might not have expected that—after the hard declaration of 1:2–26a—we would receive a promise from the mouth of the prophet. That, however, is how the canonical editors arranged the text, and we may take their arrangement with great seriousness. Thus the juxtaposition of *judgment and promise* becomes a clue about how to read the book of

Isaiah. In the first extended segment of the book (chaps. 1–12) we get four *oracles of promise*, each of which is preceded by an *articulation of divine judgment*. Thus:

> 2:2–4 follows after the judgment of chapter 1;
>
> 4:2–6 follows after the harshness of chapter 3;
>
> 9:2–7 follows after the declaration of distress, darkness, gloom, and anguish in 8:21–22; and
>
> 11:1–9 follows after 10:1–4, an announcement that God's anger has not yet turned aside.

Every such prophetic speech of judgment is sober and severe. It turns out that such judgment, however, is not finally absolute; the God who *judges* is the God who *makes promises* of an "afterward." Moreover, we can see that this same dramatic movement from judgment to promise shapes the entire book of Isaiah. In rough outline, Isaiah 1–39 consists of *divine judgment,* whereas Isaiah 40–66 concerns *gracious restoration* after judgment.

We are not told how the literature can make this abrupt reversal of utterance. It is certain that the literary reversal intends to be reflective of the reversal of God's own intent. The God of Israel is capable of harsh intention, even against God's own chosen people. This same God, however, is equally capable of moving beyond anger to fresh restorative resolve. The text of 2:4 is a first embodiment of that fresh resolve on the part of YHWH according to the tradition of Isaiah. That fresh restorative resolve is delivered with both urgency and confidence. The poet does not know when the actual lived reversal will occur, though he is certain such a reversal is in the works. There is, however, no timetable; thus the introductory formula "In days to come" is a standard rhetorical trope for a reliable assurance that lacks a predictable schedule. It is a dependable future, but not one subject to timetables.

We do best by appreciating the dramatic and complete contrast between the *new future* promised by God and the *present tense* of Isaiah in eighth-century Jerusalem. We can identify both *internal and external* elements of contrast whereby the newness of God will overcome the toxic present tense of Jerusalem.

First, concerning *the internal life* of the city of Jerusalem, it is clear that Torah instruction in the coming time will be effectively front and center, not only for the nations but for Jerusalem as well. (This is congruent with the anticipation of "the new covenant" in Jeremiah 31:31–34 wherein all will gladly embrace Torah.) It is precisely Torah instruction, understood in a very broad way, that will provide the clue to socioeconomic well-being for the city. Because the Torah tradition of Deuteronomy is the liveliest expression of Torah, we can imagine that the Torah teaching of Deuteronomy on doing justice is likely in purview here. That is, Jerusalem (and the other nations) will together be instructed in the neighborly management of the economy so that the resources of the economy are generously shared with all members of the community. While such an insight toward well-being is not the entirety of the Torah's message, there is no doubt that such instruction matters decisively for Israel's Torah and for the God who gives Torah.

This *Torah-shaped practice* in the future is in sharp contrast to the *Torah-defying regime* in Jerusalem with which the prophet had to contend. On the one hand King Ahaz receives a flat-out negative verdict for his indifference to Torah practice:

> He did not do what was right in the sight of the LORD his God, as his ancestor David had done, but he walked in the way of the kings of Israel. He even made his son pass through fire, according to the abominable practices of the nations whom the LORD drove out before the people of Israel. (2 Kings 16:2–3)

The readiness of the king to imitate the "abominable nations" is evident in his inability to trust in YHWH. As a result, he conducted foreign policy out of fear, causing him to collude with the Assyrians who, in fact, constituted the greatest threat to his regime. His fearfulness is taken by the prophet as lack of trust in YHWH, a lack that constitutes the great self-destructive failure of the king. The narrative of 2 Kings 16 details the way in which Ahaz feared his lesser enemies (Israel and Syria) and so fell into the hands of his greater enemy.

On the other hand, King Hezekiah is reckoned as a particularly good Torah-keeping king:

> He did what was right in the sight of the LORD just as his ancestor David had done. . . . For he held fast to the LORD; he did not depart from following him but kept the commandments that the LORD commanded Moses. (2 Kings 18:3, 6)

In the midst of the great Assyrian threat evoked by his father, Ahaz, King Hezekiah is counseled by Isaiah to trust in YHWH and not be afraid (19:6–7). As a pious king, Hezekiah trusts in YHWH, prays to YHWH (19:15–19), and is delivered. But of Hezekiah we may observe two things. First, he is decidedly an exception to the long line of fearful faithless kings. And second, even he, in his great fear of Babylon, naively commits himself to the rising power of Babylon, an act that the prophet denounces as an act of self-destructive foolishness (Isaiah 39:5–7). Even this great king is propelled by fear and an inability to trust in the word of the Lord. He finally could not believe the covenantal promise that Torah obedience would lead to public well-being.

The portrayal of these kings and, more broadly, the portrayal found in the words of Isaiah present the city of Jerusalem as an out-of-control political economy that was in deep contradiction to the purposes of YHWH. Thus in Isaiah we get a series of "woe oracles" that are variously introduced in the NRSV by "Ah" (5:8, 11, 18, 20, 21, 22; 10:1; 28:1; 29:1), "Oh" (30:1), and "Alas" (31:1). Jerusalem is on a path of self-destruction. In the time to come, that lethal disorder will be overcome by Torah instruction to which the city and the other nations will gladly submit.

Externally the matter is not different. The economy of Jerusalem was on a war footing. Isaiah addresses the way in which Ahaz fears his local enemies, Israel and Syria (7:1–9). The prophet assured the king that trust in YHWH will cause these threats to dissipate. But the king could not believe such an assurance and proceeded to save himself by surrendering to Assyria. Again Hezekiah is a contrast, for in his trust he watches as the city is unexpectedly rescued from the Assyrian threat. Alongside the prophet, Hezekiah is able to see that the Assyrians (and their king Sennacherib) not only threaten his regime but are mocking YHWH in a way that cannot stand (Isaiah 37:23–24). Hezekiah nonetheless remains on a war footing as he appeals to Babylon against Assyria.

Yet in time to come, Isaiah declares there will be a YHWH-given alternative. As the nations receive Torah instruction along with Jerusalem, it will become clear that the overriding governance of YHWH, surely through a public mechanism in Jerusalem, will adjudicate conflict among the nations. Something like a "world court" for a "world order" of convening nations is envisioned. And when there are peaceable ways of arbitration, the requirement of military posturing is greatly diminished. The outcome is that there can be disarmament. The economy can be otherwise imagined and enacted. There will be no need to maintain a military epidemic that shows up in bloated budgets and in absurd chauvinistic exhibits. No need to "hurt or destroy" (Isaiah 65:25).

Thus the contrast is complete:

- *internal*: from *restless self-securing* to *Torah instruction*;
- *external*: from *war fear and fever* to *disarmament*.

The move into this world of just peace is abrupt. It is not an evolutionary movement but a radical reframing of historical possibility. It is not accomplished by royal good intentions but by the irresistible resolve of YHWH who presides over the nations. All that is asked is that those who hear the poem accept that this is a real opening to a different future that is beyond conventional imagination.

A footnote: We may notice that this same familiar poem is reiterated in Micah 4:1–3, although two verses are added by Micah. First, in 4:4 this rural poet imagines a local agricultural economy to come that likely was beyond the purview of urban Isaiah. Micah entertains a local economy in which rural producers would enjoy the growth of their own crops, a simple economy that would participate in none of the aggressions of industrial agriculture of the kind the king must have sponsored. The verse is an early anticipation of the poignant witness of Wendell Berry.

And then, in 4:5, Micah adds yet another stunning verse. Both prophets have imagined a glad procession of the nations to Jerusalem for Torah instruction that makes a generous economy viable. But Micah asserts that the mark of this procession of nations in the interest of justice and peace is that each nation-group (not unlike a parade of Olympic athletes) would walk each "in the name of its god." This may be seen as a breathtaking affirmation of religious pluralism in the interest of justice and peace. The procession to Jerusalem for Torah instruction does not require conversion to Yahwism. Yahwism need not hold a monopoly on justice and peace. As a result, many peoples, with many gods, are brought together under the aegis of Torah instruction wherein the Torah is not merely or solely a "religious tract" but a guide for an alternative life in the world. Who knew that Torah instruction was the path to the world's well-being? Well, the prophets have always known that! And those who hear the prophets know that too. Those who do not hear the prophets no doubt will continue the frantic path of self-sufficiency. But since we have these poems from Isaiah and Micah, we know otherwise. We know it is a sure thing, directly from God's own lips. These poems give space for an alternative to our historical fearfulness; it yields energy for readiness and for risk. We may imagine what the poem sounded like in the ears of fearful Ahaz . . . or in the ears of faithful Hezekiah!

Questions for Discussion

1. How is the present moment marked by Torah-shaped or Torah-defying practice?
2. What is significant about the ordering of these texts, moving from divine judgment to divine promise?
3. Do you see evidence of our own world or church being on the path to self-destruction? Could attention to Torah values stop it?

Chapter 4

Four Contradictions versus the One Lord (Isaiah 2:17)

The haughtiness of people shall be humbled,
and the pride of everyone shall be brought low;
and the LORD alone will be exalted on that day.

Scripture Passages for Reference

Isaiah 2:6–21
Isaiah 30:15–17
Deuteronomy 17:16–17
Ezekiel 27:12–25
Psalm 146
Revelation 18:11–14

The word is that Jerusalem is cruising for a bruising. That is the first accent of the book of Isaiah. That hard word is given us in this text according to a prophetic *indictment* (Isaiah 2:6–8) and a ferocious *speech of coming devastation* (vv. 9–21). It belongs to prophetic assumption that the indictment is sure to evoke the speech of judgment as divine response to violation and perfidy.

The indictment against the "house of Jacob" extends through verses 6–8. It is governed by the verb "forsaken" that reprimands Israel for having abandoned the obedient ways of Torah. "Jacob" has repeatedly and systematically violated the expectations and requirements of covenantal commandment. The specificity of "forsaken" is voiced in four uses of the term "full/filled" that characterize the central preoccupations of Israel, each of which brazenly contradicts the intention of YHWH and "the way of your people."

1. The land is full of *diviners, soothsayers, and foreigners*. This cluster of terms bespeaks a passionate engagement in international commerce in which deals are made ("clasp hands"), in which buying and selling and trading work to the extreme advantage of some against others. The prophetic tradition (including Isaiah!) believes that the reduction of social life to commercial transactions causes the glue of human fidelity to dry up. The most extreme articulation of such commercialism that reduces everything to a commodity is found in the oracle against the city-state of Tyre in Ezekiel 27:12–25 (on which see also Revelation 18:11–14). In that inventory of commercial goods, notice that even "human beings" can be "exchanged" in a slave market (Ezekiel 27:13). Such commercialism, says the prophet, is a practice whereby covenantal relations are abandoned and everything is reduced to commodity transactions.

2. The land is full of *silver and gold* (Isaiah 2:7). The economy of Jerusalem is organized around greed and the compulsive accumulation of wealth at the expense of the neighborhood. In his "woe oracle" of 10:1–4, Isaiah sees that "iniquitous decrees" and "oppressive statutes" distort justice. Such "regulations" make predation legal and acceptable. Then as now, such "decrees and statutes" were no doubt concerned with regressive taxation, high interest rates, exploitative debt management, and the usual sharp practices that betray neighborliness. If one has no regard for the neighborhood, it is easy enough to manage the economy in the service of greed.

In the narrative of Israel, King Solomon is featured as the quintessential practitioner of greed who depended on high taxes and cheap labor to amass huge amounts of silver and gold. Much of his wealth was devoted to the decor of his grandiose temple, so that his wealth could be liturgically legitimated (see 1 Kings 6:20–22; 7:48–50). But of course, Solomon's wealth was not all for the temple. In addition to the temple, he managed much other silver and gold (see 1 Kings 10:10, 14–22). And of course, Solomon is not unique in the royal line. Rather, he set the "gold standard" that could be readily pursued in Jerusalem by those who came after him. Early on, the Torah of Moses knew the risk and threat posed by such preoccupation with greed, and prohibited it (Deuteronomy 17:16–17). Jerusalem, however, found easy ways to forsake and disregard the Torah, going its unfettered way in greed, all of which contradicted the ground of the covenant.

3. The land is full of *horses and chariots* (Isaiah 2:7). That is, the land is occupied by a military economy in which "horses and chariots" are instruments of war. King Ahaz, in his fearfulness, was bent on war against his immediate enemies, Israel and Syria. King Hezekiah, in his fearfulness, was assured by the prophet to trust in YHWH rather than in arms:

> In returning and rest you shall be saved;
> in quietness and in trust shall be your strength.
> 30:15

Against such counsel, the king refused the prophet and tried war:

> But you refused and said,
> "No! We will flee upon horses" . . .
> and, "We will ride upon swift steeds."
> vv. 15b–16

But the king's effort did not work:

> Therefore you shall flee! . . .
> therefore your pursuers shall be swift!
> A thousand shall flee at the sight of one,
> at the threat of five you shall flee,
> until you are left
> like a flagstaff on the top of a mountain,
> like a signal on a hill.
> vv. 16–17

The prophet insists that reliance on military might can never bring security and most often brings greater insecurity. Indeed, since the wonder of the exodus Israel has known that YHWH can avail against such arms:

> Sing to the LORD, for he has triumphed gloriously;
> horse and rider he has thrown into the sea.
> Exodus 15:21; see also vv. 4, 11–12

Or as the wisdom teachers had long since concluded:

> No wisdom, no understanding, no counsel,
>   can avail against the LORD.
> The horse is made ready for the day of battle,
>   but the victory belongs to the LORD.
>   Proverbs 21:30–31

Talk about the "fog of war"!

4. The land is full of *idols* (Isaiah 2:8). The Hebrew term used here means "worthless." The objects of worship in Jerusalem were worthless, of no value, unable to save. This fourth "fullness" is perhaps a summary of the three that precede, for commerce, gold, and arms are all worthless; they cannot make one secure. More than that, they are, in their fullness, contradictions of YHWH: commerce as commoditization contradicts neighborliness, the accumulation of gold contradicts generosity, and arms as self-sufficiency contradicts reliance on YHWH.[1] This fourfold fullness can only add up to a sorry end in Jerusalem.

At verse 9 our text makes a sharp move from indictment to divine threat (vv. 9–19). This extended poetry is crafted in a complex design:

> v. 9   humbled . . . brought low
> > v. 10   enter into the rock
> v. 11 brought low . . . humbled: *YHWH alone!*
> > > v. 12   against
> > > > against
> > > v. 13 against
> > > > against
> > > v. 14 against
> > > > against
> > > v. 15   against
> > > > against
> > > v. 16 against
> > > > against
> v. 17 humbled . . . brought low: *YHWH alone!*
> > v. 19 enter the caves of the rocks.

The poem is bracketed in verses 9–11 and in verses 17–19 by two negative phrases. The first is "humbled and brought low" (vv. 9, 17; see also v. 11). Those who "ride high" with commerce, gold, and arms imagine themselves masters of history and managers of a fail-safe economy. They fail to reckon with the social reality that they are at best penultimate in history; they finally cannot manage the outcomes of the inscrutable historical process. Second, "enter the rock . . . enter the cave of the rocks" (vv. 10, 19) traces a scenario of frantic evacuation from the city under assault to the safety of the desert, not unlike a "civil defense" evacuation. The need to flee for safety makes clear that the extravagant world of commerce, gold, and arms is an illusion that cannot stand in the face of YHWH's governance.

Sandwiched between the beginning of "humbled, brought low . . . enter the rock" and "humbled . . . brought low . . . enter the cave" at the end is a thick, insistent pounding of the particle "against" reiterated no fewer than *ten times*! The text articulates a contest. On one side are "cedars of Lebanon, oaks of Bashan, high mountains, lofty hills, high trees, fortified wall, ships of Tarshish, beautiful craft." On the other side is only YHWH—*YHWH alone*! It is, in the end, no contest. All of the icons of pride, power, wealth, and self-sufficiency are easily and readily blown away. They have no staying power. They cannot endure; they cannot make safe. They are readily overcome, vetoed, and canceled out by the insistent will of YHWH, making their advocates completely vulnerable.

Notice that the poem specifies nothing concrete. It could be that the "against" of YHWH takes the form of a mighty storm. More likely it takes the form of an enemy invasion. But we are not told. All that we are told is that, at the end of "the day," the day of YHWH's self-assertion, there will be the Lord alone (vv. 11, 17). Nothing else, no one else—all is swept away as a contradiction of YHWH. This massive dramatic "against," says the poet, is an inescapable response to a land filled to excess with all that YHWH will not tolerate.

The managers of commerce, gold, and arms are taken by surprise. They had imagined their timeless control and well-being. They had no sense of divine time. They had no awareness of the rule of YHWH that would inevitably show up in order to terminate a long, full season of self-congratulations and self-exaltation. It turns out that none of these props of self-sufficiency make any difference when the holiness of YHWH is mobilized.

Verse 22 adds a retrospect. It warns against reliance on things "mortal." Human agents have only the breath that is in their nostrils, nothing more, as Psalm 146 also asserts:

> Do not put your trust in princes,
>   in mortals, in whom there is no help.
> When their breath departs, they return to the earth;
>   on that very day their plans perish.
> Psalm 146:3–4

Human pride and power are fleeting, transitory moments. The alternative articulated by Isaiah concerns YHWH and YHWH's holiness. There is no measure of commerce, gold, or arms that can outflank the fierce mystery of YHWH.

Questions for Discussion

1. How is neighborliness betrayed in our world today?
2. How does Isaiah juxtapose trust in God over and against military power?
3. What things could be considered "false religion" now?
4. What is the Lord against? How do we know?

Chapter 5

Bad Grapes
(Isaiah 5:7)

He expected justice,
but saw bloodshed;
righteousness,
but heard a cry!

> ***Scripture Passages for Reference***
>
> Isaiah 5:1–7
> Isaiah 27:2–5
> Psalm 72
> Psalm 80
> John 15:1–17

Imagine at the outset a lover serenading his beloved. He is surely singing, perhaps also playing a lute or a zither. The song has as its object the vineyard owned by the beloved. It is a song of wooing for the vineyard, perhaps in the hope that such attentive affection would encourage the vineyard to evoke a better harvest of grapes. The singer recites all the ways in which the vineyard, object of love and devotion, has been cared for. The song is like the recital of a wounded lover who reminds the beloved of all he has done in love for the vineyard. He has generously worked to enhance the vineyard and to maximize its produce, for the vineyard has no other assignment than to produce good grapes.

> He has cultivated it and cleared it of stones;
> He has used choice vines with hope for good grapes;
> He has built a watchtower to keep the vineyard under safe surveillance, protecting it from all invaders and exploiters;
> He has prepared a wine vat in the hope of great grape production.
> (see Isaiah 5:2)

And then, like every good farmer or vinedresser, he waited. He waited for the grapes to come in, because they cannot be rushed. He waited in hope. But by the end of verse 2, the song and the singer end in disappointment. Because all that grew in the vineyard were stinky, pitiful grapes that did not look good and that tasted bad. The entire tale of the vineyard, cared for and failed, has taken only two verses!

Now in verse 3 the singer turns to his Jerusalem audience. He bids for applause for his generous actions toward the vineyard, and approval for his judgment against the vineyard. The witnesses in the city might have supported the vineyard and concluded that the owner had not done enough for the vineyard. But the singer does not wait for the vote of his audience. He issues two rhetorical questions that in fact constitute his statement of self-validation:

- *What more . . . ?* The answer is that there is nothing more he could have done to enhance the vineyard.
- *Why did . . . ?* The answer is that the "wild grapes" are not the fault of the owner; the wild grapes are the failure of the vine in its recalcitrance.

The judgment "between me and my vineyard" yields an *indictment* of the vineyard and an *acquittal* of the owner. No alternative is allowed.

From that, it follows in verse 5 that the owner is in the right and now is fully justified in destructive rage against the vineyard that failed to produce the good grapes expected. The lover has turned to an enraged, rejected speaker who now will act violently against the vineyard. That violent action is given in a series of first-person verbs in which the lover eagerly takes responsibility for the destruction now to be enacted:

> I will remove protection so that the wild animals can ravage the vineyard.

Bad Grapes (Isaiah 5:7) 27

I will take down the protective wall, so that invaders can trample.
I will make a waste. The vineyard will be abandoned; as any such
    abandoned plot it will be overrun with briers and thorns.
I will withhold rain. The vineyard will dry up in its abandonment.
(see vv. 5–6)

The devastation in verses 5–6 is a perfect counterpoint to the attentive care of verses 1–2. The negation is a point-by-point reversal of the good care initially readily extended to the vineyard.

At the end of verse 6 we may pause in our reading. So far we have been able (and have been required) to stay fully inside the imagery of the poem. Thus far there has been no identification of the vineyard and what its poetic imagery specifies. Nor has there been any identification of the singer-lover who presents the poem to us. We may take verses 1–2 and 5–6 as a perfect and complete account of *deep love extended, deep love rejected* that ends in rage. This dramatic sequence is not unfamiliar to us, because we know that love spurned may evoke great hostility.

Only now in verse 7 is the song, in its positive and negative parts, decoded for us. Perhaps we should have known from verse 3 where the people of Israel and Judah are summoned to be judges and witnesses. Nothing is made of that, however, in the poem itself. Only in verse 7 are we given the historical equivalent to the poetic imagery. The vineyard we now know is Israel. In a nice poetic inversion, Judah is the "pleasant planting." Now we know and we can read the poetic lines according to the historical reality of Israel.

The good vineyard of verses 1–2 is the community of Israel for which YHWH has done everything. Israel exists only because YHWH has made provision for its well-being:

> Israel was given food and water in the desert;
> Israel had its wars fought for it by YHWH;
> Israel is given the good land of promise;
> Israel was long protected by the providential care of YHWH.

There was every reason to hope that Israel would be a reliable covenant partner, even as there was every reason to expect that the vineyard would produce good grapes. The doxological psalm says the same of YHWH's care for Israel:

> You brought a vine out of Egypt;
>   you drove out the nations and planted it.
> You cleared the ground for it;
>   it took deep root and filled the land.
> The mountains were covered with its shade,
>   the mighty cedars with its branches;
> it sent out its branches to the sea,
>   and its shoots to the River.
>   Psalm 80:7–11

The psalm turns upon the same question as our poem: "Why then?" (Psalm 80:12). Why then, in light of such care, has there come exposure to invaders and the ravaging of wild boars? The prophetic reading of the history of Israel provides the long answer: Trouble has come on the vineyard because of the long history of recalcitrance, because of covenantal infidelity, because of Torah disobedience, because of the violation of YHWH's holiness, because of the betrayal of neighborly justice, because power and money have been substituted for trust, because of idolatrous self-sufficiency that has replaced reliance on YHWH.

The outcome for Israel was destruction and exposure to enemies who were, in prophetic horizon, dispatched by YHWH. It could have been Assyria. Later on it would be Babylon. It could have been *any* instrument of historical reality, in Isaiah's view, because all such historical instruments—all nations—are available for the performance of YHWH's lordship. The tradition of Israel, already in the eighth century, is a long-term anticipation of the time when Jerusalem will be defeated by YHWH-dispatched nations. Such an undoing is no fault of YHWH, according to Isaiah; it is the result of the failure of Israel to produce the good grapes of Torah obedience.

Thus the poem is a readout of the long view of the history of Israel that runs from *Exodus mercy* to the *demise of the city* at the hands of the enemy. It takes many centuries to perform this tale. In poetic parlance, it takes only four verses: verses 1–2 to narrate *the mercy*, verses 5–6 to narrate *the undoing*.

When we arrive at verse 7, we still do not know the identity of the singer-lover who cared for the vineyard and then destroyed the vineyard. It is all by inference that we recognize that the one who speaks is YHWH, the same one who presides over the well-being of the life of Israel who had given up that good life in savage anger. We are able to recognize YHWH as agent of both the love song and the resultant devastation by the signature marks of verse 7. In that verse, we are told that "he" (that is, YHWH) "expected." It is the same word as "expected" of good grapes in verse 4. "He" had an expectation of the vineyard Israel. YHWH expected justice and righteousness. This word pair is the most elemental marking of YHWH. (We have encountered the same word pair in 1:21. Israel was, at the outset, full of "justice and righteousness.") The word pair bespeaks full, diligent, and passionate care for the well-being of the entire community. That is what YHWH had commanded and what YHWH expects from Israel. In Psalm 72, the royal liturgy asserts the same expectation, even from the king:

> Give the king your justice, O God,
>   and your righteousness to a king's son.
> May he judge your people with righteousness,
>   and your poor with justice.
> ....
> May he defend the cause of the poor of the people,
>   give deliverance to the needy,
>   and crush the oppressor.
> ....
> For he delivers the needy when they call,
>   the poor and those who have no helper.
> He has pity on the weak and the needy,
>   and saves the lives of the needy.
> Psalm 72:1–2, 4, 12–13

This is the primary mandate assigned to Israel, to Jerusalem, and to the royal house. These are the good grapes expected by the vine keeper. These are the marks of YHWH's own life:

> But the LORD of hosts is exalted by justice,
>   and the Holy God shows himself holy by righteousness.
> Isaiah 5:16

What an expectation! The good grapes of justice and righteousness are definitional for YHWH and so are definitional for Israel.

The poem ends in verse 7 with a play in Hebrew words that is impossible to articulate in English:

> Instead of *mishpat* . . . *mispach*;
> Instead of justice . . . bloodshed;
> Instead of *tzedeqah* . . . *ze'aqah*
> Instead of righteousness . . . a cry!

Israel has only produced bloodshed and a cry. The "bloodshed" might bespeak violence, but it may also signal the slow, steady exploitation of the vulnerable through economic leverage that abuses second-class members of society. The "cry" might be the sound of distress from a victim of violence, perhaps murder or rape. But it is also a cry of despair from those vulnerable who are left behind without hope or historical possibility.

The poem ends in a brusque verdict that Israel has completely failed to live up to the expectation of YHWH. It is no wonder, in prophetic horizon, that Israel is left vulnerable to its greedy neighbors, who may now prey upon Israel because the Lord of the covenant has withdrawn protection from vineyard Israel. Israel is left exposed to the realities of international aggression. The book of Isaiah will go on to report on the demise of the city that has failed in its single mandate.

In Isaiah 27:2–5 the imagery of our poem is reiterated. Again there is the threat of "briers and thorns" when the vineyard disappoints. This time, however, the imagery arrives at a positive "or else" with an invitation to "do *shalom*" ("make peace") with YHWH (v. 5). Such peace is still on offer. The vineyard need not perish! Israel could get back to its true life with YHWH.

The same imagery of the vine is reiterated in John 15:1–17 where the branches have life because of the life-giving vine. While the imagery has advanced, the intent is not different. The purpose of the "branches" is still to produce "good fruit," which is to enact God's love in the world. And there still remains in the relationship the risk of anger and reprimand with the failure of good fruit:

> Whoever does not abide in me is thrown away like a branch and withers; such branches are gathered, thrown into the fire, and burned. (John 15:6)

In all of these uses the vine keeper is generous in giving life to the vine, making life viable for God's people. But the vine keeper has very specific intentions for the vine and its branches. The future of the relationship turns on the production of good fruit. This expectation of good grapes/good fruit from the vineyard is a summons to the people of God (Israel, the church) to be its best self, a self that reflects the good intention of the vine keeper. In Isaiah the good grapes are *justice and righteousness*. In the gospel, the good fruit is "*to love one another*." There is no compromise on this expectation. When the vine keeper is disappointed, the future will not and cannot be good for the failed branches.

Questions for Discussion

1. Why might Isaiah have used the parable of a vineyard to make his point?
2. Is our own culture also marked by "bloodshed" and "outcry"?
3. Can bad grapes be made good? How, or why not?

Chapter 6

Isaiah's Second Vision (Isaiah 6:3)

And one called to another and said:
"Holy, holy, holy is the LORD of hosts;
the whole earth is full of his glory."

> **Scripture Passages for Reference**
>
> Isaiah 6:1–13
> Exodus 2:23–25
> 1 Kings 8:27
> 2 Kings 15:1–7
> 2 Chronicles 26:1–23

The very first word of the book of Isaiah is "vision": "(the) vision of Isaiah" (1:1). The entire book is presented as "vision" wherein the prophet could see, in anticipation, what his contemporaries could not discern. On the one hand, he could "envision" the *complete demise* of the failed city of Jerusalem. On the other hand, however, he could "envision" the *inscrutable gift* of a new Jerusalem beyond the demise (65:17–25). We are not told anything of the way in which the prophet had such a visionary capacity, and there is no need for us to speculate on the matter.

Now, in Isaiah 6, the matter of "prophetic vision" is made much more specific. This narrative account of a "vision" occurs in the year of the death of the great king Uzziah (also called Azariah) in 742 BCE. The death of the great king signified the end of an era of peace and prosperity (2 Kings 15:1–7; see 2 Chronicles 26:1–23). It may be that the death of the great king opened the way for discernment of alternative reality under the aegis of "the real king." Such a newness at the point of death has an important parallel in the exodus narrative:

> After a long time the king of Egypt died. The Israelites groaned under their slavery, and cried out. (Exodus 2:23)

It was the death of Pharaoh that created space for the out-loud grief of enslaved Israel, opening the way for emancipation. Now, for the prophet, a very different season in his life is opened at the turn of royal power.

We are told nothing of the specific circumstance of his encounter with the holy God. Rather, we get a simple, straightforward report on a moment when the sheer majesty of God crowds in on his life in deeply transformative ways. The prophet says he "saw the Lord," but we are told nothing of what he saw of the Lord, for according to some traditions to "see God" is to die (Exodus 33:20). We only get a description of all that is around the Lord; decorum is in order. The prophet saw the extravagant robe worn by the royal God. He saw that the throne of God was wondrously surrounded by acolytes, ministers, and attendants, all of them serving God, honoring God, and worshiping God. The language pushes us to the extreme of imagination, for what the prophet sees has no equivalent in ordinary human vision or human discourse. The poetic imagery is an attempt to voice the unvoiceable of the wonder of God's own holiness. The extremity of reality requires the extremity of language, an extremity echoed in the singing of the church:

> Ye watchers and ye holy ones,
> bright seraphs, cherubim, and thrones,
> raise the glad strain, Alleluia!
> Cry out, dominions, princedoms, powers,
> virtues, archangels, angels' choirs:
> Alleluia! Alleluia!
> Alleluia! Alleluia! Alleluia![1]

The lyric heaps up the praise-filled inventory of the company of heaven that witnesses to God's holiness:

> Dominions, princedoms, powers, virtues, archangels, angel choirs!

None of the terms are exact. All of them together bespeak awe, astonishment, and reverence. These attendants of God are busy with liturgical duties. And then, right in the middle of the vision, we get a voice. The singing of the heavenly choir matches the overwhelming reality of God. The voice of the choir begins with "holy" and ends with "glory." These two terms articulate the unutterable majesty of God that has no counterpoint in the world of creation. The term "holy" bespeaks the radical otherness of God, a marker of God caught by Rudolf Otto and then by Karl Barth with awareness that God is "wholly other" (*ganz Anders*), without parallel or linkage to the created world.[2] The heavenly voices sing "holy" three times in order to ratchet up the superlatives of majesty.[3] The concluding term, "glory," attests to the grandeur of the royal King who has displaced the deceased king in Jerusalem. It is no wonder that the prophet experienced the temple encounter in shame and trembling, for no human construct could possibly contain the holiness of God, an awareness voiced with reference to the Jerusalem temple:

> But will God indeed dwell on the earth? Even heaven and the highest heaven cannot contain you, much less this house that I have built! (1 Kings 8:27; see also 2 Samuel 7:5–7)

The holiness of God is beyond human construction or human imagination, because the holiness of God is always again breaking out beyond the confines of human creed or ideology.

All of this the prophet witnessed. It does not surprise us that such a vision of God's holiness evoked a searing experience for the prophet. The remainder of the text in Isaiah 6 concerns response to the vision evoked by a glimpse of God's holiness. We may identify three moments in that response.

1. A vision of God's holiness evokes in the prophet a deep sense of *his own disqualification* for being in the presence of God. The vision of holiness generates an awareness of his own "uncleanness,"

ritual impurity that makes him unworthy to be in the presence of God. While this awareness may lead to a sense of guilt, his primary reality is that he is *at risk*. The holiness of God is dangerous and the disqualified are under threat because of it. In this context of holiness/uncleanness the prophet draws upon the priestly tradition of holiness that is preoccupied with all the specificities that could make one unclean and impure. Thus the inventory of the book of Leviticus provided clarity and guidance for how the disqualified may be made qualified to experience divine presence. In Christian tradition this same matter is at the center of Peter's vision in Acts 10 that led to the inclusion of Gentiles (an unclean people!) in the company of the faithful. The divine verdict given to Peter is an echo of what happens in our text:

What God has made *clean* you must not call *profane*. (Acts 10:15)

Isaiah already reported on the capacity of the holy God to make clean what is unclean.

2. The prophet reports that one from among the ministers around the throne came to him to *make him qualified* for the presence of the holy God, to move from *profane* to *clean*. That agent was dispatched from the throne by the holy God. The initiative came from God. The breach between *God's holiness* and *Isaiah's uncleanness* is unbridgeable . . . except from God's side. God finds a way, and God initiates a new possibility for the life of Isaiah. The specificity of "live coals on lips" is a sacramental act whereby the uncleanness of Isaiah is purged away. His sin is blotted out by the initiative of the holy God. The *unclean one* is now *made clean* enough to live for an instant in the presence of the holy God. (This dramatic reach toward the prophet has a parallel in the "touch" of God toward Jeremiah in Jeremiah 1:9). The holy God has a ready capacity to include into the sphere of God's holiness those whom God recruits. Now the prophet is given access for a full exchange with God.

3. This action has happened quickly, instantaneously—first "unclean," second, "made clean." And now this erstwhile unclean, disqualified man is addressed with a *divine summons*. The holy one asks two questions (v. 8). The first question concerns the "I" of God: "Whom shall *I* send?" The second question concerns "us": "Who will go *for us*?" The plural pronoun refers to the whole company of

those surrounding the heavenly throne. This is the assignment of a heavenly task. The heavenly assembly is looking for a human agent who will carry the message of the heavenly court to earthly society.

Remarkably, the erstwhile unclean man now fully qualified does not hesitate or resist. He responds readily and eagerly to the assignment. Because the work to be undertaken by the prophet is from the holiness of God, we may anticipate that the word will not be a comfortable word that will fit the safe ideology of the Jerusalem establishment. In ancient Jerusalem, as with us now, the truth of faith had been trimmed to be comfortable and convenient, easily resonating with the self-assured confidence of the Jerusalem establishment.

The holy word of God now entrusted to the prophet, however, is otherwise. We ourselves may acknowledge that in our frequent appeal to this familiar "call narrative" in Isaiah 6, we characteristically stop reading at verse 8, so happy that the prophet has signed on to his prophetic role. We are, however, obligated to continue our reading past verse 8 and the ready response of the prophet. And when we read on into verses 9–13, we cannot help but notice that the prophet is given, by heavenly initiative, very hard words to speak in Israel. The hard words reflect the reality that Jerusalem is out of sync with the will of the holy God.

Thus, in verses 9–10 the prophet articulates God's hard intention that Israel should be dull, not looking, not listening, and not comprehending, and consequently not healed. Isaiah is dispatched with very tough news to this people that has defied the purpose of YHWH. Its future consists in not being healed! The ante is upped further in verses 11–13 with its answer to the plaintive question "How long?" How long will there be no healing for Israel? The answer is a double "until." The devastation of Jerusalem will continue *until* the land is desolate and *until* its people are sent "far away." The outcome is to be only a "stump," a leftover base apparently without any growth or future. The working of the holy God in this text is twofold. First, the holy God has "cleansed" Isaiah and made him fit for a summons. But second, there is no such generous "cleansing" of the "unclean" people of Israel. Their life that violates God's holiness will only end in devastation because the holiness of God will not be mocked. This dread-filled verdict becomes a leitmotif in the early part of the book of Isaiah. The prophet can and does envision the coming devastation.

He can do so because his access to God's holiness has evidenced to him the costly consequences for all that contradicts that holiness.

This chapter constitutes a "call" to authorize the eighth-century Isaiah and his ministry. Since the latter part of the book of Isaiah, beginning at chapter 40, comes much later historically, it does not surprise us that this later poet (Second Isaiah) may also be called by God to speak. That second call for the second part of the book of Isaiah with a second word from God is found in Isaiah 40. We may reckon 40:1–11 as *a positive prophetic call* as a counterpoint to the *first negative call* of chapter 6. Both "called" prophets can envision two seasons in the life of Israel, first *a season of destruction* (6:1–11) and then *a season of restoration* (40:1–11).

Questions for Discussion

1. How has the truth of faith been trimmed down for us so that it is merely comfortable and convenient?
2. Have you ever experienced feeling disqualified and then qualified? Describe this movement from profane to clean.
3. Why is the divine destruction described in Isaiah 6 so thoroughgoing?

Chapter 7

The Holy Seed-Stump (Isaiah 6:13b)

The holy seed is its stump.

> **Scripture Passages for Reference**
>
> Isaiah 6:1–13
> Isaiah 37:30–32
> Exodus 3:12
> Judges 6:11b–17
> Jeremiah 1:4–10
> Ezekiel 1:1–3:11

We have already noted one pivotal text in Isaiah 6—namely, verse 3's vision of the thrice-holy God—but more can be said about this passage. In many ways, the entire chapter is pivotal; it is, after all, Isaiah's "second" vision (see 1:1; cf. 2:1), though some scholars interpret this chapter as Isaiah's inaugural call to ministry. Others, noting that this call comes only in the sixth chapter, not the first, think otherwise, since other inaugural calls tend to appear in first position in their respective prophetic books (see Jeremiah 1:4–10, Ezekiel 1:1–3:11; but cf. Amos 7:10–17). This debate cannot be resolved here, and perhaps little hangs on it. It is enough to note Isaiah 6's importance, whether as a kind of flashback recounting Isaiah's call to prophetic ministry or as a kind of "renewed" call, perhaps inaugurating a new stage in his work.

It should be expected that such a pivotal chapter would have more than one pivotal verse. And indeed it does! We have already seen the importance of Isaiah's vision of the holy God in our meditation on 6:3. This leads him to an awareness of his own disqualification:

> And I said: "Woe is me! I am lost, for I am a man of unclean lips, and I live among a people of unclean lips; yet my eyes have seen the King, the LORD of hosts!" (Isaiah 6:5)

Isaiah's sense of guilt leads to divine compensation for it: Isaiah is moved from disqualified to qualified (vv. 6–7). And so, perhaps without even thinking, he blurts out a response to the divine request for a volunteer to deliver YHWH's message:

> And I said, "Here am I; send me!" (v. 8b)

Up to this point, all seems well: Isaiah has been cleansed and qualified, and God has found someone to deliver the divine message. But God's message that Isaiah is tasked to deliver is harsh, even un-understandable:

> "Go and say to this people:
>   'Keep listening, but do not comprehend;
>   keep looking, but do not understand.'
> Make the mind of this people dull,
>   and stop their ears,
>   and shut their eyes,
> so that they may not look with their eyes,
>   and listen with their ears,
> and comprehend with their minds,
>   and turn and be healed."
>   vv. 9–10

God's strategy is inscrutable to say the least. It is designed to *prevent* the people from comprehending, understanding, seeing, hearing *so that they do not turn* (Hebrew *šûb*, a common word for "repent") and *so remain sick* (cf. 1:5). This hard saying is cited frequently in the New Testament, including by Jesus, who uses it to explain why he spoke in parables: precisely so that people didn't understand

The Holy Seed-Stump (Isaiah 6:13b) 41

(see Matthew 13:10–17; Mark 4:10–12; Luke 8:9–10; see also John 12:37–43; Acts 28:26; Romans 11:8)!

Small wonder that Isaiah responds to this brutal mission with a plaintive cry: "How long, O Lord?" (v. 11a). This is no polite question that courteously inquires about the duration of the messenger's appointment. This is an insistent, even impatient and indignant question, one not infrequently found on the lips of the psalmists (see Psalms 6:4; 74:10; 80:5; 90:13; 94:3; see also Psalm 82:2; Exodus 10:3, 7; Numbers 14:27; 1 Samuel 16:1; 2 Samuel 2:26). Isaiah is distressed by his newfound vocation; he may be *well qualified now*, thanks to the seraph (Isaiah 6:6–7), but he wants *immediate release* from the job—*now*!

Isaiah receives an answer to his question, or perhaps better, a reply to his plea for escape:

> And [God] said:
> "Until cities lie waste
>   without inhabitant,
> and houses without people,
>   and the land is utterly desolate;
> until the LORD sends everyone far away,
>   and vast is the emptiness in the midst of the land.
> Even if a tenth part remain in it,
>   it will be burned again,
> like a terebinth or an oak
>   whose stump remains standing
>   when it is felled."
>
>   vv. 11–13a

This is likely not the answer Isaiah hoped for. No term limit is specified, and, if anything, the divine resolve seems even more grim. Isaiah's ministry must last until cities are empty with houses and the land is abandoned. Until the exile, that is. Still more: if even 10 percent survives the coming conflagration, it must be burned again. All that will be left standing will be a stump. Not even 10 percent of the tree that is Israel is permitted to survive. It will be less than that, and will be *burned over twice*.

Prior passages in Isaiah have prepared us for this kind of despair in the mission of God, but it is still shocking in scope and force.

Even so, two things must be noted that may not be obvious on a casual reading.

1. Isaiah 6 follows a stereotypical pattern that the biblical authors frequently used in stories about famous people and their calls. Indeed, Moses's call in Exodus 3:1–12, Gideon's in Judges 6:11b–17, Jeremiah's in Jeremiah 1:4–10, and Ezekiel's in Ezekiel 1:1–3:11 all seem to follow this pattern, more or less.[1] It was apparently a kind of literary convention, a template or form authors adopted when writing these accounts. This pattern involves the following elements (with verses from Isaiah 6 and Exodus 3 provided for reference):

Divine confrontation—Isaiah 6:1–2; Exodus 3:1–4a

Introductory word—Isaiah 6:3–7; Exodus 3:4b–9

Commission—Isaiah 6:8–10; Exodus 3:10

Objection—Isaiah 6:11a; Exodus 3:11

Reassurance—Isaiah 6:11b–13a; Exodus 3:12a

Sign—Isaiah 6:13b; Exodus 3:13b

Attentive readers will note that the different elements appear in slightly different forms in Exodus 3 and Isaiah 6. Even so, the main elements are present in Isaiah 6, and when that is recognized, several fascinating things are thrown into high definition.

One has already been mentioned—namely, that Isaiah's question in v. 11a is nothing short of an objection to his prophetic calling. Once set in the larger context of this literary form and its appearance in other biblical texts, however, Isaiah's question is not only an objection. It is an *expected element* within this pattern. Those called to truly difficult tasks like prophecy and deliverance do not, typically, welcome such calls. Quite to the contrary! That is understandable because these calls are hard. Most prophets end up dead before their time, with no one to collect the life insurance. No wonder they want out—and say so! Those of us who are scaredy-cats may take solace in the fact that few are summoned to such a high calling in the Bible. Alas, the call of Christ that falls on all of us—scared or not—is no less demanding or deadly (see Matthew 10:38–39; 16:25; Mark 8:34–35; Luke 9:23–24; 17:33; cf. John 12:25). It is nevertheless no small grace that the Bible *knows* this calling is hard. The call pattern *expects* those called to *reject* it. As a result, the prophets are not chided or chastised for their objections to the call. Quite to the contrary, God anticipates such pushback.

2. That leads to the second important item—namely, that God *responds* to these objections with divine assurance. True, in the case of Isaiah 6, this reassurance is far less obvious than with Moses, who receives a promise of divine presence: "I am with you" (Exodus 3:12a). But it does appear where it belongs in the call pattern, right after Isaiah's objection. The content of this "reassurance" has been mentioned above (Isaiah 6:11–13b). God's words here are a bleak response to Isaiah's protest. Yet God nevertheless takes the prophet seriously, answering Isaiah as if Isaiah had indeed asked a question, not reached for the eject button.

God's "until" provides a time limit to Isaiah's prophetic vocation: *until . . . total devastation*. Once again there seems to be little or no positive reassurance here, only a very grim repetition of judgment. But there *is* a limit. There will be an end to this ending of Israel. God's judgment has a divine delimitation. Still further, a more pronounced trace of divine "reassurance" in this section is that God is more active in vv. 11–13a than previously in chapter 6, especially in v. 12. In the commission in vv. 8–10, *Isaiah* had to *say* things and *do* things. Now it is the *Lord's doing*. God is the one who shoulders this grim prophetic task. This may be a bitter "reassurance," but it does confirm and affirm the prophet in significant ways.

Finally, there is not only an end to God's judgment in the sense of a cessation. God's judgment also has an end in the sense that it has a goal or intention. This seems to be present in the "sign" element of the call pattern that comes at the very end of v. 13: "The holy seed is its stump." Here at last is our pivotal half-verse. And what a pivot it is! This sign is very brief and the text is rather opaque, comprising only three words in Hebrew. Besides which, v. 13 as a whole is tricky and unclear. Still, most scholars support this general translation, and two things can be underscored about our verse, which identifies the stump of the burned-over tree as the holy seed. First, within the call pattern, these three words are indeed acting as the sign element, the proof that God is acting through God's prophet.

Moses's sign is comparable, as it too came *after his obedience and the deliverance* of the people:

> And this shall be the sign for you that it is I who sent you: when you have brought the people out of Egypt, you shall worship God on this mountain. (Exodus 3:12b)

In Isaiah's case, the sign comes *after his obedience and the judgment* of the people. In both cases, the sign is *after-the-fact*, but it is proof positive nevertheless that God has sent this prophet and made good on God's divine promises. In Moses's case, those promises were for good; in Isaiah's case, those promises are for ill—but both come from the one Lord who forms light and creates darkness, who makes weal and creates woe (Isaiah 45:7).

The second thing that can be underscored about verse 13b is that, even in Isaiah's case, the sign can be understood as *for good* and *about deliverance*. The phrase "the holy seed" is found elsewhere only in Ezra 9:2, where it refers to the exiles returned from Babylon. Later, in Isaiah 65:9, "seed" refers to the faithful remnant. Still further, the presence of oracles of promise after articulations of judgment elsewhere in Isaiah (see, e.g., 2:1–4; 4:2–6; 9:2–7; and 11:1–9) has prepared us to understand that the God of Isaiah's vision(s) is never interested in punishment for its own sake, but rather in "the impossible possibility of new life," even after deep failure.[2] New life can, and will, happen again; it is the gift of God (see 37:30–32). The end of exile, what remains when the destruction is over (perhaps also the *ends* of exile, which is to say, its *purpose*), may well be something smaller, something wounded—a fraction of its former size, bearing the wounds of disobedience on its body—but it is nevertheless *holy*, not unlike "the Holy One of Israel" (see, e.g., 1:4; 5:19; 10:20; 12:6; 40:25; 45:11; 55:5; 60:9, 15), and it is a *seed*, ready to sprout again, anew and afresh. That is how things go with the God who brings dead things back to life again (26:19; Romans 4:17).

Questions for Discussion

1. What do you make of the call pattern used in Isaiah 6 and elsewhere as a kind of literary convention?

2. What do you think of the idea that objecting to God's call is expected? Is this an encouraging idea?
3. Have you ever felt God's call and objected to it?
4. Have you felt reassurance from God at such times, perhaps even receiving a divine sign of some sort?

Chapter 8

Standing Firm
(Isaiah 7:9)

*If you do not stand firm in faith,
you shall not stand at all.*

> **Scripture Passages for Reference**
>
> Isaiah 7:1–25
> Exodus 14:13–14
> Leviticus 26:36–37
> 2 Kings 16:5–7

We may learn from the book of Isaiah that prophetic utterance is not generic and universal. Rather, it is voiced with some precision in the midst of a particular historical circumstance. In the case of chapter 7, the particular historical circumstance is the crisis faced by King Ahaz in 734 BCE. The crisis is that the kingdom of Judah is under military threat from the alliance of Northern Israel and Syria, Judah's two neighbors immediately to the north. King Ahaz is not only inept, but he is terrified at the prospect of military assault before which he senses his own vulnerability. His fear is voiced with some imagination in verse 2:

> The heart of Ahaz and the heart of his people shook as the trees of the forest shake before the wind.

This phrasing of fear is reminiscent of the "curse" anticipated in Leviticus 26:36–37:

> The sound of a driven leaf shall put them to flight, and they shall flee as one flees from the sword, and they shall fall though no one pursues. They shall stumble over one another, as if to escape a sword, though no one pursues; and you shall have no power to stand against your enemies.

In this text from the old tradition, profound fear is imposed by God; this suggests that Ahaz is fearful because he is, so to speak, "under curse." That is, he is living and governing in contradiction to God and is reaping the consequences of his alienation from God. The reason for the alienation of the king—and therefore the reason for the king's fear—is that he assumed there were no resources for security except his own. Or, as the prophet has articulated it, those

> whose feasts consist of lyre and harp,
>   tambourine and flute and wine,
> but who do not regard the deeds of the LORD,
>   or see the work of his hands!
>   Isaiah 5:12

—those who engage in self-indulgence, and no doubt self-sufficiency, are unable to notice that the Lord does deeds (saving deeds!) and the Lord has hands that do work. It is the easy conclusion of powerful people that "God has no hands but our hands," an advanced seduction among us of Enlightenment rationality. Against such lowering of the ceiling of historical possibility to merely human capacity only, the prophetic tradition gives voice to a God who can and will and does act decisively in the historical process. Thus, Ahaz's fear is grounded in an illusion of royal ideology that can only end in fear and panic that will in turn evoke irresponsible, self-destructive policy formation.

The prophet is dispatched precisely to meet and counter royal panic. He connects the *most elemental assurance of covenantal faith* to the *specificity* of the two smaller states that threaten Jerusalem. The assurance the prophet utters that intends to counter royal panic is a phrasing that is deep in Israelite memory, as deep as the exodus tradition. As Israel long ago fled before the horses and

Standing Firm (Isaiah 7:9) 49

chariots of Pharaoh, Moses delivered the assurance to the fearful slaves amid escape:

> Do not be afraid, stand firm, and see the deliverance that the LORD will accomplish for you today; for the Egyptians whom you see today you shall never see again. The LORD will fight for you, and you have only to keep still. (Exodus 14:13–14)

That assurance dares to speak of deliverance, the termination of Pharaoh's army, and the ready engagement of YHWH into the struggle for emancipation. It is an extraordinary claim, but it is nonetheless a claim that pervades biblical faith. The prophetic insistence is characteristically that historical reality is never reduced to two players, "us" and "our enemies." Beyond those obvious two there is always a third party—God—who, unlike the idols who have no capacity to see, hear, speak, smell, or walk, "does whatever he pleases" (Psalm 115:3–7). Thus, the assurance of the prophet is not simply a practical consideration. It is a vigorous theological claim that intends to upend the entire world that King Ahaz and his contemporaries assumed. This prophetic faith, in this instance, is not only addressing a particular issue but is insisting upon the reality and freedom of God amid the historical process that has so far eventuated in royal paralysis.

The prophet alludes to the two threatening neighbor states who are about to attack Judah. This allusion leads to the prophetic "therefore" in Isaiah 7:7 that introduces the prophetic oracle. It is as though the planned attack against the city of David has evoked the "therefore" and the oracle that follows. The oracle begins in specificity. In prophetic horizon the planned attack cannot happen. This conclusion that seems to contradict the facts on the ground is confirmed by the historian:

> "Then King Rezin of Aram and King Pekah son of Remaliah of Israel came up to wage war on Jerusalem; they besieged Ahaz but could not conquer him." (2 Kings 16:5)

Imagine, "They could not conquer him"! The historian does not say why, nor does Isaiah (Isaiah 7:1). It is likely that the failure of these threats could be explained by geopolitical reality. Perhaps the Edomites mentioned in 2 Kings 16:6 distracted Ahaz's enemies, or perhaps it is the threat against these minor states from Assyria that caused this failure (see 2 Kings 16:7). It is important, however, that neither the historian nor the prophet offers an explanation. The failure to conquer lingers in the air. It vindicates the prophetic anticipation of such a failure. But it leaves open the tacit claim that YHWH is central to the protection of Jerusalem.

The prophetic oracle anticipates that these two threatening states will fail because they have poor leadership. Syria is led by Rezin; Northern Israel has as king Pekah, son of Remaliah, a nobody without pedigree who seized the throne in Samaria in a coup and who was promptly killed in turn during a second coup (2 Kings 15:25–31). It is as though Isaiah could say of these nobodies, "Don't worry about them. They have no royal mandate and no royal capacity and are about to be overrun by Tiglath Pileser III and Assyria." An editor has added to Isaiah 7:8 the retrospective notation that within sixty years—more precisely, in 722 BCE—the Northern Kingdom (Ephraim) will be obliterated. The intent of the prophetic oracle is to assert that the panic of Ahaz is disproportionate to the real threat; what appears to be a real threat amounts to nothing. It amounts to nothing because of geopolitical reality—or it amounts to nothing because the God whom Ahaz has "disregarded" (see Isaiah 5:12) will have the decisive say in the historical process. Without reference to YHWH, the king cannot possibly discern his true situation.

And then, at the end of his oracle, Isaiah delivers his decisive conclusion on the reality of faith. It is not evident in English translation, but in the Hebrew the words rendered as "stand firm in faith" and "stand" are the same term that is the root of our term "Amen." The prophetic word to the king is that having trust (being found reliable) is the prerequisite for being kept faithfully by God. Thus Isaiah is the great articulator of what faith means in the actual life of the world and in the actual realm of Ahaz. It turns out that "faith" is not concerned with doctrinal teaching, a set of propositions, or confident certitude. It is rather an attitude that yields a reliable relation to God that will permit God to govern and respond in faithful, steadfast ways. Such confidence is the antithesis of panic and fear. The prophet is summoning the king beyond his myopic governance toward the mystery of God's governance that goes under the rubric of God's providential care. "Providence" is the prophetic conviction that in hidden but decisive ways God's governance operates in, with, and under historical-military-geopolitical processes. Gerhard von Rad formulates it this way:

> And this is what Isaiah called faith—leaving room for God's sovereign action, desisting from self-help. . . . This work of Jahweh thus enfolds the whole realm of world history as it was understood at the time; and the way in which the great world empires who were proudly strutting about on this very stage of history came into collision with God's plan.[1]

When we read on in Isaiah 7, the prophet moves promptly beyond the "minor" crisis of 734 BCE. In a series of oracles, Isaiah declares that YHWH will have "a day" that will settle accounts for recalcitrant Jerusalem. There are four such oracles (excepting vv. 21–22, which is curiously a message of hope). The first of these four oracles reckons with the threat of Assyria (vv. 10–17). The second oracle anticipates the threat of the "bee" of Assyria (vv. 18–19); Jerusalem is sure to be stung! The third oracle imagines a "close shave" by Assyria (v. 20), and the fourth oracle anticipates "thorns and briers" in the abandoned land (vv. 23–25). Thus verses 10–25 confirm the immense threat of Assyria. Before that, in verses 1–9, the prophet asserts deliverance from minor threats. In both cases, the prophet treats of the governance of YHWH: it is YHWH who will deliver from trouble (vv. 1–9) and who will bring trouble (vv. 17, 19, 20).

When we read these staggering oracles, we are left with a sense that our grasp and our governance of history are, at best, penultimate. It is that hidden providence of God, so boldly voiced by Isaiah, that renders our best thinking and our best actions as less than absolute. It is the burden of the witness of Isaiah that a larger governance is at work, that, when recognized, curbs our pride as well as our fear. When our pride is not curbed, however, it evokes destructive foolishness.

It requires no keen imagination to see such foolishness and arrogance now—for example, in much US foreign policy in recent decades. As one of few remaining superpowers, we in the United States have imagined, on the one hand, that we could have our unfettered way; on the other hand, we have imagined we have responsibility (as indispensable) for the management of all of history. The tradition of Isaiah does not, of course, champion specific policies. It rather bears witness to the freedom of God that may curb both our pride and our fear.

Here is one cunning instance of acute awareness of God's curb on our pride and fear: At a moment of urgent international decision-making concerning Japan, H. Richard Niebuhr penned a remarkable warning entitled, "The Grace of Doing Nothing."[2] His theme was that military policy must reckon with the work of divine providence, and that even great military power cannot preempt that reality. Niebuhr's argument is an important modern echo of Isaiah's counsel to King Ahaz.[3] This witness, ancient or more recent, depends on a vigorous affirmation of the reality and governance of God. Such an affirmation is strenuously demanding in every crisis and any crisis. It is offered by the prophet an as antidote to panic. Later on in the book of Isaiah, the same "fear not" of divine assurance will be voiced in different circumstances (41:13; 43:1, 5). The book of Isaiah, in all of its parts, attests the governance of YHWH. As we will see, this governance concerns the "design" of God for the disposal of the several international superpowers that seek ultimacy beyond any curb of holiness. It is no small matter to assert faith in the face of such terrifying predation.

Questions for Discussion

1. How do you define providence? Do you trust that God's governance works in, with, and under various human processes?

2. Do you agree that our grasp and governance of history are "at best, penultimate"? Is that encouraging or discouraging in your opinion?

3. Imagine yourself in Ahaz's situation (or another dire predicament). How might you stand firm in faith?

Chapter 9

"God-with-Us" and the "Virgin" (Isaiah 7:14)

Therefore the Lord himself will give you a sign. Look, the young woman is with child and shall bear a son, and shall name him Immanuel.

> **Scripture Passages for Reference**
>
> Isaiah 7:10–17, 20–25
> Isaiah 8:1–10
> Matthew 1:18–25
> Luke 1:26–38

As with Isaiah 6, chapter 7 also contains more than one pivotal passage. In the case of the present verse, it must be admitted that it is probably the most familiar text to Christians who may otherwise know little of Isaiah. This is, of course, because our verse is used in the birth account of Matthew's Gospel, which is so important in Advent. The importance of Matthew's birth account, in turn, has no doubt led to the wide use of Isaiah during the Advent season.

In Matthew 1, an angel appears in a dream to Joseph to dissuade him from divorcing Mary quietly (1:18–20). The angel explains the situation: "Joseph, son of David, do not be afraid to take Mary as your wife, for the child conceived in her is from the Holy Spirit. She will bear a son, and you are to name him Jesus, for he will save his people from their sins" (1:20b–21). Matthew then offers a bit of commentary that connects this remarkable moment to the plans of God that have come before:

> All this took place to fulfill what had been spoken by the Lord through the prophet:
>
> "Look, the virgin shall conceive and bear a son,
>   and they shall name him Emmanuel,"
> which means, "God is with us." (1:22–23)

The prophet in question is, of course, Isaiah. The slight difference in spelling of the child's name—Immanuel versus Emmanuel—is purely the result of how the English and Greek translations, respectively, have rendered the original Hebrew. (In the ancient Greek translation of Isaiah 7:14 that Matthew would have had access to as a Greek speaker, the spelling is identical to that in Matthew 1:23.) That Hebrew original can be represented graphically as *imma-nu-el*, which highlights the three parts of the name: "with" (*'im*) "us" (*nu*) "God" (*'el*). Theophoric names—names that contain God's name or a divine title—were very common in biblical times, and in this case, the name is best understood as a sentence: "With us (is) God" or, using common English word order, "God (is) with us." Matthew earns extra points: he got the meaning of the name I/Emmanuel just right!

But what about the "virgin" part? As with his spelling of "Emmanuel," Matthew seems to be following the Greek translation of the Hebrew Old Testament. In Isaiah 7:14, the Greek reads "virgin" (*parthenos*). In Matthew's account, *parthenos* is a technical word, employed almost scientifically, as it were. We are first told that after Mary and Joseph had been engaged but before they lived together (at which point marriages were typically consummated), Mary "was found to be with child from the Holy Spirit" (Matthew 1:18). Next, after the dream, we learn that Joseph followed the angel's instructions—he did not divorce Mary despite this illicit conception—but Matthew adds that the two "had no marital relations" until Mary had "borne a son; and he named him Jesus" (vv. 24–25). Luke 1 supports this technical understanding of *parthenos*. There, upon receiving her own angelic visitor who delivers the news of her divine conception, Mary questions the biology: "How will this happen since I haven't had sexual relations with a man?" (Luke 1:34, CEB). According to both Matthew and Luke, therefore, it seems clear that, when it comes to Mary, *parthenos* means "virgin."

But what of Isaiah 7? Does the technical use in the Gospels mean that our verse, too, refers to a miraculous, virginal conception of a child? The answer is "Yes" according to the King James Version, which reads, "Behold, a virgin shall conceive." But with all due respect to that venerable translation, the answer to the question in the original Hebrew seems to be "No" or at least "Not necessarily." Isaiah 7:14 uses a Hebrew term that appears broader than "virgin" in Matthew's more technical sense. The word, *'almāh*, refers to a young woman, especially of marriageable age, with some scholars believing the term was used even of a married woman prior to the birth of her first child. "A young woman of marriageable age" often coincided with virginity in antiquity, but "a married woman prior to parturition" obviously did not—only virgin births occur without sexual relations first! Alas, *'almāh* does not occur often in the Hebrew Bible, so certainty eludes us as to its precise meaning (Genesis 24:43; Exodus 2:8; Psalm 68:26; Song 1:3; 6:8; Proverbs 30:19). Moreover, words for various stages of life are also rather unspecific in Hebrew, as is evident later in Isaiah 7, which is vague about some point in time when the child Immanuel will know how "to refuse the evil and choose the good" (vv. 15–16). Inquiring minds would like to know the precise age at which that happened in ancient Israel. Perhaps it coincided with the magical time of confirmation in Christian circles: twelve years old (or so)! More likely, given the language used, the age of the child in mind in Isaiah 7 would have been two to three years, maybe four at most.

An important factor to consider is that there are other Greek versions of Isaiah besides the one that translates *'almāh* with *parthenos*. Some of these, including ones known to be more wooden, chose a different Greek word, *neanis*. This other Greek term is a generic one for "young woman" and thus *not* a technical term having to do with sexual relations. If that is what *'almāh* means, too, then *neanis* is a very good translation and *parthenos* a less good one.[1]

Words certainly mean things, but words mean things most clearly in larger contexts, alongside other words, in sentences and paragraphs, and so forth. At this point, then, the larger context of Isaiah

7 must be recalled to help us decide what translation and interpretation is best. According to chapter 7, Isaiah is standing before King Ahaz of Judah, who is shaking like a tree in a heavy wind in the face of a serious military threat (v. 2). Two foreign powers have made an alliance and turned hostile toward Jerusalem. They have plotted evil, planned a coup, and now stand at Ahaz's door (vv. 5–6). This is the conflict known as the Syro-Ephraimite war (ca. 734–732 BCE), which occupies parts of Isaiah (7:1–8:18) and obviously occupied King Ahaz and his people. But, Isaiah prophesies, these plans "shall not stand" and "shall not come to pass" (7:7).

Right after this word of hope and deliverance (vv. 7–9), God tells King Ahaz to request a sign—one that would presumably confirm the divine promises (vv. 10–11; cf. 2 Kings 19:29). Ahaz refuses (Isaiah 7:12). We do not know why but we may posit that it was due to a kind of false piety, because Isaiah responds to Ahaz in apparent frustration:

> Then Isaiah said: "Hear then, O house of David! Is it too little for you to weary mortals, that you weary my God also?" (7:13)

Then comes our verse with its mention of a "young woman" (*'almāh*) or "virgin" (*parthenos*), followed by the nonspecific age of accountability for baby Immanuel. This latter bit proves to be of great importance to resolving our question about the meaning of *'almāh* as "virgin" or something else:

> For before the child knows how to refuse the evil and choose the good, the land before whose two kings you are in dread will be deserted. (7:16)

Put differently: "Don't worry, Ahaz, because by the time this child Immanuel reaches an unspecific-but-presumably-not-too-old age, the hostile powers at your gates, who want to depose and replace you, will be gone."

That is a positive word to be sure, but if the Immanuel in question is Jesus, with the "virgin" Mary of Nazareth, it loses most of its force since Ahaz reigned in Judah ca. 743–728 BCE but Jesus isn't born until approximately seven centuries later. Of course Ahaz's rivals will be long gone by then, but so will he! Isaiah's sign of Immanuel

"God-with-Us" and the "Virgin" (Isaiah 7:14)   57

must apply first and foremost to Ahaz and his time, since it is a sign that confirms God's assurance in the midst of his pressing military conflict. Three items are important at this point.

First, a number of scholars have noted that the prophet Isaiah has a penchant for children with symbolic names. Already in chapter 7, there is mention of his son Shear-jashub, which means "a remnant shall return" (v. 3). In the very next chapter we hear of another son with the name Maher-shalal-hash-baz—a mouthful to be sure!—which means "the spoil speeds, the prey hastens" (8:3). The first son's name seems hopeful, indicating there will be survivors from the coming divine judgment who will return to the land; the second is obviously more punitive, specifying—not unlike 7:16—how quickly the capital cities of Damascus and Samaria will be deposed by Assyria (8:4). Maher-shalal-hash-baz's mother is identified as a "prophetess" (8:3). Many assume this is a reference to Isaiah's wife, in which case she would also be the mother of Shear-jashub. In context, our verse comes between these two symbolically named children, increasing the likelihood that Immanuel, too, is a second of three symbolically named sons, and thus another of Isaiah's own children. (Hosea, too, has three children with symbolic names.) If so, the 'almāh of our verse would be the same as "the prophetess" of 8:3 and is none other than Isaiah's wife.[2] Her conception and birth of Immanuel is thus imminent, and so Immanuel's reaching the age of accountability is not too far off—within Ahaz's lifetime—just a few years off at most. This soon-to-pass sign does indeed confirm the divine promise of deliverance. This shows once more that the prophetic word is not generic or unspecific but uttered in the midst of particular circumstances as a word on target.

Second, even if the above is quite right about 'almāh and the timing of the sign of Immanuel, Matthew nevertheless finds in our verse a text about Jesus, his conception, and his mother. Even so, we would do Isaiah 7 a great injustice if we believe it was *originally and only* about the Christ child. Believing that this text is about the coming of Christ seven centuries after Ahaz's emergency would make Isaiah 7 a word *not* on target, but something else altogether, something far more akin to the future-telling Nostradamus than Isaiah the son of Amoz. But we would also do a great injustice to Matthew if we did not take seriously his sense that our verse *nevertheless somehow also* applies to the birth of Jesus. How this is so is a complicated matter. Theologians sometimes speak of a "fuller" sense or meaning of Scripture (the *sensus plenior*). In such a perspective, our verse meant one thing in Ahaz's time, but, in a fuller sense, it meant something else, something *further*, in the first century at the turn of the eras. Matthew's own language is revealing at this point. He states, "This took place *to fulfill* [*plērōthē*] what had been spoken" by God through Isaiah (Matthew 1:22). Throughout his Gospel, Matthew is at pains to show how Old Testament texts are fulfilled, sometimes mentioning Isaiah by name (see 2:15, 23; 4:14; 8:17; 12:17; 13:35; 21:4; see also 3:3; 13:14). But Matthew's language also recognizes that this fulfillment isn't the same as a one-for-one identicalness. Note how the angel who addresses Joseph specifies the child's name as *Jesus*, relating that name to salvation from sin (1:21). That is, in fact, what Joseph names his son (v. 25). But Matthew's editorial comment, which works so hard to connect this moment back to Isaiah, does not use *Jesus* but *Immanuel*, a name that is related, not to salvation, but to divine presence.

We should note, finally, that our verse appears in a passage that seems somewhat double-edged. Yes, there is deliverance from Aram and Samaria, but the means of that deliverance—the razor that is the king of Assyria—cuts both ways (see Isaiah 7:20–25). Promise can be laced with threat, judgment with deliverance. Ahaz and all others must keep that in mind. "A remnant shall return" may mean that "*only* a remnant shall return" (cf. 10:20–23; 11:11–16). The name Imma-Nu-El might be more of the same. It promises divine presence, but that, too, can be two-sided (see 8:8, 10). Much later, a young woman discovered the same about another, belated Immanuel:

> Then Simeon blessed them and said to his mother Mary, "This child is destined for the falling and the rising of many in Israel, and to be a sign that will be opposed so that the inner thoughts of many will be revealed—and a sword will pierce your own soul too. (Luke 2:34–35)

Questions for Discussion

1. Have you ever heard of a translation other than "virgin" in Isaiah 7:14?
2. What do you make of the sign of Immanuel in King Ahaz's day?
3. Can you think of other instances in the Bible that seem to reflect a "fuller" or "further" sense of the Old Testament?

Chapter 10

A Child Has Been Born for Us! (Isaiah 9:6)

For a child has been born for us,
  a son given to us;
authority rests on his shoulders;
  and he is named
Wonderful Counselor, Mighty God,
  Everlasting Father, Prince of Peace.

> ### Scripture Passages for Reference
>
> Isaiah 9:2–7
> Isaiah 2:2–4
> Isaiah 4:2–6
> Isaiah 8:20–22
> Isaiah 11:1–9
> Judges 6:4–6
> Psalm 72
> Psalm 89

This familiar poem of Isaiah 9:2–7 is one of four promises in the first section of the book of Isaiah. The others are 2:2–4, 4:2–6, and 11:1–9. In each of the four promises the *oracle of hope* follows immediately upon a *harsh prophetic denunciation or threat*. In each of these cases, the promise that follows prophetic harshness makes clear that the assertion of prophetic judgment is a penultimate utterance and not the final word. The same move *from judgment to hope* is reflected in larger scale in the structure of the book of Isaiah: chapters 1–39 mostly concern judgment, and chapters 40–66 anticipate restoration. Thus the smaller texts voice *in nuce* the large claim of the book of Isaiah.

In our prophetic oracle of promise, the prophetic harshness that precedes is voiced in 8:20–22; it speaks of "distress, darkness, gloom, anguish, and thick darkness." While the terms are generically negative, most interpreters judge that, in context, the terms refer to the threat of Assyria that kept Jerusalem in distress. Thus there is reference to the threat of Assyria in 7:17, 18, 20; 8:4, 7. Assyria was an aggressive superpower that threatened all of the smaller states of the Fertile Crescent, including both Northern Israel and Judah in the south. In 8:4, there is reference to the Assyrian assault on Samaria, the capital city of Northern Israel.

In 9:1, the narrative commentary juxtaposes the "former time" of contempt and the "latter time" of well-being. That "former time" was the time when Assyria was contemptuous of the minor vulnerable states; the latter time is an anticipation that life will be good beyond the time when the Assyrians have been decisively rebuffed.

The way in which the poetry of 9:2 follows the prose of 9:1 suggests that 9:2–7 is a set poetic piece that has been placed here to illuminate what is meant in 9:1 by the "latter time." The "latter time" anticipated by the prophet is a time when Jerusalem has been delivered from the "deep distress" of the Assyrian threat. This set poetic piece may have been a liturgical piece used in the Jerusalem temple. That temple was unmistakably a venue in which the centrality of the Davidic dynasty for the life of Israel was legitimated and celebrated. Thus it is possible, given 9:6, that we have a liturgical piece set in the temple that celebrated the birth of a new "son" of the Davidic dynasty, assuring that the dynasty would continue as carrier of YHWH's royal promises (see 2 Samuel 7; Psalm 89:3–4, 35–37). Or, alternatively, the liturgical celebration could have been for the coronation of a new Davidic king so that the lyric of "birth" in Isaiah 9:6 is simply an affirmation that Jerusalem has a royal heir. Whether it is celebration of a birth or a coronation, it is either way an affirmation that the

A Child Has Been Born for Us! (Isaiah 9:6) 63

core hope for the well-being of Jerusalem depends upon the effective governance of the Davidic house. The dynasty has a chance, with the blessing of YHWH, to withstand the Assyrian threat. Like all such liturgical legitimacy, this poem is partly an *affirmation of faith* as it is partly an *act of propaganda* for a particular political claim. Given all of that, it is most plausible that the "son" who is celebrated at birth or at coronation is King Hezekiah, son of Ahaz, who will in the end preside over the rescue of Jerusalem from the Assyrian threat (see chaps. 36–37).

The first part of the poem, addressed to YHWH as "you," celebrates a new sense of well-being made possible by the "great light" of royal recovery. The celebration of recovery for that threat is not unlike "joy at the harvest," as when peasant farmers got a good crop with their entire annual income in one season harvest. Or we might imagine the exuberance at delivery is not unlike Victory in Europe (VE) Day in London when the threat of German assault was eliminated. We can imagine there was dancing in the streets of Jerusalem, much happy drinking and feasting, and great celebration. The poem likens this unrestrained joy to the great ancient victory over the Midianites in the book of Judges. In that narrative the Midianites constituted an immense threat to Israel:

> They would encamp against them and destroy the produce of the land, as far as the neighborhood of Gaza, and leave no sustenance in Israel, and no sheep or ox or donkey. For they and their livestock would come up, and they would even bring their tents, as thick as locusts; neither they nor their camels could be counted; so they wasted the land as they came in. Thus Israel was greatly impoverished because of Midian; and the Israelites cried out to the LORD for help. (Judges 6:4–6)

That narrative tells how YHWH empowered Gideon, who marshaled a sufficient military force to defeat the Midianites and so gave relief to the Israelites (Judges 7:24–8:21). This present relief from Assyria is "as the day of Midian" (Isaiah 9:4). Isaiah 9:5 offers a dramatic scene wherein all of the military equipment of the Assyrians is captured and burned in a way that eliminated the threat of Assyria. It is a glorious moment of relief for Jerusalem. We notice, moreover, that thus far in the poem (vv. 2–5) the action of triumph is credited only to God; there is no human agent, not even a Gideon (as in the narrative of Judges). Only in verse 6 do we get our first reference to a human agent in deliverance. It is always a blessing and a relief when the dynasty gets an heir. It ensures that the family line will continue. (For the sad catastrophe of the end of the royal line, see Jeremiah 22:30.) As already noted, it is possible that we may take this celebrative declaration, in context, with reference to Hezekiah, either to his birth or his coronation. In the common chronology, the reign of Hezekiah began in 715 BCE. On the basis of 2 Kings 18:1 this would date his birth to 744 BCE, near the end of the reign of Uzziah (Azariah), but we lack precision about such data.

What is clear in verses 6–7 is that the birth or coronation of the new king was cause for great liturgical affirmation. Like every monarch, even a most modest one, liturgical celebration tends to pile up honorific titles. In this case the liturgical exuberance yields four such titles.[1] The first is "Wonderful Counselor." (We note that Handel in his familiar *Messiah* made a mistake by placing a comma between the two words.) The phrase sees in the new king a quite astonishing royal wise one. The other phrases gladly overstate the reality of the new king. To call the king "Mighty God" does not suggest divinity, but only a matter of uncommon power and authority. The king is "Everlasting Father" of the realm, provider of well-being and security in a patriarchal setting. He will, moreover, be "Prince of *Shalom*," a term that means not only "peace" but general social well-being. These four titles assigned to the new king are like the expectation of every political campaign that assures that the new governance will be one of "peace and prosperity." We may refer to the royal Psalm 72 that links care for the poor and needy to "prosperity" (*shalom*, v. 3), expanded domain (v. 8), long life (v. 15), and agricultural flourishing of "amber waves of grain" (v. 16). All of that flourishing is expected of the new king because the new king is dispatched by the God who wills only good for Israel and for Jerusalem.

It is further anticipated in 9:7 that the territory of the Davidic house would expand and that expansion would lead to a broader peace characterized by "justice and righteousness." Thus the song anticipates that the regime will enact the preferred prophetic word pair that we have seen in 1:21 and 5:7. Israel will, as a result, prosper without restraint or limitation.

Finally, this promissory oracle seals the deal of this future time by the concluding line, which asserts that YHWH has intense passion to fulfill this hope. Notice that the ultimate assurance is not in the effectiveness of the king per se but is rather in the fidelity of YHWH, who keeps promises. It is YHWH as creator who will ensure the success of the agricultural economy, because that economy depends upon "justice and righteousness" so that the creation may be willingly and gladly generative. It is YHWH who will ensure political advantage and necessary military success to the regime. This liturgical piece of hope comes at a moment in the life of Israel when it had great hope for well-being after the threat of Assyria had been repelled. As we will see, Hezekiah was able to deliver on that hope. Like every such liturgical exuberance, no one at the moment could foresee that these extravagant expectations would not be perpetual for the house of David. It turns out eventually that these promises ran out in the face of the failure of the regime:

> Lord, where is your steadfast love of old,
>   which by your faithfulness you swore to David?
>   Psalm 89:49

But not now! Not for a long time! Jerusalem had miles to go before its failure caught up with its ruling class. For now, all is well; at the very least the governing class could take great heart as it departed the liturgy.

As the most Jewish of the early Christian evangelists, Matthew found this poetic text a useful way to render the entry of Jesus into his ministry. Thus Matthew places Jesus in the territory of "Zebulon and Naphtali," surely an anachronism in the first century (4:13). That geographical placement then permits Matthew to appeal to our Isaiah text in order to assert that it is now Jesus who enters into history as "a great light." Jesus brings the new governance ("kingdom") that will end the darkness. Matthew does not specify the darkness. Maybe it is Rome that stands in for Assyria, or, in conventional Christian parlance, the darkness is to be understood as the rule of death, so that Jesus is the ultimate hope that death cannot and will not win. It has subsequently become easy for the Christian tradition (helped along by Handel's *Messiah*) to assign the four titles of Isaiah 9:6 to Jesus. The "increase of his government," moreover, is reflected in the conclusion of Matthew in his ultimate commissioning of the disciples:

> All authority in heaven and on earth has been given to me. Go therefore.... (Matthew 28:18–19)

That mandate later gave impetus for the worldwide missionary movement, an attempt to implement the mandate in Isaiah in the form of the Christian movement, which was unfortunately sometimes deeply and uncritically marked by Western (American) values. In some (certainly not all!) of this missionary activity, it is clear that the church was better at remembering the titles assigned to Jesus by appeal to expansion of "territory" than it was at remembering the imperative to seek "justice and righteousness." The latter has too often been forgotten in the church; no doubt that dreadful neglect is now coming home to roost in much of the Western church. Not unlike ancient Israel, the church has often forgotten *the imperative mandate* of the creator God while embracing *the lavish promises* from the utterance of God.

Questions for Discussion

1. How do you see Isaiah's four titles applying to a faithful king like Hezekiah?
2. How do you see the four titles applied to Christ in the New Testament?
3. How best can we embrace God's lavish promises without forgetting God's imperative mandates?

Chapter 11

The Rod of God's Anger (Isaiah 10:15)

Shall the ax vaunt itself over the one who wields it,
or the saw magnify itself against the one who handles it?
As if a rod should raise the one who lifts it up,
or as if a staff should lift the one who is not wood!

> **Scripture Passages for Reference**
>
> Isaiah 10:5–11
> Isaiah 45:9
> Isaiah 47:6

Isaiah practices his prophetic imagination on an expansive international scale. To be sure, Jerusalem is always at the center of his concern. At the same time, however, the prophet has no doubt that YHWH governs the international community and every nation-state, including the superpowers of his time: all are subject to YHWH's purposes. In the context of the eighth century BCE, that expansive international scale inescapably drew attention to the empire of Assyria, the superpower to the north of Israel that was matched in power only by Egypt to the south. With the reign of Tiglath-pileser III (745–727) Assyria exercised its primacy of power in the region with a strong reach of economic leverage and military aggressiveness (see 2 Kings 16:7–10). Consequently, Assyria was a continuing threat to Israel and Judah through the rule of Tiglath-pileser III, Sargon II, and Sennacherib.

It is Isaiah's contention that the threat of Assyria toward Jerusalem was evoked by YHWH as punishment against wayward Judah, and so Assyria was dispatched by YHWH for that purpose. This Yahwistic explanation for the threat makes clear that the prophet has no interest whatsoever that there might be geopolitical reasons for the aggression of Assyria. Assyria destroyed the state of Northern Israel and its capital city, Samaria, in 722 BCE under Sargon II (2 Kings 17:5–6). This was during the time when Ahaz was king in Judah. In the time of Ahab's son Hezekiah, Jerusalem just barely escaped capture in 701 BCE by Sennacherib in what was understood by Isaiah to be a miraculous delivery by YHWH (Isaiah 37:36–38). It may be that this dramatic failure of the Assyrian invasion is the context for our present verse.

Our poem begins in 10:5. This verse begins with "Woe" (NRSV has "Ah"), a term that bespeaks big trouble coming upon the one addressed. Assyria at the moment is said by the prophet to be under threat by YHWH. But before that, Assyria is identified by YHWH as YHWH's "rod," that is, an instrument of leverage or a weapon. Assyria is a club that YHWH is ready to wield. That "club" is dispatched by YHWH against a "godless nation" (v. 6). The term "godless" means "transgressed my commandments." Thus it is Judah that is "godless," that has rejected the will and purpose of YHWH. No particulars are given about Judah's transgression, but we know from other texts that the failure of Judah is the refusal to enact "justice and righteousness" in the political economy. Because of that disobedience, YHWH is provoked to "fury." As a consequence, furious YHWH summons Assyria, one of YHWH's available tools, to "take spoil and seize plunder," that is, to invade and occupy the city. The phrasing of verse 6 is informed by what every invading army is sure to do. The Assyrians are to "tread down" Judah in defeat, humiliation, and shame. Thus the prophet can see an overarching divine purpose in which we might otherwise see only the violent way in which a superpower may overrun a vulnerable state. It is exactly the work of the prophet to insist that a "normal" reading of history according to Realpolitik is inadequate, because such a reading disregards the purpose and work of the Lord of history.

The poetry of Isaiah pivots on the conjunction of verse 7, "but." The term is an adversative whereby Assyria contradicts YHWH's purpose for which Assyria was dispatched against Jerusalem. Isaiah declares that Assyria failed to be in sync with the purpose of YHWH. The contradiction between YHWH's purpose and Assyria's action is one of scale, intent, and intensity. YHWH authorizes "spoil, plunder, and treading down." But Assyria, a relentless superpower, did not stop at that. It went beyond this specific mandate of YHWH and went on to far more brutality than YHWH intended (v. 7). Isaiah does not explain to us how Assyria was to have known the limit of YHWH of brutality against Judah, but as YHWH's "rod" Assyria should have known better. Notice the close reasoning by the poet that is operative here. It is a distinction between "treading down" that YHWH intends and the "cutting off" that Assyria performed. The "cutting off" is more brutal than "treading down," and YHWH will not tolerate action that exceeds YHWH's intent.

In the verses that follow, the poem at some length narrates why it is that Assyria exceeded its mandate from YHWH (vv. 8–14). In a self-congratulatory boast that Isaiah puts into the mouth of the Assyrians, we get a glimpse of imperial reasoning that justifies brutal behavior. All the peoples are just alike. They are all to be conquered. The several conquered peoples are all adulterers. Jerusalem and Samaria are just like all other capitals. Thus in the Assyrian calculus, these two capital cities and their states merit the same destruction as all the others. The superpower will not pause to discriminate one such state for any other. All are subject to immense brutalizing power. The prose of verse 12 makes the point clear. Assyria, like every superpower, thinks it is a law unto itself. It is filled with "arrogant boasting" and "haughty pride" that leads it to act without restraint by YHWH's will, not held in check by any abhorrence of brutality. It is shameless in its work of devastation and suffering.

In verses 13–14 the arrogance of Assyria is brought to speech with lines filled with the braggadocio of first-person pronouns:

By the strength of *my* hand *I* have done it
By *my* wisdom, for *I* have understanding
I have removed . . . plundered
I have brought down

> *My* hand has found
> *I* have gathered

Every superpower imagines it is a law unto itself. Or as one White House official asserted not so long ago, "We don't react to history. We make history." Assyria was busy "making history" through its brutalizing capacity without reference to any limitation imposed by human suffering, by the distinctiveness of Judah that it never recognized, or by the restraint of the Lord of history.

Thus our sequence: (1) *YHWH dispatches* Assyria against Judah; (2) *Assyria oversteps* its mandate from YHWH by not being restrained by YHWH's purpose. And now in our verse, (3) *YHWH responds* to Assyria's arrogance. In our verse the metaphor of "ax" and "wielder of ax" refers to Assyria as ax and YHWH as one who wields the ax. And now Assyria rejects its role on behalf of YHWH and acts without reference to the one who would wield it. (A similar image is offered in Isaiah 45:9 with the clay asserting its autonomy from the potter.) Such autonomy is unthinkable and impossible, for it yields an ax that is destructively out of control.

These rhetorical equations lead to the ominous "therefore" of verse 16. For that reason because of the defiance of Assyria against the intention of YHWH, YHWH will now act decisively against Assyria. The mighty superpower cannot contradict the purposes of YHWH and so will end in wasting sickness and fire that destroy body and soul (vv. 16–19)! The imagery is breathtaking. Even superpowers must come to terms with the rule of YHWH. Like every superpower, Assyria learned that the hard way—the only way superpowers (can) ever learn.

This astonishing claim is reiterated later in the book of Isaiah with reference to Babylon, the superpower that succeeded Assyria. In Isaiah 47, it is asserted that YHWH had dispatched mighty Babylon against Judah. Babylon was given free rein to seize the city of Jerusalem and its temple. Again, however, we have a reversal in the midst of verse 6:

> You showed them no mercy;
> on the aged you made your yoke
> exceedingly heavy.

Babylon showed no mercy to Judah. It should have known better! Once again, Isaiah does not tell us why or how Babylon should have known about YHWH's limit on brutality against Jerusalem. Perhaps Babylon should have known because YHWH's purpose was correction and not destruction. But the superpower Babylon, not unlike the superpower Assyria, failed to take into account that the action of YHWH against Jerusalem was an act of faithful governance. And for that reason Babylon, like Assyria, will be terminated.

This prophetic reasoning is not easy in our modern world. We may, however, consider how this theological limitation and restraint on a superpower might be translated into modern parlance. Paul Kennedy, in his remarkable study *The Rise and Fall of the Great Powers*, has traced the way in which the empires of Portugal, the Netherlands, and Great Britain have successively fallen apart.[1] His careful judgment is that, in every case, the superpower of the time overreached and destroyed itself by overspending on military adventurism. Kennedy has no interest in theological claims. His analysis is not unlike that of Isaiah, however; there are *intractable givens* in historical reality that all the power and smarts in the world cannot outflank. In Isaiah's horizon, those givens are identified as the resilient, nonnegotiable purpose of God. That resilient purpose is "justice and righteousness," which must prevail. In modern parlance those same givens might be taken as the economic reality of budgetary limitation that will not yield to exploitative money, power, or wisdom. There is in this reasoning, ancient or modern, theological or secular, a sober alert for the United States that is one of the major superpowers in our present day. Our own local superpower, for all of its confidence in its exceptionalism, does not make or merit exemption from such God-given givens.

Thus Assyria (or any of its replications) comes to a sorry end. The inverse side of that sorry ending concerns YHWH's passionate commitment to Israel. Even in the face of the "godlessness" of ancient Israel, YHWH nonetheless persists in particular attentiveness to Judah and Jerusalem. It turns out, according to Isaiah, that there is a limit to what can be imposed on Israel. In the end, Israel is given "mercy" even in the world of Realpolitik.

Questions for Discussion

1. Can you think of historical events that could be seen as evidence of God's hand at work?
2. Did those events ever go too far—farther, that is, than you imagine God would want?
3. Which "givens" ought we to recognize today? Are they God-given? Are we overstepping these divine limits in some fashion? How so?

Chapter 12

The Shoot from Jesse's Stump (Isaiah 11:1)

*A shoot shall come from the stump of Jesse,
and a branch shall grow out of his roots.*

> **Scripture Passages for Reference**
>
> Isaiah 11:1–9
> Isaiah 2:2–4
> Isaiah 4:2–6
> Isaiah 9.2–7
> Deuteronomy 17:14–20
> 1 Samuel 16:13
> Psalm 72
> Psalm 146
> Mark 10:47–48
> Luke 1:52–53
> Luke 7:22
> Colossians 1:17–20

This well-known poem of 11:1–9 is the fourth promise in early Isaiah after 2:2–4, 4:2–6, and 9:2–7. As with the other three promises, this one also follows after and reverses the negative imagery that precedes it. In 10:27b–34 the poetry traces the movement of a terrifying invading army that will threaten Israel. The poetry tells of the movement of the army from north to south until it come to "shake his fist" in the face of Zion and Jerusalem (10:32). In context, it is most plausible that this poetry pertains to the advance of the Assyrian army of Sennacherib, though the poem does not provide any specific identity. In verse 33 the poem affirms that it is the "Sovereign, the LORD of hosts" who is doing the harsh work of lopping, cutting down, bringing low, and hacking down (vv. 33–34). Yet again, an invading army is portrayed as a vehicle for the action of YHWH. The imagery of the poem could accommodate other crises as well, but here it seems to refer to the Assyrians.

Then in 11:1 the poetry voices a sharp reversal that contradicts what has just gone before. The God of promises begins to act. The reference to "Jesse," David's father, indicates that the subject of the poem is the dynasty of David. That the dynasty is a "stump" refers to a time when Davidic rule had been brought low and humiliated, or even maybe terminated. The affirmation of the poem is that this "stump," hopeless and without a life or a future, now will generate a "shoot," a new beginning in the way a shoot may appear inexplicably from a stump taken for dead. The poem is an anticipation or celebration of a revival or restoration of the Davidic line after its dramatic and seemingly irreversible failure. The poem, in three moves, traces the wondrous and immense impact that the restoration of the house of David will effect.

First, it is affirmed that the new unnamed king will be empowered and authorized by the "spirit of the LORD" (v. 2). This is indeed a God-sent, God-authorized ruler, a relative of the first David. At the anointing of the first David as king, it is reported,

> The spirit of the LORD came mightily upon David from that day forward. (1 Samuel 16:13)

Now this belated representative of the same family receives the same spirit. When it is remembered that the Hebrew word for "spirit" (*ruah*) is also "breath," these lines may indicate that the new king has great vitality. In this regard, this new David is contrasted with the other rulers:

> Do not put your trust in princes,
>   in mortals, in whom there is no help.

When their breath departs, they return to the earth;
on that very day their plans perish.
                                        Psalm 146:3-4

The spirit-breath of the new king is marked by all the best ingredients of good rule: wisdom, understanding, counsel, might, knowledge, and fear of the Lord. This is perhaps in contrast to recently remembered kings in Jerusalem who pitifully lacked all these qualities. Jerusalem will now have a Davidic king who rules in a way attentive to YHWH.

Second, this wise ruler is now fully characterized as one who works according to the expectations of Torah (vv. 3b–5). While the imagery of verse 5 may be metaphorical, it refers to particular formal dress donned by the king for coronation in which his robes bear belts with names: righteousness and faithfulness. It could be that the Davidic king actually dressed in that way for such an occasion. And if not, the liturgy of coronation would have indicated as much. That is, the proper markings of the new king are not money or power or knowledge but the ancient commendations of covenantal fidelity. It is further anticipated in these verses that the new king will rule according to the neighborly requirements of the Torah. The new king will not be misled by the appearances of money and influences (v. 3) but will be attentive to the poor and meek who have no attractive appearance at all. The king will adjudicate economic matters by his "wisdom and understanding" in order to rule justly, and he will weigh in on the side of economic justice and equity for the vulnerable (cf. Deuteronomy 17:14–20).

It follows in verse 4 that the king must stand decisively against the "wicked," those who are arrogantly self-serving and self-seeking in a way that contradicts the common good of the community. This is nothing less than a government that is in the service of the poor. Or in the parlance of liberation theology, this is a king who exercises a "preferential option for the poor." Obviously, in the governance imagined here, there could be no court case like *Citizens United* that turned the government over to concealed big money and gave domination to the oligarchy of the wealthy. Isaiah envisions government "from below."

Third, in the ancient world of kingship, the work of the king was to cause all of creation to function in healthy, abundant ways. Thus the Davidic king plays the role of "Adam" from the Genesis story who has the responsibility to "keep and till" creation in order that it should flourish (Genesis 2:15). In verses 6–9 of our poem, it is anticipated that the new king will revivify a functioning harmonious creation. The royal Psalm 72 alternates between care for the poor (vv. 2, 12–14) and the full functioning of creation (vv. 3, 6–7, 16). That psalm dares to affirm a decisive linkage between *care for the poor* and the *proper work of creation*. That is, a just *human economy* is a precondition of a just, *harmonious, functioning creation*. To hold the king responsible for this is to suggest that governmental rules and decisions can indeed make a difference in how creation works. The responsibility of the king for this is not unlike a common assumption in the United States that the executive branch is responsible for the economy and the maintenance of the stock market. And, given the crisis of climate change, it is easy enough to see that when the human economy is organized to serve only the interests of big money and big power, two things are sure to happen: *The environment is violated* and will, perforce, suffer; and *the human community will be disordered* through exploitation and injustice.

We may wonder at the particulars of the reconciliation in verses 6–8: wolf-lamb, leopard-kid, calf-lion, cow-bear, lion-ox, child-asp, child-adder. All of those old enmities become functioning friendships. All of those seeming impossibilities now can be enacted under the aegis of the new king who will reorder human economy and restore the proper functioning of creation that is no longer at odds with itself because of greedy exploitation. If we imagine such reconciliation of wolf and lamb is not possible, then we do not yet grasp the radicality of the new king, for the reconciliation of wolf and lamb is no more unthinkable than justice for the poor.

While we may be dazzled by the particulars of this imagery of reconciliation, we should not lose sight of the primary claim of the poem—namely, that all of creation, human and animal, will be restored to full relationality intended by the creator. This is the work of the new king. It is the work of government! It is clear that such *restoration of the environment* and such *reordering of the human economy* necessitate an activist government with the effective use of regulation to curb every impetus for human exploitation or the destruction of the environment.

We may note in passing that, after the completion of our poem, the next verses in Isaiah anticipate that the "root of Jesse" will recover the remnant of scattered exiles (11:11) and "assemble the outcasts of Israel" (11:12). This is in every way a radical new beginning! It is easy to see why the Christian tradition has found this poem in Isaiah to be an anticipation of the coming of Jesus as the ultimate "son of David" who will enact the *restoration of creation* and *recovery of the human economy*. Such a look toward Jesus was not on the horizon of Isaiah in his original historical context. As the early church looked back at Isaiah, however, it found this poem helpful in understanding the identity of Jesus. Thus Mary at the outset sings of a radical inversion of the economy wrought by her son:

> He has brought down the powerful from their thrones,
>   and lifted up the lowly;
> he has filled the hungry with good things,
>   and sent the rich away empty.
>   Luke 1:52–53

Luke can summarize the restorative work of Jesus:

> Go and tell John what you have seen and heard: the blind receive their sight, the lame walk, the lepers are cleansed, the deaf hear, the dead are raised, the poor have good news brought to them. (Luke 7:22)

In the witness of Paul, moreover, Jesus's effective role pertains not only to the "poor and meek" but to the governance of all creation for its flourishing and harmony:

> He himself is before all things, and in him all things hold together. . . . For in him all the fullness of God was pleased to dwell, and through him God was pleased to reconcile to himself all things, whether on earth or in heaven, by making peace through the blood of his cross. (Colossians 1:17–20)

In all of these dimensions of reality—*socioeconomic* and the *whole created order*—Jesus is portrayed as the one who fully executes the rule of the righteous king portrayed in our poem. Thus in its witness to Jesus, the early church appealed to all of the claims made for the Davidic house. And while Jesus occasionally exhibits some unease about that identification, that unease did not stop needy people from making the connection. Thus Bartimaeus made precisely such an appeal:

> When he heard that it was Jesus of Nazareth, he began to shout out and say, "Jesus, Son of David, have mercy on me!" Many sternly ordered him to be quiet, but he cried out even more loudly, "Son of David, have mercy on me!" (Mark 10:47–48)

Nor does it stop the church in its liturgy from making that same claim derivative from David today. While Jews continue to await the coming of the Messiah, the church does not doubt that the poem of Isaiah has come to its fulfillment. Either way, in Jewish hope or Christian confession and continuing hope, God's purpose in the world is seen to be linked to the project of the Davidic house and its "branch."

Questions for Discussion

1. How might Isaiah's vision of government relate to our own context? Can it?
2. Why are righteousness and faithfulness key markers of the obedient life?
3. How do you see the New Testament applying Isaiah 11 to the person and work of Jesus?

Chapter 13

The Lord's Plan
(Isaiah 14:27)

For the LORD of hosts has planned,
and who will annul it?
His hand is stretched out,
and who will turn it back?

> **Scripture Passages for Reference**
>
> Isaiah 14:1–23, 24–27
> Psalm 2
> Psalm 96
> Daniel 4:35, 37

No doubt Isaiah had participated in the liturgies of the Jerusalem temple (see 6:1). Because of that participation he likely would, over time, have become familiar with the "psalms of enthronement" that affirmed and celebrated YHWH as the king of all creation, as the one who in majestic sovereignty presides over the affairs of all nations. That liturgy regularly made the bold claim that the covenantal *Lord of Israel* is at the same time *the Lord and ruler of all the world*. Thus it was affirmed in his hearing,

"Say among the nations, 'The Lord is king!'" (Psalm 96:10)

He might have heard, moreover, the royal psalm that made grand claims for the house of David:

> Why do the nations conspire,
>   and the peoples plot in vain?
> The kings of the earth set themselves,
>   and the rulers take counsel together,
>   against the LORD and his anointed, saying,
> "Let us burst their bonds asunder,
>   and cast their cords from us."
>
> He who sits in the heavens laughs;
>   the LORD has them in derision.
> Then he will speak to them in his wrath,
>   and terrify them in his fury, saying,
> "I have set my king on Zion, my holy hill."
>   Psalm 2:1–6

The liturgy readily presented the Davidic king as an instrument of YHWH's rule in response to the mocking of the nations.

Because of such affirmations that framed the imagination of Isaiah, the prophet could poetically articulate the reality of YHWH's rule of the nations. As a result, chapters 13–23 gather together a series of "Oracles against the Nations" wherein the several nations, named one by one, are said to be accountable to YHWH. The charge against each nation is that it has failed to adhere to the requirements of YHWH. The requirements of YHWH are not explicitly said to have been given to the nations in specific commandments. Rather, they seem to be inherent in the very fabric of creation, readily discernible to any and every nation-state that pays attention. Thus John Barton can conclude of Isaiah,

> Isaiah, then, begins with a picture of the world in which God is the creator and preserver of all things and occupies by right the supreme position over all that he has made. The essence of morality is cooperation in maintaining the ordered structure which prevails, under God's guidance, in the natural constitution of things, and the keynote of the whole system is order, a proper submission to one's assigned place in the scheme of things and the avoidance of any action that would challenge the supremacy of God or seek to subvert the orders he has established.[1]

YHWH's requirements are thus not limited to explicit commandments but are evident in what Barton terms "natural law." The most explicit example Barton cites is torture. One does not need an explicit commandment to know that torture is intolerable and never, ever acceptable. Any nation-state should know this. See, for example, Amos 1:13, which Barton cites elsewhere as a case of violating something like "natural law":

> For three transgressions of the Ammonites,
>   and for four, I will not revoke the punishment;
> because they have ripped open pregnant women in Gilead
>   in order to enlarge their territory.

In the long series of oracles against foreign nations, every nation is held accountable to YHWH and the way in which YHWH has structured creation. In turn, every nation is brought under judgment. No nation is autonomous and free to do as it pleases. Thus the oracles speak vigorously against the temptation to arrogance of every powerful nation-state. As Nebuchadnezzar in the book of Daniel (a model of arrogance) finally learned,

> All the inhabitants of the earth are accounted as nothing,
>   and he does what he wills with the host of heaven
>   and the inhabitants of the earth.
>   Daniel 4:35

There is, accordingly, no nation that has the capacity to question the way in which YHWH governs. In the Isaiah collection of such oracles, the most interesting and important are the oracles against Babylon (chaps. 13–14), Egypt (chap. 19), and Tyre (chap. 23). These were the states that most aggressively sought to promote their own autonomy and so were also the ones that most fully collided with the rule of YHWH.

We may consider the oracle against Babylon as a case in point (Isaiah 13–14). Under Nebuchadnezzar, Babylon was the dominant superpower for a time in the sixth century BCE. Babylon will be a dominant figure in the middle section of the book of Isaiah (see chap. 46 on Babylonian gods and chap. 47 on Babylonian failure). In the present oracle within chapters 13–14, Babylon is dramatically portrayed as a failed power that in weakness must descend to Sheol, the place of the dead (14:9). When Babylon arrives in Sheol, it is greeted by other failed powers that also end up weak, dormant, and irrelevant. The now dead powers greet Babylon with recognition that Babylon has now become as weak and irrelevant as they (14:9–11). The poet exposes the inescapable fate of every such arrogant power.

At the end of this oracle in a stunning passage, Isaiah states the theological conclusion toward which the oracle has been pointing (14:24–27). One may well note that this brief oracle concerns Assyria and not Babylon as one would expect. One interpretive approach understands that this is a mistake in the tradition and that the oracle was intended to cite Babylon. Our own judgment is that Assyria and Babylon, the two dominant superpowers in the north, are poetic equivalents for every nation that imagines its own unfettered autonomy. As a result, the specific citation of Assyria does not matter, because the prophetic verdict pertains to every such state.

In verses 24–27, one notes that at the beginning and the end we have the divine title "LORD of hosts." This phrase means that YHWH, as the creator, has massive troops available. The imagery is thus militaristic: YHWH has sufficient military resources (in poetic imagination) to prevail against every nation-state. Sandwiched between these two citations of the "LORD of hosts," the oracle speaks of YHWH's "plan" for the future of the world (vv. 24, 26, 27). The word "plan" need not lead us into a scholastic calculation about the exact design and blueprint whereby God has "predestined" the outcome of the world. Rather, the term may simply mean that YHWH has a will, purpose, and intentionality to which YHWH is vigorously committed, about which YHWH will not relent. In prophetic imagination, this divine intentionality is not congruent with the ideology of any nation-state, not even Israel's. At the core of prophetic imagination is the conviction that YHWH is a real agent with a real purpose and thus not captured by or confined to any human ideology. The accent is on YHWH's freedom to act in the historical process to bring about YHWH's own purpose. Once again, Nebuchadnezzar, the Babylon ruler, learned this lesson well as recorded elsewhere in the tradition:

> All his works are *truth*,
> and his ways are *justice*;

and he is able to bring low
those who walk in pride.
Daniel 4:37

Thus YHWH's "plan" is for truth and justice—truth that exposes the fraudulence of every autonomous state, and justice that contradicts the injustice of every state.

The inescapable consequence of this claim is that the Lord of hosts must stand against every state that mocks the truth and twists justice. In verse 25 the specific outcome of this affirmation is that YHWH will "break" the Assyrians. This reference to Assyria could be an allusion to the threat of Sennacherib that we have seen earlier. In that case, the inexplicable rescue of Jerusalem amounted to the breaking of Assyria. Or if we read the poem with reference to Babylon, then by the end of the book of Isaiah YHWH has broken that power by instigating the rise of Cyrus the Persian. With reference to either superpower, its long-range aggressive ambition could not be sustained. In turn, Assyria fell before Babylon, and Babylon fell to the Persians. In the vista of Isaiah all such turns of history ought to be referred to the rule of YHWH. The result is that the "yoke" or "burden" of the superpower is repelled. These two terms variously concern military threat or imposed taxation. The "yoke" of the superpower violates the intent of YHWH and cannot endure. In subsequent Christian tradition the "yoke" and "burden" of the gospel are light and easy (Matthew 11:28–30). In the context of Matthew, the yoke that is displaced by the gospel could be the yoke of Rome or of excessively demanding religious punctiliousness. Either way, the God of the gospel who is, perforce, the God of Israel, is the God of freedom.

At the end of Isaiah's brief poetic unit, the poet asks two rhetorical questions:

- Who will annul the plan of the Lord of hosts? *The answer is, "No one," not Assyria, not Babylon, not any nation-state.*
- Who will turn back YHWH's hand? *The answer is again, "No one," not any power that imagines it has the capacity to have history on its own terms.*

The questions are echoed in the fresh learning of Nebuchadnezzar in Daniel 4:35. No one can stay the hand of YHWH! No one can call

God to account. No one can question YHWH. No state can live out a policy that in the end contradicts YHWH.

In context, the counterpoint to this strong insistence is that the defeat of the superpower will cause the emancipation and restoration of Israel that has been abused and deported by the superpowers. Thus in 14:1–2 the prophet anticipates such restoration:

> But the LORD will have compassion on Jacob and will again choose Israel, and will set them in their own land. (Isaiah 14:1)

But then in what appears to be a somewhat characteristic extrapolation, the oracle goes on to anticipate that restored Israel can now exercise domination that in its brutality seems to replicate the brutality of the erstwhile superpower:

> The house of Israel will possess the nations as male and female slaves in the LORD's land; they will take captive those who were their captors, and rule over those who oppressed them. (14:2)

That, of course, is the too-often-reiterated pattern of history in which emancipated peoples become the new overlords, repeating the same mistake and seeming to learn nothing in the process. A most blatant example of this in our time is the case of Daniel Ortega in Nicaragua. He had been the bold leader of a great liberation movement against a brutalizing regime. Later, however, after succeeding to the presidency of Nicaragua, he ended up becoming a brutalizing tyrant himself.

We now live in a world of three superpowers—China, Russia, and the United States—each of which competes economically and militarily with the other two. It is the great temptation of each power, including the United States, to imagine that, in its unfettered power, it is free to do whatever it wants in order to overcome its fears and achieve its ambitions. Such superpowers learn, over and over, that such autonomy is not sustainable in the end. It is not sustainable—not simply due to some vague reality imposed "from above." Rather, it is not sustainable because justice arises "from below" and will, finally and definitively, have its say. It turns out, in prophetic imagination, that the life story of the world is not written by the superpowers. It is, rather, sketched out by the voices of truth and justice that finally cannot be silenced. Isaiah is one such voice, but by no means the first or the last one.

Questions for Discussion

1. Do you agree that all turns of history "ought to be referred" to the rule of God?
2. What is the Lord's plan, and how can it be discerned?
3. If God is consistently against all superpowers, what does that mean for contemporary politics, including those within the church?

Chapter 14

"Egypt, My People; Assyria, the Work of My Hands"? (Isaiah 19:24–25)

> *On that day Israel will be the third with Egypt and Assyria, a blessing in the midst of the earth, whom the LORD of hosts has blessed, saying, "Blessed be Egypt my people, and Assyria the work of my hands, and Israel my heritage."*

> ***Scripture Passages for Reference***
>
> Isaiah 19:1–25
> Exodus 2:23–25
> Exodus 15:21
> 1 Kings 14:25–28
> Jeremiah 46:13–19
> Psalm 107
> Revelation 5:9
> Revelation 7:9
> Revelation 11:9
> Revelation 14:6
> Revelation 17:15

Midway through the Oracles against the Nations is the oracle against Egypt (19:1–25). Egypt of course occupies a central position in the memory and imagination of Israel. Egypt under Pharaoh is remembered as the great tyrannical force that subjected Israel to slavery.

Egypt was, moreover, the venue in which YHWH showed passion for enslaved Israel and the capacity to override the power of Pharaoh (Exodus 15:21). In more recent times, Egypt functioned as the great superpower to the south that was always a threat to Israel, sometimes dormant but always lingering and lurking at the border (see 1 Kings 14:25-28).

In this oracle against Egypt, the prophet does not make any comment about the transgression of Egypt against YHWH or the grounds for YHWH's fierce resolve against Egypt. Perhaps the name "Egypt" is sufficient to evoke that ancient bondage. Or perhaps it was simply understood that Egypt is the classic adversary of YHWH. More likely it simply belongs to the genre of prophetic oracle to assume the negative and let YHWH respond to it.

In verses 1-15 the threat of YHWH is fairly conventional. In verses 1-4 YHWH intends to "stir up" internal dissension and cause civil unrest. That divine "stirring up" will disrupt the "plans" of the superpower because it will have to turn its attention to the internal turmoil (v. 23). But then the internal dissension is matched by a threat of an invasion (v. 4). This likely refers to the advance of a northern power against Egypt, perhaps Assyria or perhaps Babylon, when Israel no longer functioned as a buffer to protect Egypt from northern aggression (see Jeremiah 46:13-19).

In verses 5-10 our oracle against Egypt anticipates a severe drought in the land that will cause a deep disruption of the economy of the state. And in verses 11-15 YHWH will show the vaunted wisdom of Egypt to be futile and ineffective foolishness. The so-called wisdom of Egypt and its plan for control will be overrun by YHWH's "plan" against Egypt, a plan for trouble and disorder (v. 12). As we have seen elsewhere, Isaiah took what might be regarded as geopolitical realism and reframed it as YHWH's governance of the nations. The sum of verses 1-15 is that Egypt, the great superpower, will be reduced to irrelevance. According to the conventional genre, the oracle against Egypt might properly have ended with verse 15. There is no more to be said, because YHWH has decided a fierce and final verdict against Egypt.

Because of our familiarity with the genre, we are more than a little surprised that the oracle does not end with the seeming finality of verse 15. Instead of an expected ending, the oracle continues for

"Egypt, My People; Assyria, the Work of My Hands"? (Isaiah 19:24–25)

ten more verses in which the utterance of YHWH abruptly reverses field. There is nothing like this in any other prophetic oracle against the nations, because these final unexpected verses articulate the renewal and restoration of Egypt after a decisive divine judgment. Every other such oracle ends in devastating judgment. Thus against Babylon there is only a final negativity:

> I will rise up against them, says the LORD of hosts, and will cut off from Babylon name and remnant, offspring and posterity, says the LORD. And I will make it a possession of the hedgehog, and pools of water, and I will sweep it with the broom of destruction, says the LORD of hosts. (14:22–23)

And against Tyre the oracle ends with anticipation that the wealth of Tyre will be devoted to Israel and to YHWH (23:17–18). But here expectation for Egypt is positive because there is a coming "day" when YHWH will prevail and do good for Egypt. In what follows there are five terse oracles. In the first (19:16–17), the "plan" of YHWH is against Egypt and will reduce Egypt to fear, trembling, and terror. This oracle extends the divine threat against Egypt. But then in what follows in the second oracle it is anticipated that the Egyptian population will come to serve YHWH:

> On that day there will be five cities in the land of Egypt that speak the language of Canaan and swear allegiance to the LORD of hosts. (v. 18)

In the third oracle concerning "that day," Egypt in its dismay will "cry out" to YHWH because of its oppression (vv. 19–22). This is a staggering change of tone. Egypt will have nowhere else to turn for help and so finally will acknowledge YHWH by asking for relief and deliverance. In the very same verse, YHWH will send a deliverer (v. 20). Thus the structure of this exchange is classic in Israel: the oppressed cry out and YHWH hears and delivers. This pattern of *"cry out . . . hear"* occurs repeatedly in the Israelite tradition. The defining use, of course, is when the Hebrew slaves in Egypt cried out (Exodus 2:23–25) and YHWH responded by dispatching Moses to Pharaoh (3:10). In intentional irony here, Egypt now replicates the patterned speech that Israel had uttered in a plea against Egypt. Now the erstwhile oppressor has become the oppressed and must make the same appeal to the same God who delivers. The pattern is familiar in Psalm 107:

Concerning desperate wandering,
"They *cried* to the LORD . . . he *delivered*" (v. 6).
Concerning imprisonment,
"They *cried* to the LORD . . . he *saved* them" (v. 13).
Concerning sickness to death,
"They *cried* to the LORD . . . he *saved* them" (v. 19).
Concerning a storm at sea,
"They *cried* to the LORD . . . he *brought them out*" (v. 28).

Only now it is *Egypt* that cries out and is saved! Egypt comes to "know the LORD," that is, acknowledges YHWH as sovereign, the one who will heal Egypt. Unheard of! Unimaginable!

In our verses at the end of the oracle, the positive anticipation of the prophet becomes even more bold, even more vigorous. In the fourth oracle, the prophet anticipates the remaking of the political map of the Near East (v. 23). Heretofore the Near East was ordered with competing superpowers in the north (Assyria, Babylon) and Egypt to the south, with tiny Israel located between as a buffer state. Because the superpowers were characteristically in opposition and competition, each regularly sought to control Israel so that it had protection on its exposed border. But now, in prophetic imagination, the opposition and hostility will be completely negated. The nations together will construct a highway from one end of the Fertile Crescent to the other. This project intends a free flow of traffic and commerce with no more border impediments, no barriers of any kind. This is an astonishing vision of a sociopolitical possibility that recognizes that the ancient habit of hostility is not a necessary or required one.

The clue to the breaking of hostility, moreover, is that the several nations will worship together. The text does not say that they will together worship YHWH, but that is surely implied. Thus worship of YHWH is affirmed as a way to overcome and terminate old hostilities and old national-tribal identities. In this oracle, YHWH is not presented as the God of Israel but as *the God of all the nations* who makes peace and commercial prosperity possible. Thus we may see in this highway project an echo of the earlier promise in Isaiah 2:4 about not learning war anymore, along with the end of spears and swords. As Egypt is invited to a new way in the world, so something happens as well to YHWH, who runs out beyond what had been a specific commitment to Israel to a larger vista of sovereignty.

That remarkable anticipation in the fourth oracle of verse 23 is reinforced by the fifth oracle concerning "that day" (vv. 24–25). This oracle imagines a time when the God who presides over the peaceable highway that connects the nations now issues a stunning inexplicable blessing. The poet imagines the three nations—Egypt in the south, Assyria in the north, and Israel in between—all together in worship before the one God of all nations. Before that new international worship is ended, the God of all nations issues a blessing. In the blessing the Lord of hosts names all three nations. This shows how all three nations are subject to that Lord, but what is interesting is how, in the blessing, God assigns a specific title of chosenness to each. The first named is Egypt, the subject of this entire chapter. Egypt had been in an earlier time the great nemesis of YHWH; only in verse 21 was Egypt able to acknowledge YHWH and offer worship and sacrifices to YHWH. Now, in verse 25, Egypt is identified by YHWH as *my people*.

Second, the God who blesses names Assyria, the empire that had been a constant threat to Jerusalem, as *the work of my hands*—that is, the beloved creature willed and crafted by the creator God. We may imagine that the Egyptians and the Assyrians who were present for that blessing could hardly believe their ears. And we may imagine that the Israelites present for that blessing could hardly believe their ears either. What all who listened heard was that the Lord who chose and loved Israel was now choosing and recognizing other peoples. The God who blesses finishes the blessing with reference to Israel, who is named, consistent with the tradition, as *my heritage*. Now everything has changed in the Near East; the sovereign Lord of history has declared, via the blessing, that there is a plurality of chosen peoples. In the blessing, the Lord of hosts has taken the phrasing used for chosen Israel—"my people," "the work of my hands," "my heritage"—and has generously strewn these monikers across the Near East to acknowledge chosen peoples who now, along with Israel, enjoy status as the special recipients of YHWH's fidelity.

This breathtaking affirmation on the lips of God is clearly out beyond any narrow construal of the tradition of ancient Israel. At the same time, however, it is the culmination of the radical prophetic imagination of Isaiah in which the prophet cedes nothing of the claim of Israel as God's own but manages at the same time to include in that gracious governance other peoples who now share in that peculiar blessing. There is in the Bible, to be sure, a trajectory of narrow, almost sectarian religious claims. That trajectory, however, is vigorously contested here. Isaiah had come to see that his promise of "not learning war anymore" required a more expansive vision of the role and vision of God. It is that more expansive vision that challenges the "normal" tribalism of religion. That wondrous vision, in Christian tradition, eventuated in the inclusion of Gentiles in the early church (see the struggles in Acts 10–15) and in the final anticipation of the New Testament that includes every "nation, tribe, tongue, and people" (Revelation 5:9; 7:9; 11:9; 14:6; and 17:15).

We in the United States are now in a season of xenophobia that wants to exclude from our national community all those who are "other" and unlike us. This tendency, now attested broadly among Christians in the United States, is vigorously contested by this oracle. On offer in this oracle is a God who does not linger in tribal fearfulness but who generously extends the blessing of life and well-being to all parties. We are invited to entertain the awareness that those we most fear turn out to be also among God's chosen peoples. We dare not exclude those to whom God's blessing and identity as part of "the chosen" extend.

Questions for Discussion

1. What do you make of God calling Assyria and Egypt—often bitter enemies of Israel—names that are otherwise reserved for God's covenant people?

2. Can you imagine a similar treatment of people groups or some sort of parallel elsewhere in the Bible or today?

3. What does this say about the character of God, in general, and what will happen in the "days to come"?

Chapter 15

Apocalyptic Pollution
(Isaiah 24:5)

*The earth lies polluted
    under its inhabitants;
for they have transgressed laws,
    violated the statutes,
    broken the everlasting covenant.*

> **Scripture Passages for Reference**
>
> Isaiah 24:1–13
> Isaiah 54:9–16
> Genesis 9:9–10, 16
> Hosea 4:1–3

Chapters 24–27 of Isaiah are often regarded as the latest material in the book of Isaiah. The label often placed on these chapters is "apocalyptic." Apocalyptic literature arises when the current circumstance of society is so unbearable and terrible that there can be no hope for restoration or recovery; for that reason the poet must reach outside of and beyond any hope in this world order and articulate a more radical hope for a newness that is quite beyond any present reality. Theologically, apocalyptic literature turns to the decisive action of God, who abruptly terminates *all that is old* and just as suddenly initiates *a new world order*. The accent on "old and new" means that nothing of newness will be derived or extrapolated from what is old. There will be a clean and radical break between old and new, because God has decisively rejected what is old and dysfunctional. This radical theological perspective is, perforce, matched by a radical rhetoric of extremity in which the failure of the old is given elaborate expression and the coming newness to be wrought by God is given equivalent extreme articulation. The whole of such literature is thus an exercise in extremity of thought, speech, and expectation. Nothing good can be expected from what presently is; everything that is good can be expected from the newness that God will soon (but not quite yet!) enact.

In these four chapters of Isaiah, it is evident that chapter 24 is an extreme negative statement of the ending that is sure to come. The three chapters that follow give voice to the newness that YHWH will enact. When we consider chapter 24, we notice that the poetry begins with the name of YHWH. YHWH will be the agent of the judgment that follows in the poem. In this rhetoric there is no room for any human agent to implement divine judgment. YHWH will act directly. In the Hebrew text the initial naming of YHWH is intensified by the opening word *hinneh*, which the NRSV translates as "now." The term is traditionally rendered as "behold." It is used to call attention to something following that merits great attention. Thus great attention must be paid to what is now to be announced by the poet. What follows the name of YHWH is the devastation that YHWH will work on the whole earth. This inventory of destruction and loss continues through verse 13. In verses 14–16 the devastation is interrupted by a doxology to YHWH, but the doxology is to be sung by those who witness the dreadful work of YHWH just declared. YHWH is praised for this exhibit of divine power and governance, hymned by those who affirm this "alien work" of YHWH (cf. 28:21). After this interlude of doxology, the poetry continues the devastation to the end of the chapter. The devastation to come is so sweeping that it will, by the end, include the shaming of the sun and the moon (v. 23).

If we read the book of Isaiah knowingly, we recognize that the harsh judgment of YHWH is a central theme of the book. Such a theme is very difficult for our modern ears, as it conjures up an old, angry man in the sky who acts without emotional restraint. That image, of course, is unacceptable to our modern sensibilities. If, however, we begin, as Isaiah did, with the conviction that God, in creation, is passionately committed to *shalom* for the entire world, then it may follow that whatever violates, contradicts, or refuses that God's goodwill for *shalom* will be offensive to the Lord, who has ordered the world for good. That affront to God and God's properly ordered world evokes a biting comeback to those who settle for ignoble or lesser purposes. The order intended by God is not indifferent to human engagement or inert but anticipates good human performance of that will. This extremity of negatively presented rhetoric is offered by those (Isaiah among them) who trust deeply in the moral coherence of YHWH's governance.

This conviction concerning YHWH's refusal to accept what contradicts the divine will for *shalom* is articulated in two primary forms in the Bible. On the one hand, particularly in apocalyptic rhetoric, the response of YHWH to such contradictions is by *direct agency*. So here in verse 1, YHWH, as direct agent, will "lay waste." But alternatively (as in much of our chapter) the Bible also articulates the notion that the world is so ordered that the violation of its good order will itself evoke negative consequences, because the linkage between human choice and action and world outcomes is guaranteed by the fabric of creation and requires *no direct divine intervention*.[1]

Thus verse 5 clearly states the connection between human choice and negative outcomes. The choice made by the inhabitants of the earth (*all* of them, not just Israel) is to violate the covenant and its Torah commandments. For accent we get the triad "Torah, statute, and covenant." This triad of terms features the covenant here violated as an "everlasting covenant." This phrase is surely an allusion to the covenant made with Noah concerning the order and well-being of all the earth after the flood:

> As for me, I am establishing my covenant with you and your descendants after you, and with every living creature that is with you, the birds, the domestic animals, and every animal of the earth with you, as many as came out of the ark. . . . When the bow is in the clouds, I will see it and remember the everlasting covenant between God and every living creature of all flesh that is on the earth. (Genesis 9:9–10, 16)

This covenant ensures the reliable, life-giving structure of all creation. That assurance pertains to all creatures and is by YHWH's guarantee "everlasting." But now, in our verse, that everlasting covenant guaranteed by YHWH has been broken by the inhabitants of the earth. It is important to recognize that in rabbinic reflection, the covenant with Noah has imposed commandments on all creatures.[2] These are not the commandments of Sinai, but they are commandments that are required by and congruent with the ordering of creation. They cannot be violated with impunity—neither by Jews nor Christians.

But now, in our passage, these commandments intrinsic to the structure of the universe have been violated, and the consequence is that "the earth lies polluted." In context, the notion of "pollution" was that life has become so impure and unclean that the holiness of God can no longer abide there. The earth, as a result, will be God-abandoned. It is no far stretch of the term to segue to our contemporary crisis of pollution that fouls the earth and renders life unlivable. That "a curse devours the whole earth" (v. 6) is not a result of divine agency but is the sure consequence of human decision-making that runs against the will of the creator and the given order of creation.

It is fundamental to how the prophets understand divine judgment that human actions contrary to the will of the creator lead to dire outcomes. The most succinct articulation of this linkage is in Hosea 4:1–3:

> Hear the word of the LORD, O people of Israel;
>   for the LORD has an indictment against the inhabitants of
>   the land.
> There is no faithfulness or loyalty,
>   and no knowledge of God in the land.
> Swearing, lying, and murder,
>   and stealing and adultery break out;
>   bloodshed follows bloodshed.
> Therefore the land mourns,
>   and all who live in it languish;
>   together with the wild animals
>   and the birds of the air,
>   even the fish of the sea are perishing.

The indictment is expressed first in the general terms of covenantal fidelity (faithfulness, knowledge of God), but then the indictment is precisely keyed to the Ten Commandments in verse 2. The disobedience is enough to evoke the harsh "therefore" of verse 3 that leads to inescapable consequence. These *acts of infidelity* result in *a severe drought* that causes all of creation to shrivel and dry up without hope. Thus, in shorthand, violation of the commandments leads to a devastating drought. The linkage is, of course, prescientific, shocking to the rationalistic mind. The linkage nonetheless pertains, not only in prophetic imagination, but in our own context as well as we brood over the high costs of climate change. The prophets knew, as we are learning, that the givens of the structure of creation cannot be violated with impunity.

In our passage in Isaiah 24, the climate crisis of "pollution" pertains to everyone, slave and master, buyer and seller, lender and barrower; none is exempt (vv. 2–3). The crisis, moreover, will disrupt all of social life. There will be an end to social merriment (v. 8). Every house will be assaulted by the drought (v. 10). Kings will become like prisoners, trapped like everyone else (vv. 21–22). The reasoning of this oracle is quite simple. The poetic rendering, however, is extended, elaborate, and shrill. After one is clear about the linkage of *violation and consequence*, then one must listen for the poem to be read out loud in order to sense the emotive force of the whole. The rhetoric matches the crisis; the poet intends to bring listeners to full awareness of the depth of the crisis. And indeed, in our own situation, we have not yet begun to face the depth of the climate crisis because we will witness the displacement of huge masses of people so that our current "immigration crisis" may well seem like a walk in the park. By the end of our poem, there is no positive prophetic word, no resolution, no hope. In this case, the prophet is capable of ending the utterance in death and despair, so great is the violation here brought to speech.

We may notice one other use of the imagery of the everlasting covenant with Noah. In 54:9–10 belated Isaiah alludes to *the flood* and likens *the exile* of Israel to the flood, for both are matters of profound chaos. The difference is that in chapter 54, the threat of the flood is overridden by the fidelity of YHWH:

> For the mountains may depart
>   and the hills be removed,
> but my steadfast love shall not depart from you,
>   and my covenant of peace shall not be removed,
> says the LORD, who has compassion on you.
>
> 54:10

In Isaiah 24 there is no such steadfast love or covenant of peace. There is only chaos and disaster. Yet these two texts together exhibit the agile way in which the prophet can manage the remembered tradition. In the latter case, YHWH's fidelity will override the threat of the flood of chaos. In chapter 24, by way of contrast, YHWH acts destructively in and through the flood. In our text YHWH is transactional; in the later text, YHWH responds with a different kind of gracious freedom. YHWH is capable of both and either response. In each case, YHWH's response is given prophetic articulation. In our oracle there is no relief. We can only wait for the counter-utterance to come.

Questions for Discussion

1. How is God's concern for *shalom* different from "an old, angry man in the sky who acts without emotional restraint"?
2. What are your thoughts and feelings about the climate crisis? Can you imagine it as something that is against God's willed order for creation? How so?
3. What have been your impressions of apocalyptic literature? How has reading this chapter informed those impressions?

Chapter 16

Your Dead Shall Live
(Isaiah 26:19)

Your dead shall live, their corpses shall rise.
O dwellers in the dust, awake and sing for joy!
For your dew is radiant dew,
and the earth will give birth to those long dead.

> **Scripture Passages for Reference**
>
> Isaiah 26:6–19
> Isaiah 25:6–9
> Isaiah 27:1–13
> Isaiah 65:21–25
> Isaiah 66:22
> Daniel 12:2
> Romans 4:17

Isaiah 24 introduces what is often thought to be the "apocalyptic" corpus of chapters 24–27. After chapter 24 we have visionary poetry that voices an immense reversal from the gloom and doom of chapter 24. In chapters 25–27, with rich variation, we get poetic affirmation about the saving power of YHWH and the consequent good future for Israel and for all creation.

In chapter 25 we are offered a doxology that confidently waits on YHWH's saving power:

> It will be said on that day,
>> Lo, this is our God; we have waited for him so that he might save us.
>> This is the LORD for whom we have waited;
>> let us be glad and rejoice in his salvation.
>
> 25:9

Verses 10–12 suggest the rescue of Israel is from the threat of the Moabites (on which see also Isaiah 15). But the more familiar imagery of verses 6–8 is that the threat from which the faithful are rescued is death itself. It is no wonder that the church appeals specifically to these verses in the lectionary, and that these verses serve well in times of death. The promise is that on "this mountain," presumably Zion, there will be a lavish banquet of celebration. The ground for that celebration is that YHWH will prevail against the power of death:

> And he will destroy on this mountain
>> the shroud that is cast over all peoples,
>> the sheet that is spread over all the nations;
>> he will swallow up death forever.
>
> vv. 7–8a

The imagery of "swallowing death" is an appeal to very old mythic imagery of one great gulp that ends the threat of the enemy monster. In 27:1 we also have an appeal to mythic imagery with reference to Leviathan. The outcome of this victory over the monster death is the end of sadness:

> Then the Lord GOD will wipe away the tears from all faces,
>> and the disgrace of his people he will take away from all the earth,
>> for the LORD has spoken.
>
> v. 8b

It is evident in this text that the imagery moves easily between the mythic and the historical as the poet seeks to give voice to an expectation that is not yet in hand. Placement of the coming banquet on "this mountain" permits Jerusalem and its temple to be, at one and the same time, a historical assurance and a mythic allusion.

Your Dead Shall Live (Isaiah 26:19) 101

In chapter 27 after the reference to Leviathan in verse 1, the imagery is much more historical. Verses 2–6 pick up the imagery of the Song of the Vineyard in 5:1–7. While the vineyard Israel was devastated in chapter 5, here the vineyard is invited to cling to YHWH and so to live in peace:

> Or else let it cling to me for protection,
>   let it make peace with me,
>   let it make peace with me.
> 27:5

The remainder of the chapter is historical in its reference to "Jacob." The confusing imagery of verses 7–11 seems to end with judgment against Jacob. But the prose conclusion of verses 12–13 envisions a gathering of scattered Israel from "the land of Assyria" and "the land of Egypt." It is worth noticing that the juxtaposition of Israel-Jacob to Assyria-Egypt here is very different from the promise of 19:24–25. In that vision, the three peoples are allies in faith. Here Assyria and Egypt continue to be places of hostility and displacement from which rescue is required. Both texts attest to both YHWH's sovereignty and YHWH's attentiveness to Israel.

This overview of chapters 25 and 27 serves to highlight the context of hope for chapter 26. In chapter 26, hope-filled poetry is less ambiguous than in the surrounding chapters. Here all is positive, for on "that day" YHWH will directly assert rule over creation. YHWH is "an everlasting rock" (v. 4) who acts for the sake of the "poor and needy" (v. 6) and casts down oppressors who are the proud in the city. This poetry is partly confident *affirmation*, but it is also partly *petition* from a people not yet delivered. That petition takes the form of a lament that portrays for God the sorry, helpless situation to which the poetry bears witness:

> The dead do not live;
>   shades do not rise—
> because you have punished and destroyed them,
>   and wiped out all memory of them.
> v. 14

Life has come to a full stop without any prospect for a future. Israel has become vulnerable and helpless. Israel is without a future like a woman who is unable to birth a child:

> Like a woman with child,
>> who writhes and cries out in her pangs
>> when she is near her time,
> so were we because of you, O LORD;
>> we were with child, we writhed,
>> but we gave birth only to wind.
> We have won no victories on earth,
>> and no one is born to inhabit the world.
>>> vv. 17–18

Thus in both "death" (v. 14) and "birth" (v. 18) the poetry bespeaks helplessness and voices an urgent petition to YHWH as the only one who can move beyond death and failed birth.

But then in our verse 19 there is an inexplicable but glorious response to that vulnerable helplessness. It is an affirmation that the dead shall live, thus exactly countering the phrasing of verse 14:

> The dead do not live. (v. 14)
>
> Your dead shall live. (v. 19)

We notice that the negative statement is generic, "*the* dead," whereas the positive statement is specific, "*your* dead"—that is, the dead of Israel. What matters even more, however, is that the power of YHWH is mobilized. YHWH's power is against Israel's enemies, and death is the final enemy. The proper response to this wonder of life is a surge of joy and praise for the complete reversal of despair.

This verse is pivotal in the book of Isaiah for two reasons. First, because it voices the extreme hope of Isaiah and of Israel, and second, because it is one of only two unambiguous witnesses to resurrection in the Old Testament, the other being Daniel 12:2. Two things are clear in this remarkable text. First, the poetry of Isaiah 25–27 is filled with elusive images and metaphors that are not always clear in their reference. Thus we must take this affirmation of resurrection in the midst of a field of metaphors and not assume that we have exhausted its meaning by simply affirming that "a dead person can come back to life." Second, this imagery of resurrection (as also in Daniel 12:2) is situated in a field of apocalyptic thought and cannot be extracted from that mode of thinking and speaking. This means that "resurrection" belongs to a world of imagery in which God presides over all that is old and failed; God presides, with equal authority, over the generation of something new that is possible only by the power of God. It is profound *despair, helplessness, and loss* that evoke from God an equally profound act of *hope, buoyancy, and restoration*. In the book of Isaiah, that unutterable capacity of YHWH to create newness (which *is* ultimately uttered!) is mobilized in order to imagine and evoke the restoration of Jerusalem that will be part of a new heaven and a new earth (see 65:21–25; 66:22). The God to whom Israel attests is the God who will make all things new, precisely in a context where no newness seems to be possible. It is the great temptation of faith to assume that the most God can manage and will give will be in the order and categories of present world reality. Thus we are always wont to domesticate God's capacity for newness to our explanatory categories and capabilities. Such containment of God's power, however, leaves us fully without hope in a world governed by the mighty force of death. That is why the only appropriate response to resurrection faith is not explanation but doxology: "Sing for joy!" in our verse.

From this remarkable affirmation of hope we may trace two extrapolations. The first is that Jewish faith is redolent with resurrection hope. In a series of books, Jon Levenson has explored the depth and richness of that faith.[1] Two outcomes from his work may be mentioned. First and most important is the theme of *the resurrection of Israel* in the oracle of Ezekiel 37. The question "Mortal, can these bones live?" (Ezekiel 37:3) is answered with a vigorous affirmation. God remains faithful to Israel and is capable of bringing new life to Israel in every circumstance of vulnerability and despair. Second, Levenson compellingly shows that *the temple is an antipode to Sheol*, the place of the dead. Thus Israel's hope is for a restored temple that will be the vehicle for Israel's best hope from God:

> In the Temple, instead of want, they found surfeit; instead of abandonment, care; instead of pollution, purity; instead of victimization, justice; instead of threat, security; instead of vulnerability, inviolability; instead of change, fixity; and instead of temporality, eternity. If this sounds like the World-to-Come or the Garden of Eden of rabbinic tradition, or the heaven of Christianity, that is surely no coincidence, for the Temple is the source of much of the imagery out of which these ideas grew.[2]

The second extrapolation we can trace from the expression of resurrection hope in our verse is that Christian tradition, focused on Easter, also posits resurrection hope in the wake of Isaiah's testimony. In speaking of the faith of Abraham, Paul can assert a wondrous parallel between the grace of which he writes—and the resurrection of the dead—and the creation of that which does not exist:

> in the presence of the God in whom he believed, who gives life to the dead and calls into existence the things that do not exist. (Romans 4:17)

It turns out that resurrection, creation, and grace are ways of speaking about the unfettered capacity of God to generate newness that is beyond everything extant heretofore. In Christian tradition it is the gift of life and new historical possibility in and through Jesus that proves pivotal for faith.

It is most unfortunate that such resurrection faith, grounded in apocalyptic hope and rhetoric, has been misunderstood and domesticated as though it concerned merely the resuscitation of a dead man from Nazareth. Resurrection is rather an attestation to the power of God to give new life beyond all the capability of our imagination. This faith, rooted in Israel's (and Isaiah's!) testimony, will require a fresh embrace of an apocalyptic sensibility that takes seriously the vulnerability and despair of the world and then gives doxological voice to the wonder of God's ready capacity for alternative. Even the greatest forces of evil and despair have no chance in this world of inexplicable newness that we have only to receive and call forth in praise.

Questions for Discussion

1. How are we as humans "wont to domesticate God's capacity for newness," over history and in our own time?
2. How does apocalyptic thinking help explain the idea (and doctrine) of the resurrection of the dead?
3. How is grace like (new) creation and resurrection?

Chapter 17

The Strange Work of God (Isaiah 28:21)

For the LORD will rise up as on Mount Perazim,
he will rage as in the valley of Gibeon
to do his deed—strange is his deed!
and to work his work—alien is his work!

> **Scripture Passages for Reference**
>
> Isaiah 28:14–22
> Isaiah 31:6
> Ezekiel 18:23, 30

The extended prophetic oracles in Isaiah 28–31 and 33 may be taken together as series of invectives concerning those who live in contradiction to the ordered structure of YHWH's creation. These oracles have in common that they are variously introduced by the Hebrew term *hôy*, which is often translated in an old-fashioned way as "woe" (28:1; 29:1, 15; 30:1; 31:1; and 33:1; see also 5:8–23 and 10:1–4 for another series of "woe oracles"). In the NRSV this recurring term is variously rendered as "ah," "ho," "ha," and "alas." It is not entirely clear why the NRSV has not chosen one translation to use consistently; we will in any case do well to notice the recurrence of the term, even if it is variously rendered.

105

The old translation, "woe," is of special interest for understanding the oracles of Isaiah 28–31 and 33, even though the NRSV translation seems to take the term only as an attention-getter. Two features of *hôy* are worth noticing. First, the term refers to the sadness of death. It is an anticipation of coming grief because of loss. Second, it can refer to big trouble to come that is not the result of any direct agency but that simply arises from a set of circumstances that make the anticipated loss inescapable and inevitable. The term reflects the conviction that creation is ordered so that *bad outcomes* are certain to arise from *bad choices, bad practices,* and *bad policies.* Behind that guaranteed structure of moral coherence is the God of Israel, who need not directly intervene to produce such grievous outcomes. The *consequences* are inchoately present in the *choices* already made. Thus this series of oracles concerns coming bad outcomes because of choices, practices, and policies that are inimical to the ordered governance of YHWH.

In chapter 28 those addressed with the "woe" are the proud and self-indulgent who will be overwhelmed by coming trouble. Those who live that way have in effect made a "covenant with death" that cannot yield life and certainly not life abundant (28:15, 18). The positive alternative in verse 16 leaves a way out by "YHWH's cornerstone of assurance." This invitation is an echo of 7:9 addressed to King Ahaz. Jerusalem, however, is unable or unwilling to trust God's assurance and goes its own fearful, destructive way.

Chapter 29 begins with a lament over Jerusalem ("Ariel") for its coming judgment and devastation. The oracle, however, is a mixed one; in addition to judgment it also anticipates a rescue for the city, a mixed theme that recurs throughout Isaiah. After the second "woe" in 29:15, the continuing oracle becomes one of hope and promise. The "meek and needy" will rejoice in the Holy One of Israel (v. 19), and the people of Abraham will be sanctified to God (vv. 22–24). The juxtaposition of *threat and promise* reiterates a motif common to Isaiah. It is to be noted, nevertheless, that the restoration is only *after* the devastation, that is, after the "woe"—evoking trouble to come.

Chapter 30 provides the same juxtaposition of *threat and hope.* The oracle begins with a condemnation for reliance on Egypt rather than reliance on YHWH. The indictment of this rebellious, faithless people (v. 9) is because of oppression and deceit (v. 12). But then the

The Strange Work of God (Isaiah 28:21) 107

prospect of hope is raised. The summons to trust in verse 15, however, is promptly rejected in verse 16 with an option for self-reliance that is sure to fail. The chapter ends with a strong assurance that Assyria will be "terror-stricken" and devastated (vv. 31–33).

The oracle in chapter 31 has the same mix of *judgment and hope*. The judgment again arises from reliance on Egyptian military protection (vv. 1–3). But again the threat of verses 1–3 is answered in verses 4–9 with an assurance that Assyria cannot succeed against Jerusalem because YHWH is like a lion that will protect the city. In chapter 33 the "woe" is turned away from Israel and Jerusalem and addresses a "destroyer," perhaps Assyria. The poem ends, moreover, with well-being and forgiveness for Zion (vv. 23–24).

The sum of this rather confusing material in chapters 28–31 and 33 is that YHWH will be the ultimate ruler over Jerusalem and over the nations—Egypt and Assyria—who variously assault Israel. This inescapable governance of YHWH offers to Israel both a "No" and a "Yes." The "No" is that the ordering of life willed by YHWH will not finally accept a system of choices, practices, and policies that contradict YHWH's intent. The "Yes" that seems mostly to prevail in the end is that in spite of YHWH's consternation over recalcitrant Jerusalem, YHWH will remain faithful to Israel and save it. This *Yes/No* of *judgment and hope* is intrinsic to the theology and rhetoric of the book of Isaiah; behind Isaiah, moreover, that same *Yes/No* is definitional for covenantal Israel. We get that dialectic pattern because YHWH is, at the same time, utterly *for Israel* and also passionately *for YHWH*. "All things work together for good" (Romans 8:28) when the *pro-Israel* and *pro-YHWH* impulses converge. When they do not converge, as often did not happen in the horizon of Isaiah, we get prophetic oracles that articulate the profound tension that shows up in historical reality. Just so, the prophetic tradition must return always again to the awareness that God's people and God's city, in recalcitrant disobedience, always reap the whirlwind set in motion by contradiction to YHWH's purpose.

Finally we come to our verse, 28:21, in which the poet anticipates the harsh judgment against Israel that is marked by YHWH's "rage" (*rāgaz*). The term, in almost onomatopoeic fashion, bespeaks intense agitation. YHWH is agitated by Israel's "covenant with death" (vv. 15, 18), which may be an allusion to an alliance with Assyria, and to Israel's refusal to "trust," choosing, rather, to panic, which in turn causes self-destructive decisions (v. 16). YHWH has offered Jerusalem "a sure foundation" (v. 16)—likely a commitment to the Davidic house—but it has refused to trust that foundation. The church has taken over the phrasing of this verse in its singing of Christ as the sure foundation of faith:

> Christ is made the sure foundation, Christ the head and
>   cornerstone,
> chosen of the Lord and precious, binding all the church in one;
> holy Zion's help forever, and her confidence alone.[1]

Israel's rejection of God's "sure foundation" and its choice of a covenant with death have evoked enraged hostility from YHWH. That harsh response is what we have in the "woe" oracles of these chapters. What interests us in our verse is that Isaiah refers to this harsh response of YHWH as "strange" and "alien work." The terms "strange" (*zār*) and "alien" (*nokriyyāh*) indicate that this work is incomprehensible, but they may also suggest that it is not natural, normal, or congruent with YHWH's typical character or propensity. If such harsh work is strange and alien, then we may recognize that YHWH's more familiar and normal work is exactly the opposite—namely, faithful, forgiving, and restoring. Thus the "No" of YHWH is not YHWH's preferred stance toward Israel. YHWH's "Yes" is what YHWH is prepared to do and prefers to do. This seems a most welcome declaration, because readers of prophetic texts are often puzzled or offended by the harshness of prophetic judgment. That puzzlement or affront leads one to wonder why the prophet speaks so or, behind that, why YHWH would act so. The answer here is that Isaiah speaks so and YHWH acts so not because of pleasure in it, but because Israel's recalcitrance so contradicts YHWH's intent that some response appropriate to the recalcitrance is required. It is surely reassurance to recognize that YHWH has no delight in such negative action.

Thus in 31:6 YHWH makes a bid for Israel to turn to fidelity:

> Turn back to him whom you have deeply betrayed, O people of Israel.

The Strange Work of God (Isaiah 28:21)

Such turning will require the rejection of the idols of silver and gold that are markers of self-sufficiency and self-reliance. This summons is closely parallel to the bid of YHWH according to Ezekiel:

> Have I any pleasure in the death of the wicked, says the Lord GOD, and not rather that they should turn from their ways and live? . . . Therefore I will judge you, O house of Israel, all of you according to your ways, says the Lord GOD. Repent and turn from all your transgressions; otherwise iniquity will be your ruin. (Ezekiel 18:23, 30)

These verses make clear that YHWH is engaged in a clear transactional relationship in which *deeds* bespeak *consequences*, and YHWH is the guarantor of that equation. This is not, to be sure, the whole of YHWH's initiative toward Israel, but it is an important part of it. It is the case that YHWH, in prophetic utterance, breaks out of and beyond such a transactional mode toward graciousness. That, however, does not eliminate the reality of "deeds and consequences" reflected in the "woe" oracles.

The dual capacity of YHWH in these oracles is not unlike the work of an attentive parent. Almost every parent is committed to love and cherish the child. But responsible parenting also entrusts to the parent discipline for the child that sometimes leads to unwelcome and painful actions. Not many parents delight in such discipline of the child. Indeed, it is "strange and alien" to many parents. The British psychoanalyst D. W. Winnicott has carefully delineated the work of a parent in nurturing the true self of the child by permitting the child to "gradually abrogate omnipotence."[2] It is this "strange and alien work" that causes the true self to emerge. To be sure, Winnicott has in mind a gentle intentionality that was not yet on the horizon of Isaiah. There is evidence, however, in the oracles of Hosea 11:1–9 and Jeremiah 31:20 that the gentleness of YHWH functioned to override harshness (see also Isaiah 49:14–16; 66:13). But the point is the same. A healthy child is neither fearfully conformist nor grandiose in autonomy, but learns to live in faithful, responsible interaction. So the prophet of YHWH does the work of YHWH that is normally and naturally restorative, but also does the work that is "strange and alien"—punitive and consequential. Both kinds of work are essential to Israel's good life. These complex oracles invite us to reflect on the ways that God wills a "Yes" toward us and the "No" of God that is evoked by our failure of fidelity.

Questions for Discussion

1. How do you understand God's "strange and alien work" of discipline?
2. How do you experience or think about God's "Yes" and "No" in Scripture and in life?
3. Does it help to know that "Yes" is God's preferred disposition? How so?
4. What is the ongoing place and role (if any) of God's "No" in your life or the world around you?

Chapter 18

Salvation by Returning and Rest Alone (Isaiah 30:15)

For thus says the Lord GOD, the Holy One of Israel:
In returning and rest you shall be saved;
  in quietness and in trust shall be your strength.

> ### *Scripture Passages for Reference*
>
> Isaiah 30:15–18
> Isaiah 7:9
> Isaiah 28:16
> Isaiah 31:1–3
> Exodus 15:21
> Leviticus 26:36–37

In our reflection on chapters 28–31 and 33 we have noticed two matters regularly placed in juxtaposition. On the one hand, each of these oracles begins with "woe," a term bespeaking the coming of *big trouble*. On the other hand, these oracles move toward *unconditional promise* through which YHWH will engage in restoration:

> No longer shall Jacob be ashamed,
>   no longer shall his face grow pale.
> For when he sees his children,
>   the work of my hands, in his midst,

> they will sanctify my name;
> they will sanctify the Holy One of Jacob,
>   and will stand in awe of the God of Israel.
> > 29:22–23
>
> Therefore the LORD waits to be gracious to you;
>   therefore he will rise up to show mercy to you.
> For the LORD is a God of justice;
>   blessed are all those who wait for him.
> > 30:18
>
> So the LORD of hosts will come down
>   to fight on Mount Zion and upon its hill.
> Like birds hovering overhead, so the LORD of hosts
>   will protect Jerusalem;
> he will protect and deliver it,
>   he will spare and rescue it.
> > 31:4–5
>
> But there the LORD in majesty will be for us
>   a place of broad rivers and streams,
> where no galley with oars can go,
>   nor stately ships can pass.
> For the LORD is our judge, the LORD is our ruler,
>   the LORD is our king; he will save us.
> . . . .
> And no inhabitant will say, "I am sick";
>   the people who live there will be forgiven their iniquity.
> > 33:21–24

This move from *threat* to *unconditional promise* is characteristic of Isaiah. In 30:15, however, we have quite a different prophetic impulse. In this verse there is no threat, nor is there any unconditional promise. Rather, the verse is a summons to an alternative that will require intentionality and that will result in altered practice and policy.

The invitation addressed to Jerusalem is to engage in "turning" (returning) and "rest," the practices essential to being saved. The first term, "turn/return," is a call to revise policy and practice. The second, "rest," is to cease all anxiety, agitation, and panic. Both of these terms become a tacit reference to YHWH even though the summons does not mention YHWH. To "turn" is to order life in sync with *the purpose of YHWH*. To be at rest is to stop frantic activity by trusting completely in *the saving governance of YHWH*. To turn means to embrace the requirements and disciplines of the covenant. To have rest is to engage in calm patience without seeking in aggressive ways to be self-sufficient and self-securing. The implied negative counterpoint is that if there is no turn and if there is no rest from agitated anxiety, there can be no "saving." In the context of Isaiah "turn" and "rest" likely constitute a summons to the royal house of David to cease its anxious policies that consist, on the one hand, in *making war* and, on the other hand, *seeking refuge and relief* from either Egypt or Assyria (31:1–3).

In the parallel line of our verse, the summons is to *quiet* and *trust* that yield hero-like "strength" (*gĕbûrāh*). Both *quiet* and *trust* bespeak serenity and freedom from disturbance. The same word pair occurs twice in Judges 18 to characterize a society that enjoys well-being. In these cases our term "trust" is translated as "unsuspecting":

> When they came to Laish, they observed the people who were there living securely, after the manner of the Sidonians, *quiet and unsuspecting*, lacking nothing on earth, and possessing wealth. (Judges 18:7)

> The priest who belonged to him came to Laish to a people *quiet and unsuspecting*. (v. 27)

The stance of "quiet and trust" yields real strength that is lacking among those who live in agitation and anxiety.

By the end of the verse, however, the prophet obviously indicts the royal house for its negative response to the summons: "You refused." The royal house in Jerusalem was no longer capable of such a *turn* or such a *rest,* and knew nothing of *quiet* or *trust*. The prophet puts into words what the royal impulse had expressed in action. The refusal of Jerusalem, according to Isaiah, is in two statements:

> No! We will flee upon horses.
> We will ride upon swift steeds.

That is, "No, we will not turn and we will not rest. We will continue our futile military efforts." Mention of "horses and swift steeds" alludes to war, for these are the indispensable armaments for battle. Thus we may imagine either King Ahaz or King Hezekiah reiterating his military policy that is a gesture of self-sufficiency: "We will not abandon our military preparedness nor will we give up our itch for battle."

These two lines of defiance by royal Jerusalem are answered in the two lines of prophetic response. First, the royal resolve to "flee on horses" will result, says the prophet, in flight: "Therefore you *shall* flee!" That is, you shall retreat in panic and defeat, for your horses and chariots cannot save you (see already Exodus 15:21). Second, the royal resolve for swift *steeds* will result, says the prophet, in swift *pursuers*: "Your pursuers shall be swift." In each of these two cases the prophet turns royal resolve against the king. Military aggression will not work! Military preparedness is futile!

The prophet then adds in verse 17 a reprise on the verdict of verse 16. The prophet anticipates that current military policy in Jerusalem will end in disaster and will generate more fear and more anxiety that are in fact quite disproportionate to the actual threat. That is, Israel's panic will not be connected to any military reality; it will be grounded in and energized by alienation from YHWH. This conclusion voiced by the prophet is a reiteration of an ancient covenantal curse:

> As for those of you who survive, I will send faintness into their hearts in the lands of their enemies; the sound of a driven leaf shall put them to flight, and they shall flee as one flees from the sword, and they shall fall though no one pursues. They shall stumble over one another, as if to escape a sword, though no one pursues; and you shall have no power to stand against your enemies. (Leviticus 26:36–37)

Jerusalem's foolish policies will evoke some of the oldest curses that are sure to follow from alienation from YHWH. In that alienation the royal house will completely misread military reality.

It should be noted that the prophet does not delineate a precise practical policy. Rather, the prophet is engaged in metahistorical claims concerning the foolishness of the royal house, because Isaiah does not and cannot tell the kings what to do. His metahistorical claim, however, has immediate implication for real historical action. Thus Norman Gottwald can conclude,

Salvation by Returning and Rest Alone (Isaiah 30:15)

> The quality in political leadership which Isaiah prized above all others was calmness of spirit and possession of mind, rooted in a deep trust in Yahweh's control of history. All that smacks of haste and fear is stamped by impermanence and only evokes its own forces of disintegration.[1]

This calmness of spirit is the exact opposite of the "fog of war" that has seduced the United States into various conflicts in Vietnam, Iraq, and Afghanistan. This same motif becomes a signature conviction for the prophet:

> If you do not stand firm in faith,
> you shall not stand at all.
> Isaiah 7:9

> One who trusts will not panic.
> 28:16

The better wisdom for policy is the recognition that human players are penultimate in the historical process. They are not permitted the *hubris* that imagines they may take ultimate action. Nor are they permitted *despair* to imagine that nothing practical can be done. The prophet seeks to articulate Jerusalemite policy in a wholly different frame of reference. It is a frame of reference that must have seemed foolish to those who had long since forgotten the crucial claim of Sinai that YHWH is the savior God who can emancipate even from superpowers like Egypt.

There is obviously no ready or easy "application" of this prophetic teaching to contemporary political realities. We can note, however, that much US military posturing has been based on miscalculation that is grounded in fear and/or pride. In Vietnam, it was an unfounded fear of the expansion of Communist China that propelled the war, when the reality of history has shown that Southeast Asia was not in a rush to submit to China. More recently, panic before "terrorism" or before the "onslaught of Islam" has generated military crises for the United States that have taken forms of aggression quite disproportionate to historical reality.

The tradition of Isaiah offered no easy advice to royal Jerusalem. Nor does it, in contemporary reading, make things easy or obvious for us now. It is clear, nevertheless, that confidence in YHWH's rule of history permits a different frame of reference for sane, sober, judicious policy formation. When that grounding in divine governance is absent, fearful governments are likely to be engaged in self-destructive foolishness. Thus the call of Isaiah is to turn from self-destructive foolishness. Such a turn would entail the curbing of anxiety and agitation in a way that permits centered calmness, a calmness that does not rely excessively on the strength of horses or the speed of swift steeds, or the size of military spending or of a church's budget. It might be the hope of the prophet that the policy-makers in Jerusalem back then and among us now would pause for this prayer:

> O LORD my heart is not lifted up,
> > my eyes are not raised too high;
> I do not occupy myself in things
> > too great and too marvelous for me.
> But I have calmed and quieted my soul,
> > like a weaned child with its mother;
> > my soul is like the weaned child that is with me.
> O Israel, hope in the LORD
> > from this time on and forevermore.
>
> Psalm 131

Questions for Discussion

1. Do you agree that "human players are penultimate in the historical process"?
2. How might we consider returning and resting now—in our lives, in our churches, and in our country?
3. How do you navigate between hubris and despair?
4. How does confidence in God's "rule of history" permit a different and more sane, sober, and judicious frame of reference for your life?

Chapter 19

Exodus 2.0
(Isaiah 35:10)

*And the ransomed of the LORD shall return,
and come to Zion with singing;
everlasting joy shall be upon their heads;
they shall obtain joy and gladness,
and sorrow and sighing shall flee away.*

> **Scripture Passages for Reference**
>
> Isaiah 35:1–10
> Isaiah 40:3–5
> Isaiah 43:18–21
> Luke 9:28–36

Isaiah 34–35 seems to strike a different tone from the chapters that precede it, and it is set off from what follows in 36:1–39:8, which is almost entirely a run of prose material that is also found in 2 Kings 18:13–20:19. After chapter 39, of course, come chapters 40 and following, which for a number of reasons—tone being a major one—are identified as new sections in the Isaiah tradition: Second Isaiah in chapters 40–55 and Third Isaiah in 56–66. According to many, what is found in chapters 34–35 is quite similar to Second Isaiah, so much so that many believe these chapters once belonged to Second Isaiah but have been moved forward in the book for some reason—invading First Isaiah, as it were—perhaps as a way to anticipate what is coming in chapter 40 after the prose insert of chapters 36–39. The judgment that these two chapters are similar to Second Isaiah is especially true for chapter 35, a text of promise containing our verse that speaks of the joyous return of the exiles, called here "the ransomed of the LORD" (see also 51:11).

This return, both here and in Second Isaiah more broadly, is presented as a new and improved exodus (see 40:3–5; 43:18–21). In our technological society, we might call it "Exodus 2.0"—the upgrade! Both the similarities and dissimilarities (the latter representing improvements) between the "old" exodus and the "new" one should be observed.

The most obvious similarity is that in both instances the people move through wilderness, dry land, and desert. In Exodus–Numbers, the wilderness stretching between Egypt and Canaan proved formidable for Israel's trek. Here, however, we find a major dissimilarity between Exodus 1.0 and Exodus 2.0. In the "new and improved" exodus

> The wilderness and the dry land shall be glad,
>   the desert shall rejoice and blossom;
> like the crocus it shall blossom abundantly,
>   and rejoice with joy and singing.
> The glory of Lebanon shall be given to it,
>   the majesty of Carmel and Sharon.
>   Isaiah 35:1–2a

This sentiment is repeated, and extensively, elsewhere in chapters 40–55. For example,

> A voice cries out:
>
> "In the wilderness prepare the way of the LORD,
>   make straight in the desert a highway for our God.
> Every valley shall be lifted up,
>   and every mountain and hill be made low;
> the uneven ground shall become level,
>   and the rough places a plain.
> Then the glory of the LORD shall be revealed,
>   and all people shall see it together,
>   for the mouth of the LORD has spoken."
>   40:3–5

> I am about to do a new thing;
>   now it springs forth, do you not perceive it?
> I will make a way in the wilderness
>   and rivers in the desert.
> The wild animals will honor me,
>   the jackals and the ostriches;
> for I give water in the wilderness,
>   rivers in the desert,
> to give drink to my chosen people,
>   the people whom I formed for myself
> so that they might declare my praise.
>
>   43:19–21[1]

The upgraded version of the exodus helps explain the idea expressed in 43:18–19 (and elsewhere) that God is doing a "new thing" such that the "old" or "former things" do not need to be remembered anymore (see also 42:9; 43:18; 48:6; cf. 65:17; 66:22). That's how spectacular and transformative God's new work is!

The "old" exodus witnessed divine provision in the desert: first bitter water made sweet, then manna from heaven (which in some traditions was nothing less than the bread of angels but in others grew tiresome to the palate—see Psalm 78:24–25; Numbers 11:6), then quail, and more water from a rock. Yet none of these miraculous instances of divine beneficence come close to what is imagined in the "new" exodus. In the upgrade, the wilderness is no longer only a place where, despite all evidence to the contrary, God satisfies human needs. No, now God transforms the wilderness itself. The desert blooms, something that normal deserts can in fact do, but not at this level. "The glory of Lebanon," the abundant forests of Israel's northern neighbor, will be given to this desert, which would mean it should probably not be called a "desert" anymore. So also "the majesty" of the rich geographical areas of Carmel and Sharon are handed over to what was formerly (but no longer rightly) considered "dry land." Still further, the wilderness that the returnees traverse in Exodus 2.0 is personified: it not only blossoms, as flora are wont to do; it *feels* and *exults*. It is "glad," it "rejoices," not unlike what we find in the Psalms:

> Let the heavens be glad, and let the earth rejoice;
>   let the sea roar, and all that fills it;

> let the field exult, and everything in it.
> Then shall all the trees of the forest sing for joy
> > before the LORD; for he is coming,
> > for he is coming to judge the earth.
> He will judge the world with righteousness,
> > and the peoples with his truth.
>
> Psalm 96:11–13

> Let the sea roar, and all that fills it;
> > the world and those who live in it.
> Let the floods clap their hands;
> > let the hills sing together for joy
> at the presence of the LORD, for he is coming
> > to judge the earth.
> He will judge the world with righteousness,
> > and the peoples with equity.
>
> 98:7–9

Like the psalmists, the prophet sees the "inanimate" world fully animate; even barren land is suddenly the "theater of God's glory" (Calvin). No wonder Isaiah 35:2 ends with

> They shall see the glory of the LORD,
> > the majesty of our God. (Isaiah 35:2b)

The "they" here is the wilderness, dry land, and desert!

This seeing, accompanied by rejoicing, suggests a kind of theophany, a revelatory appearance of God on earth. That is what Psalms 96 and 98 imagine as well, and they rejoice that this divine arrival is accompanied by divine judgment (!) marked by *righteousness*, *equity*, and *truth*. Our linkage of the prophet to the psalmists at this point is confirmed by what follows in Isaiah 35, where our poet shifts from observing the desert in flower to addressing the audience. They should be strong, take heart, and fear not (vv. 3–4a) because

> Here is your God.
> > He will come with vengeance,
> > with terrible recompense.
> > He will come and save you.
>
> v. 4b

Vengeance and *recompense* are not polite words, at least in church. If we are honest, however, they are always present whenever we look in the mirror, and they are more and more accepted—to a disturbing degree—in recent politics, entertainment, and media. Importantly, in Isaiah's vision, vengeance and recompense are *divine*, which immediately distances them, and drastically so, from any and all human forms with which we are familiar. God's vengeance and recompense are, moreover, for salvific ends. That is why, returning to Psalms 96 and 98, the natural world is thrilled at the coming judgment of God: because it will set everything straight.

In the case of the new and improved Exodus 2.0, this "setting straight" involves the healing of human sickness (vv. 5–6a) and the further transformation of nature (vv. 6b–7). This will facilitate the return of those who are weak and weary or otherwise incapacitated to make the return (see 40:27–31; it also reverses the damning verdict found in 6:9–10). Further facilitation is provided by the smooth road that will run from the place of exile back home:

> A highway shall be there,
>   and it shall be called the Holy Way;
> the unclean shall not travel on it,
>   but it shall be for God's people;
>   no traveler, not even fools, shall go astray [on it].
>   35:8

Even those who are the absolute worst with directions won't get lost on this road! Furthermore, this road is completely safe:

> No lion shall be there,
>   nor shall any ravenous beast come up on it;
> they shall not be found there.
>   35:9a

Instead, "the redeemed shall walk there" (v. 9b) undisturbed, at peace, and at leisure.

Finally comes our verse, which summarizes what has come before and clarifies a good bit in the process. This highway is for those redeemed (v. 9) and ransomed (v. 10), they who return to Zion from parts unspecified in the poem but known to the reader of the larger

Isaiah tradition—from exile! They return, neither wounded nor scarred, but healed (vv. 5–6) and full of song (v. 10a). Instead of sorrow, they will have "everlasting joy" (v. 10b; cf. Psalm 30:5, 11). They will "obtain joy and gladness" according to Isaiah 35:10b, or perhaps better (in the CEB translation), "happiness and joy will overwhelm them"! Either way, the final line (repeated in 51:11 for good measure) is clear: those who take "Holy Highway 1" from exile to "Zion Exit" do so in the complete absence of sadness and depression, grief and groaning. Those are long gone; those things have fled for their lives (35:10c)!

By the end of Isaiah 35, the transformation of the exiles is thus as drastic as the transformation of the desert at the start of the chapter. On the face of it, each transformation seems impossible. But the poetry summons us to see the very "glory of the LORD, the majesty of our God" (v. 2). This is the God who brought Israel out of Egypt. The slavery in Egypt was due to no fault of Israel's own; God's miraculous deliverance from a tyrannical pharaoh and his politics of oppression was (and is!) worth commemorating from the first Passover (Exodus 12) to the present, celebrated annually in the Passover Haggadah. But this deliverance is commemorated not only in the Passover; the exodus event is a fundamental paradigm for the life of Israel's faith, referred to explicitly or alluded to implicitly throughout the pages of the Old Testament and New. Isaiah's "new exodus" is one such instance, and a very important one. The *continuities* between the old exodus and the new demonstrate that the same God is at work in both. The *discontinuities* are not at odds with what has come before—antithetical in some way—but, rather, are improvements. These upgrades may be present because the situation has changed: "Egypt 2.0" is Babylon, and the sojourn there is not due to a tyrannical pharaoh but the despotic heart of one (or rather many) in Israel and Judah who was unfaithful, disobedient, recalcitrant. And within that first cause for the sojourn of exile there was a second cause: God's punitive hand. Since it was in part (but only in part!) God who put Israel in exile, it makes sense that the God who now delivers from that exile does so with extra panache. In no small way, therefore, the "extras" in Exodus 2.0—the healing and joy of both the wilderness and the exiles—serve as nonverbal assurance of God's accompaniment and goodwill. Yes, YHWH played a role in the exile, but YHWH is ultimately the exodusing God. To prove this yet again and once more, the big picture of this new exodus is the same: crossing a wilderness to return home. Only this time there is so much *more*: a desert so overfull with beauty and fecundity that it might as well be a different biome, through which runs a highway so straight and smooth (see 40:4) that no one could possibly get off track, and certainly not for forty years!

Three points of connection between our text and the New Testament can be noted briefly: First, in response to John the Baptist's query if Jesus is indeed "the one to come," Jesus alludes to the healing promised in Isaiah 35:5–6 as proof of his identity (Matthew 11:5; Luke 7:22; see also Mark 7:37). This means that Jesus's work in the Gospels is part of the highway of holiness back home to God. Second, further testimony to the exodusing God and the fundamental import of the exodus event is found in the fact that Christ's passion takes place during Passover. Third, the second point casts light on a fascinating detail in the story of the Transfiguration. Luke 9:31 provides details about what Moses and Elijah say to Jesus when they appear alongside him: they "spoke of his departure, which he was to accomplish at Jerusalem." In Greek, "his departure" is *exodon autou*, woodenly translated, "his exodus"!

Questions for Discussion

1. Why do you think God's new deliverance is portrayed with imagery drawn from the earlier deliverance of God's people from Egypt?
2. Can you think of other passages in the Bible that also draw on the imagery of the exodus?
3. Why do you think the exodus is so foundational to the biblical imagination?
4. What new things might God be doing now? What do you make of the use of "exodus" in the Transfiguration account of Luke 9?

Chapter 20

The Lord Said to Me: Destroy (Isaiah 36:10)

Moreover, is it without the LORD that I have come up against this land to destroy it? The LORD said to me, Go up against this land, and destroy it.

> **Scripture Passages for Reference**
>
> Isaiah 36:1–37:38
> Isaiah 7:3
> Isaiah 10:5–19

It must be stressed, first and foremost, that our verse is not found on the lips of the prophet Isaiah, who, like all of the Old Testament prophets, speaks for the Lord and in the Lord's name, even in the Lord's voice. It is, rather, part of the speech attributed to an Assyrian official known as "the Rabshakeh." *Rabshakeh* is the Hebrew equivalent of what was originally two Akkadian words meaning "chief cupbearer." (Akkadian was the language used in Assyria.) This title did not designate some sort of waiter or palace servant but was reserved for a very high administrative official—indeed, the only official listed in Isaiah 36 as the king's designee (cf. 2 Kings 18:17). In brief, the Rabshakeh is nothing less than the chief and official spokesman for the Assyrian king, which in the present circumstance is Sennacherib (36:1). The Rabshakeh would have had a

126 Unwavering Faithfulness

personal name, but the Old Testament is uninterested in that. Only the title matters; this person is identified entirely and exclusively with his role. The Rabshakeh is Sennacherib's "Press Secretary" or, likely better, "Minister of Propaganda."

Before proceeding, we should recall that chapters 36–39 are a mostly prose inset that interrupts the poetry of Isaiah and that appears also, in virtually identical fashion, in 2 Kings 18:13–20:19. It may be that these chapters were drawn directly from 2 Kings, or vice versa, or that both, in turn, derive from a third account that preceded both. Why this material is duplicated here is not clear; perhaps it was felt necessary to round out "First Isaiah" with a historical appendix. Whatever the case, in its current form, chapters 36–39 intervene between what is historically later material—namely, Isaiah 34–35 and 40–55. Such an interlude is likely by design, and we do well to ponder it rather than dismiss it as the work of a lazy editor.

Chapter 36 begins with the specific time of the Rabshakeh's speech: it happened in the fourteenth year of King Hezekiah, or 701 BCE, a date confirmed by Assyrian annals. The text also specifies the circumstances in considerable detail: in this year, Sennacherib "came up against all the fortified cities of Judah and captured them" (v. 1). The Assyrian campaign is described as *thoroughly successful*, as even fortified cities stood no chance. But Jerusalem, still standing, does have a chance. And so, while Sennacherib is occupied with Lachish (to the southwest), he sends the Rabshakeh "with a great army" (v. 2) to parley with Hezekiah. Given the success recounted in v. 1 and the sheer size of the army accompanying the Rabshakeh, it is clear that Hezekiah and Jerusalem are in dire straits.

The location of the parley may have been strategic for the Assyrians, but perhaps this detail is intended to call our minds back to Isaiah 7:3 since the same location is mentioned there. In chapter 7, Isaiah encouraged King Ahaz in the face of a similarly tense military stand-off. Will a later king also receive a promise of divine deliverance?

The Rabshakeh begins the negotiations, speaking extensively and directly (vv. 4–20). He is interrupted only once, and briefly, by the Jerusalemite delegation (v. 11), who subsequently answer with silence (vv. 21–22). The Rabshakeh's speech is not only lengthy and straightforward, it is also a masterful piece of rhetoric, one that is delivered in the Hebrew language (called "Judahite" in vv. 11, 13) so that all within earshot can understand it (v. 12). This is much to the chagrin of the Judean officials, who would prefer to conduct these negotiations in Aramaic (v. 11), the official language of the Assyrian Empire in the west. The Rabshakeh sticks to Hebrew because he knows his message—and his threats—are for everyone, not just Hezekiah or his officials, but all who are facing the worst conditions in the imminent siege when they will be forced to consume their own feces and urine (v. 12).

The situation is dismal, as war always is, but the Rabshakeh offers a way out, shrewd rhetor that he is. He begins by using the messenger formula commonly used by the prophets: "Thus says the great king," he begins, "the king . . . *of Assyria*" (v. 4a)! The empire's name occurs in final position, as if held in reserve for maximum effect. The true king, according to the Rabshakeh, is not YHWH, "high and lifted up," as in 6:1. Nor is it "the LORD, the Most High . . . awesome . . . great king over all the earth" (Psalm 47:2; see also Malachi 1:14) who is "a great God, and a great King above all gods" (Psalm 95:3). YHWH has been demoted, according to Assyria, as has Jerusalem, which is no longer "beautiful in elevation . . . the joy of all the earth, Mount Zion . . . the city of the great King" (Psalm 48:2; see also Matthew 5:35). In the Assyrian calculus there is only one who can be "great king." It is Sennacherib. The very way the Rabshakeh's speech begins, along with its content, is sure to remind us, however, that there is another King who stands above and beyond Assyria, mighty as the empire might appear (and truly is).

The Rabshakeh proceeds to dismantle every hope that Hezekiah and Judah might possibly entertain.[1] Egyptian aid is the most proximate military option, but Pharaoh is a worthless ally (vv. 4b–6). Next addressed is divine assistance, but the Rabshakeh comes prepared, perhaps with military intelligence that suggests all is not well within the political landscape of Judah. The Rabshakeh notes that the people of Jerusalem might say, "We trust in YHWH," but it was Hezekiah himself who dismantled a good bit of YHWH worship by shutting down high places and altars and centralizing worship in Jerusalem. These reforms are mentioned in 2 Kings 18:3–6, where they are explicitly said to be "right in the sight of YHWH." The Rabshakeh thus misunderstands Hezekiah's reform or intentionally misconstrues it (cf. 10:10–11). Alternatively, perhaps some in ancient Israel believed the various cult sites throughout the land were Yahwistic in some fashion, though the historian responsible for 2 Kings clearly thought otherwise. Whatever the case, the second "point" in the Rabshakeh's speech sows or reflects internal dissension—something shrewd colonizers capitalize upon.

Next, the Rabshakeh conducts a thought experiment: Assyria will pony up 2,000 horses if Hezekiah can provide riders for them. Since Hezekiah does not have such forces available, he stands no chance (vv. 8–9). The final, climactic point in the Rabshakeh's brilliant propaganda returns to the question of divine aid. As it happens—according to Assyria—the only reason Sennacherib has come to conquer and destroy Judah is *because YHWH wills it* (v. 10). Assyria comes with the Lord's assistance and at the Lord's command! This is a stunning and devastating theological claim and is surely what prompts the Jerusalemite officials to request further negotiations to be more discreet, conducted in a language less widely known (v. 11). But it is too late; the claim that YHWH is behind Sennacherib is out in the open, which is exactly how the Assyrians want it. All will suffer should Hezekiah choose the wrong path (v. 12). And so the Rabshakeh doubles down, shouting this time in a loud voice—and in Hebrew—the message of the great Assyrian king (v. 13). The message is even more direct this time, with yet another possible source of confidence dismantled. Jerusalem may trust in the good king Hezekiah, but he, too, is unable to deliver (v. 14). Don't fall for Hezekiah's piety either, the Rabshakeh adds; don't believe any pie-in-the-sky "God will deliver us" message. Don't listen to Hezekiah, because, to the contrary, "thus says the king of Assyria" (vv. 15–16). After this come several false promises of peace and prosperity from the Assyrian king, all of which are given the lie by verse 17's "until I come and take you away," followed by further lies about how idyllic life in exile will turn out to be.

Religion matters deeply in conflicts like this, so the Rabshakeh further undermines Hezekiah and his trust in YHWH's deliverance (vv. 18–20a; repeated, to further effect, slightly later in 37:10–13). Look around, the official says. All of the gods of all of Assyria's enemies are gone; they are powerless in the face of Assyrian might. There is no track record of divine deliverance to even consider. Sennacherib has won every battle against every god, every country,

The Lord Said to Me: Destroy (Isaiah 36:10)   129

every king. Why should YHWH or Hezekiah or Judah be any different? Jerusalem is already within his grip (36:20b).

The Jerusalem envoys say nothing in response (v. 21). Hezekiah had ordered their silence, but even if he hadn't, the brilliance of the Assyrian's rhetoric and its (apparent) truthfulness likely left them dumbfounded. Shaken, they return to the king, tearing their clothes as a sign of mourning.

The narrative continues on through the end of chapter 37, which is followed by an account of Hezekiah's illness (chap. 38) and a later visit from a Babylonian contingent (chap. 39). The rest of the story shows that Hezekiah and Jerusalem survive. But our verse still gives us pause. How should we evaluate the Rabshakeh's comment that it was YHWH himself who gave aid to Sennacherib and who commanded his mission to attack and destroy?

On the one hand, we would no doubt wish to dismiss this comment. Assyria is the "bad guy," with Hezekiah, Jerusalem, Judah, and all the rest "the good guys." Bad guys lie, and so we are tempted to dismiss the Rabshakeh's remark as unadulterated, self-serving political propaganda, which no doubt it is. And yet we who read Isaiah know that things are not so simple. The Rabshakeh is not all wrong. Earlier in the book, we have repeatedly heard of YHWH using other nations as punitive instruments against God's people, including, especially, Assyria, which God calls, "the rod of my anger—the club [of] . . . my fury" (10:5; cf. Babylon's mention in 39:6–7). This, then, is the "on the other hand"; we cannot dismiss the Rabshakeh's comment as total fabrication. He speaks truth, somehow, even if he doesn't know it in the same way that we who read Isaiah do.

In the Assyrian's mouth, this comment may be pure mendacity, little more than a ploy to discourage and dissuade Hezekiah and Jerusalem from further resistance. But in Isaiah's mouth—and in YHWH's own mouth—the comment is *not* all falsehood. Isaiah along with other biblical prophets can see the unseen hand of YHWH in the geopolitical events of the day. They go so far as to say that YHWH takes credit for those events or, at least, for many of them, and to a degree that often makes us uncomfortable.

This receives shocking confirmation in chapter 37, where Isaiah sends a lengthy message back to Hezekiah about Sennacherib. It is sent to Hezekiah, but it is really an oracle against Sennacherib. That "great king" has messed with the wrong God! As for Jerusalem, the city isn't worried in the least about Sennacherib; it mocks him (37:22), perhaps because he has mocked "the Holy One of Israel" (vv. 23–24). Assyria has overestimated itself, thinking that its many accomplishments were its own doing (vv. 24–25):

> *My* many chariots
> *I* have gone up . . .
> *I* felled . . .
> *I* came . . .
> *I* dug . . .
> *I* dried up . . .

But no. All this was the Holy One's plan. Hadn't Sennacherib heard as much—heard that all of this was determined by YHWH "long ago" (v. 26a)?

> I planned from days of old
>   what now I bring to pass,
> that you should make fortified cities
>   crash into heaps of ruins.
>   v. 26b

This stunning claim is entirely in line with the Rabshakeh's comment, only this time it comes not from an Assyrian propagandist but from the Lord God of Israel, who here claims total responsibility for Assyria's path of destruction (see also 10:6). So is the Rabshakeh right after all?

We who read Isaiah know that there are limits to any and all worldly power, including Assyria's. And we know that Assyria is in the habit of overestimating its power and importance (see 10:13–14). No ax, however, can "vaunt itself over the one who wields it" (10:15). YHWH is intimately acquainted with Sennacherib and his ways (cf. Psalm 139:1–4), which includes "your raging against me" (Isaiah 37:28). Assyria is not only mistaken and overconfident about the true source of its power; it is now in active rebellion against it. "Raging" is mentioned twice (vv. 28–29a), but the offenses also include mockery and reviling (vv. 23–24; cf. vv. 4, 6, 17) and arrogance (v. 29b), exemplified by a raised voice and haughty eyes (v. 23).

Sennacherib and all his company ought to know better (v. 26a); they should not be deceived because YHWH is not a God who will be mocked (Galatians 6:7). Hezekiah's hope, expressed in a message to the prophet, has been realized: YHWH has indeed heard the words of the Rabshakeh, YHWH does indeed rebuke those words, YHWH receives the prayer for the remnant (v. 4). The Rabshakeh has been clever with his speech containing many compelling points, but the divine response is equally clever and multipronged:

- *To Hezekiah*: Do not be afraid, I will cause Sennacherib to fall by the sword back home in Assyria (vv. 6–7).
- *To Sennacherib*: I'll treat you like you treated so many other kings, putting a hook in your nose and a bit in your mouth, sending you back to where you came from (v. 29; see also v. 33).
- *To the remnant*: As a divine sign, your stump shall grow again thanks to the zeal of YHWH of hosts (vv. 31–32; cf. 6:13; 7:14–17).
- *To the Assyrian army*: An angel strikes down 185,000 troops (37:36).

We do not know how all this happened, especially the loss of Assyrian troops. The prophet doesn't say, perhaps because miracles cannot be fully explained. But we know from both the Bible and Assyrian records that Jerusalem was not taken and that Sennacherib did indeed die in a coup back home (vv. 37–38).

In sum, the Rabshakeh got part of it right—those who deceive us typically do. That is what makes their deception so powerful. As a result, on the ground, it is often very hard to know if one's confidence is rightly placed (36:4), and so we worry if "mere words" will suffice for "strategy and power for war" (v. 5). Most likely they will not. But the Word of the Lord is a very different matter. That Word says, "Fear not!" (37:6), and that Word cares for the remnant such that there is always a word after and beyond "destroy." As the later Isaiah tradition asserts: the Word of our God will stand forever (40:8).

Questions for Discussion

1. What do you make of the Rabshakeh's speech and how he gets some things about God's purpose right?
2. How do you imagine making hard decisions about what to do in the midst of difficult situations like that facing Hezekiah and Jerusalem? What does it mean to call on God in situations like that?
3. How is God's perspective on geopolitics and the warring empires different from the Assyrian one when they look so similar?

Chapter 21

Hope (in/for) the Lord! (Isaiah 40:31)

Those who wait for the LORD shall renew their strength,
they shall mount up with wings like eagles,
they shall run and not be weary,
they shall walk and not faint.

> ***Scripture Passages for Reference***
>
> Isaiah 40:27–31
> Isaiah 8:17, 19–20
> Isaiah 33:2, 22
> Isaiah 44:24–28
> Isaiah 51:5
> Isaiah 55:12
> Isaiah 60:9
> Isaiah 61:1–2
> Mark 13:35–37

After the shameless sellout of King Hezekiah to the Babylonians (39:1–8), most biblical scholars believe that the Isaiah tradition went silent for 150 years. During that long silence, Jerusalem was sacked by the Babylonians, the temple was razed, what was left of the royal family was deported, and leaders of the Jerusalem community were displaced into exile (see 2 Kings 24–25). Only after that long silence does the Isaiah tradition speak again, now in a very different idiom (40:1).

Here, in a mighty eruption of poetry, a new voice of the tradition (called Second Isaiah) speaks to announce a new era in the life of Israel and in the history of the world. As the introduction to this mighty new declaration, chapter 40 is like an overture to a vigorous fugue, which sounds themes and then circles back to reiterate the same themes in different, fresh forms. Here the recurring themes are hope, restoration, and homecoming.

Chapter 40 opens with a declaration that the quid pro quo requirements of *sin and punishment* in the tradition of Deuteronomy—or, earlier, in First Isaiah!—have been satisfied (vv. 1–2). Israel has served its time in the big house! There follows a discussion among the angels and messengers who surround the throne of the Holy One of Israel (vv. 3–8). The outcome of that discussion, imagined by the poet, is the designation of a prophetic speaker to announce the new decision made by the heavenly court of YHWH that concerns the future of history on earth and the future of Israel. This imagery is a poetic strategy whereby the poet can assert the governance of the world by YHWH. The new decree of YHWH entrusted to the prophetic speaker is good news, a "gospel." The one who utters it is a "gospel herald" (v. 9). The substance of the new assertion of God's gospel is this: "Here is your God!" (v. 9). Behold YHWH! See YHWH! Notice YHWH! That is the sum of the new voicing of Isaiah, a declaration articulated differently in 52:7 as "Your God rules!" (CEB).

This announcement of the fresh emergence of YHWH is an astonishing declaration. Heretofore in the Isaiah tradition, YHWH had dispatched Sennacherib and the Assyrians (10:6; 36:13–20; 37:1–13) and Nebuchadnezzar and the Babylonians (47:6; see Jeremiah 25:9; 27:6) in order to enact the divine intention against Jerusalem. That divine intention in both cases was to punish Israel for its covenantal disobedience.

But now YHWH makes a new appearance. In what follows in Isaiah, it turns out that YHWH's new historical intention is through the work of Cyrus the Persian (44:24–28; 45:1). But it is all YHWH! It is all the fresh intention, will, and purpose of YHWH that formerly displaced Israel should now return home to Jerusalem. Cyrus is at best a bit player in this dramatic divine initiative.

Hope (in/for) the Lord! (Isaiah 40:31) 135

What follows in chapter 40 is a doxological rendering of YHWH. He is a mighty warrior (v. 10) and a gentle shepherd (v. 11). In 40:12–17 YHWH is a mighty sovereign before whom the nations are "a drop in the bucket" (v. 15). So Sennacherib, Nebuchadnezzar, and Cyrus are each one tiny drop in the bucket of divine sovereignty. There is no one like YHWH, certainly no god with such authority (vv. 18–20, 25). There is no god like YHWH because YHWH is the creator of the world before whom all royal and divine pretenders are as "grasshoppers" of insignificance (v. 22).

As chapter 40 reaches its culmination, the poet acknowledges and responds to the complaint of Israel in exile. Israel in exile had complained that YHWH was inattentive and uncaring concerning its plight (v. 27; see the book of Lamentations). To the contrary, says the poet. This God is neither inattentive nor uncaring. This God announced in the gospel of verse 9 is the God who empowers and who strengthens. The targets of divine empowerment are the powerless and the faint, the despairing Judean exiles who imagined they had no future and who, as a result, were perhaps ready to give up on YHWH. But YHWH does not settle for the status quo. YHWH, by immeasurable power and unflinching purpose, can and will invert Israel's situation of hopelessness and helplessness.

In verse 30 the poet repeats the same words of verse 29 in order to counter them. The targets of YHWH's new intervention are "the faint" (*yā'ap*) and the "weary" (*yāga'*). This deflated, despondent population includes young people whom we do not expect to be faint or weary or exhausted. We expect them to have energy and exuberance. But they too are weary and faint, because despair wears out even the best and the strongest. That sorry condition, however, is countered exactly by YHWH in verse 28. It is YHWH, none other, who is *not* faint (*lō' + yā'ap*) and *not* weary (*lō' + yāga'*). YHWH has not given in to or come to terms with the condition of Israel in exile. YHWH is otherwise! YHWH is an agent with endless resources. YHWH is an emancipator with wide historical reach. YHWH is covenant partner of Israel with acres of energy for well-being.

Thus chapter 40 is a lyrical sketch of YHWH who is now to be seen and beheld in the midst of international affairs. This God, who is warrior and shepherd without parallel, is back in play after a long dormancy. And now, in verse 31, the final one in the chapter, Israel is summoned to engage this God and to take seriously the reality of this God who alters the prospects of everything in the life of Israel. YHWH is not an add-on or an afterthought to Israel's plight. YHWH is the key to transformation in a historical circumstance where no transformation appears to be possible. It is not hard work that evokes faintness and weariness. It is despair! It is the conviction that there is no possible future available. And now, in this sweeping utterance, the poet intends to override all such weariness by making palpable and available the God who makes all things new.

Israel is summoned to "wait YHWH." In the Hebrew text there is no connecting preposition, just the imperative verb and the divine name. "Wait" might convey that Israel should have some patience until YHWH is ready to intrude into its life in transformative ways. But "wait," in conventional rendering, is too passive. Rather, this "wait" in the mood of command is better translated as "hope." "Hope YHWH!" Hope *in* YHWH! Hope *for* YHWH! Expect YHWH! The poet has voiced this long chapter as a sketch of YHWH in order to issue this imperative summons to despairing Israel in exile. It is this God, and none other, who is the ground for Israel's expectation that is to counter the despair dictated by circumstance.

While the term "wait/hope" is not frequent in the book of Isaiah, it is possible to notice the theme in all parts of the book. In First Isaiah, the verb occurs twice in 8:17: "I will *wait* for the LORD, who is hiding his face from the house of Jacob, and I will *hope* in him." The speaker, the prophet Isaiah, will wait for YHWH, will hope in YHWH in the midst of the Assyrian threat against Jerusalem. The prophet will hope, even though YHWH is hiding his face from Israel in the same terms voiced later in 40:21–23. Israel (and the prophet) does not hope in YHWH when YHWH is obvious, easy, and available. To the contrary, hoping must be done when God's face is hidden and God is not present. With this declaration of hope in 8:17, the prophet goes on to describe those who hope falsely, who wrongly appeal to ghosts or to the gods of the dead (8:19). Such false hope will provide "no dawn" (8:20). Such false hope, rather, will end in distress, darkness, gloom, and anguish. In contrast to such dismal prospects from false hope, however, are those who hope in YHWH. For those who hope, there follows the great familiar "messianic" vision of Isaiah 9:2–7 that anticipates a new royal rescue. Hope lodged elsewhere will fail. Hope addressed singularly to YHWH will be assured a new governance of justice and righteousness that will continue to expand (9:7).

The same term of hope is utilized in the poetry of Isaiah in 33:2:

> O LORD, be gracious to us; we *wait* for you.
> Be our arm every morning,
> our salvation in the time of trouble.

In this lyrical chapter those who wait for and expect from YHWH will see God arise in power (33:10) and come in beauty (33:17). They will have confidence to know this:

> The LORD is our judge, the LORD is our ruler,
> the LORD is our king; he will save us.
>
> 33:22

The same theme of hope occurs in exilic usage in 51:5. God issues an assurance to people in exile:

> I will bring near my deliverance swiftly,
> my salvation has gone out
> and my arms will rule the peoples;
> the coastlands wait for me,
> and for my arm they hope.

The imagery concerns exiles eager to go home. They have their bags packed for the journey. They are standing waiting in hope, at the edge of the water, with no doubt that God will come to rescue them. The same imagery is reiterated in 60:9:

> For the coastlands shall *wait* for me,
> the ships of Tarshish first,
> to bring your children from far away,
> their silver and gold with them,
> for the name of the LORD your God,
> and for the Holy One of Israel,
> because he has glorified you.

And finally, in what is likely the latest part of the book of Isaiah—the apocalyptic unit of chapters 24–27—the same theme of "wait/hope" is sounded. This belated voice of Isaiah imagines a great feast of well-being when the ultimate enemy, death, is defeated. In response to the great divine triumph of this rescue, Israel will say,

> Lo, this is our God; we have *waited* for him, so that he might save us.
> This is the LORD for whom we have *waited*;
> let us be glad and rejoice in his salvation.
>
> 25:9

And again in 26:8, Isaiah has complete confidence in YHWH:

> In the path of your judgments,
> O LORD, we *wait* for you;
> your name and your renown
> are the soul's desire.

All over the book of Isaiah, in all its parts, hope in YHWH is the ground for the future. The Isaiah tradition does not speculate on how YHWH will act. It has a memory of the mobilization in turn of Sennacherib, Nebuchadnezzar, and Cyrus as tools for the purposes of YHWH, but it leaves the matter completely open in confidence that God will find a way to act. God's good purpose is the offer for Isaiah.

In our verse, the poet knows what may happen when there is active, courageous, energetic hope in circumstances of despair. When waiting actively for YHWH, hopers are not weary ($lō$ ' + $yāga$ ') and not faint ($lō$ ' + $yā$ 'ap). They have become like YHWH, who is also not weary ($lō$ ' + $yāga$ ') and not faint ($lō$ ' + $yā$ 'ap)! Thus we may observe an artistic triad of uses in 40:28–31:

> YHWH is *not* faint or weary.
>
> Youth without hope *are* faint and weary.
>
> Those who wait on YHWH *are not* faint or weary.

The poet also constructs a triad of speeds for those who hope: they may *soar* (like eagles), they may *run*, or they may *walk*. They may go at the speed appropriate to them. But they will all be able to move, able to return, able to go home. Such energy and courage come from an active hope in the God who keeps promises. Such hope never

Hope (in/for) the Lord! (Isaiah 40:31)

means sitting around passively. It means making plans; it means mobilizing resources. It means being on the ready for the newness that may be given at any moment. It is no wonder that the hope of Isaiah 40–55 is all about homecoming. It is the hopers in YHWH who have the energy and courage for the arduous task of homecoming and restoration.

Not the others! Those who are *faint and weary* are the ones who do not hope. They are the ones who would have reduced YHWH to a lifeless totem, who have trimmed YHWH down to the size and shape of the empire or the tribe. Perhaps they are the ones who have for too long engaged in excessive nostalgia for the way it used to be, or the way they falsely remember it having been. They have, as in Psalm 137, constructed in their imagination an old Jerusalem, and all the while the poet of YHWH has declared, "Do not remember former things" (43:18–19)—get your mind off such old imagining! Perhaps they would excessively bet on Cyrus and the Persians, and so engage in cunning stratagems to curry Persian favor. Or, alternatively, on the basis of a misjudged YHWH or a falsely imagined Persian regime, they have settled into despair and have tried to "make the best" of an unbearable situation—*faint, weary,* and *without hope.*

The poet will have none of that! It is the work of Isaiah 40 and this final verse 31 to challenge and refute all such easy, comfortable settling down. The poet awaits YHWH's new thing. The poet intends his listeners to bet on this new thing from YHWH. He assumes that such a bet does not end in faintness or weariness or exhaustion, but with the capacity to fly, run, or walk—on the move! The God for whom Israel waits is holy in God's elusiveness. That elusiveness, however, does not end in the darkness and gloom of unbearable alienation. It culminates, rather, in bold, daring, and active anticipation. It is no wonder that those who wait and hope in verse 31 are the very ones who at the end of Second Isaiah go out in joy:

> For you shall go out in joy,
>   and be led back in peace;
> the mountains and the hills before you
>   shall burst into song,
>   and all the trees of the field shall clap their hands.
>   55:12

These are the ones who are anointed to, eventually,

> bring good news to the oppressed,
> to bind up the brokenhearted,
> to proclaim liberty to the captives,
> and release to the prisoners;
> to proclaim the year of the LORD's favor,
> and the day of vengeance of our God.
> 61:1–2

Christians, belatedly, are heirs to this same summons. It is the summons that Jesus issues to his disciples:

> Therefore, keep awake—for you do not know when the master of the house will come, in the evening, or at midnight, or at cockcrow, or at dawn, or else he may find you asleep when he comes suddenly. And what I say to you I say to all: "Keep awake." (Mark 13:35–37)

It is no time for sleepiness or fatigue, or faintness or weariness, or exhaustion. Newness is on its way!

> Wait for the Lord,
> whose day is near.
> Wait for the Lord,
> keep watch, take heart![1]

Questions for Discussion

1. Have you ever had to wait for and hope in God along the lines described in this chapter?
2. Have you ever trimmed God down too much, to something human sized rather than God sized?
3. How is waiting on God not the same as total passivity or just "making the best" of a bad situation?

Chapter 22

I Am He!
(Isaiah 43:10–11)

You are my witnesses, says the LORD,
  and my servant whom I have chosen,
so that you may know and believe me
  and understand that I am he.
Before me no god was formed,
  nor shall there be any after me.
I, I am the LORD,
  and besides me there is no savior.

> **Scripture Passages for Reference**
>
> Isaiah 43:1–25
> Isaiah 37:14–20
> Isaiah 44:9–20
> Deuteronomy 4:32–40
> John 18:1–11

Twice in his prayer under the threat of Sennacherib in chapter 37, Hezekiah asserts the uniqueness of YHWH. The Lord *alone* (*lĕbaddĕkā*), he says, is God (vv. 16, 20). This sentiment is nothing new in the Isaiah tradition. We have had occasion to note the incomparability of God at several points in the book prior to chapter 37. Already in Isaiah 2, for example, we read twice that YHWH *alone* (*lĕbaddô*) will be exalted "on that day" (2:11, 17). Later, Isaiah 26 recounts lyrics that will be sung in Judah "on that day" (26:1):

> Other lords besides you have ruled over us,
> but we acknowledge your name *alone* [*lĕbad-bĕkā*].
> 26:13

These texts are connected in part by the use of the compound word *lĕbad*, which means "solitude, alone" and, when combined with additional grammatical elements, "except, apart from, beside." However constructed in Hebrew, the point is that YHWH stands alone, apart, singular. Since that is true, a number of corollaries follow: YHWH is the sole creator, for instance (see 41:4 and 48:12–13; also 44:24; 45:7), and also the only living (that is, *real*) God, as Hezekiah recognizes in his prayer:

> O LORD of hosts, God of Israel, who are enthroned above the cherubim, you are God, you *alone* [*lĕbaddĕkā*], of all the kingdoms of the earth; you have made heaven and earth. Incline your ear, O LORD, and hear; open your eyes, O LORD, and see; hear all the words of Sennacherib, which he has sent to mock the *living* God. . . . So now, O LORD our God, save us from his hand, so that all the kingdoms of the earth may know that you *alone* [*lĕbaddekā*] are the LORD. (37:16–17, 20)

Given the function of chapters 36–39 as a kind of bridge between First and Second Isaiah, it is unsurprising to see that Hezekiah's appeal to YHWH's singularity is also found in the second major section of the book. Indeed, in the opening chapter of this second unit starting in chapter 40, God's incomparability is stated clearly by the prophet to the people:

> To whom then will you liken God,
> or what likeness compare with him?
> 40:18

Later, God asks the same question directly:

> To whom will you liken me and make me equal,
> and compare me, as though we were alike?
> 46:5; cf. v. 9

I Am He! (Isaiah 43:10–11) 143

The answer to these rhetorical questions is obvious: no one and nothing, a point underscored by other texts from Second Isaiah, many of which employ some form of *lĕbad*, its near homonym *bil ʿădê* ("apart from, besides, except"), or its synonym *zûlāh* ("except, only"):

> Is there any god besides me [*mibbal ʿāday*]?
> There is no other rock; I know not one.
> 44:8b

> I am the LORD, and there is no other;
>   besides me [*zûlātî*] there is no god.
> I arm you, though you do not know me,
> so that they may know, from the rising of the sun
>   and from the west, that there is no one besides me [*bil ʿādāy*];
> I am the LORD, and there is no other.
> 45:5–6

> They will make supplication to you, saying,
>   "God is with you alone, and there is no other;
>   there is no god besides him."
> 45:14b

> For thus says the LORD,
> who created the heavens
>   (he is God!),
> who formed the earth and made it
>   (he established it;
> he did not create it a chaos,
>   he formed it to be inhabited!):
> I am the LORD, and there is no other.
> 45:18

> Declare and present your case;
>   let them take counsel together!
> Who told this long ago?
>   Who declared it of old?
> Was it not I, the LORD?
>   There is no other god besides me [*mibbal ʿāday*],
> a righteous God and a Savior;
>   there is no one besides me [*zûlātî*].
> Turn to me and be saved,

all the ends of the earth!
For I am God, and there is no other.
45:21–22

Two grammatical observations might be made. First, in addition to words meaning "except," "besides," or "alone," the texts above often stress the point by means of a simple clause that is only two words in Hebrew: "and there is no other" (*wĕ'ên 'ôd*). Second, 45:18 is particularly illuminating in showing how an assertion of God's singularity can erupt in doxology, "He is God!" which, in context, surely means, "He *alone* is God!" This same predication-become-doxology is made by greats like Moses (Deuteronomy 7:9), David (2 Samuel 7:28; 1 Chronicles 17:26), Solomon (1 Kings 8:60), Elijah and the people after the showdown with Baal (1 Kings 18:24, 39), Hezekiah (Isaiah 37:16; 2 Kings 19:15), and even the Persian emperor Cyrus himself (Ezra 1:3)!

This predication doesn't quite work, of course, if placed on God's own lips and so must be differently articulated: from "He is God" to "I am LORD" (Isaiah 42:6; 48:17; 49:23, 26; see also 51:15; 60:22). Indeed, several instances of "I am the LORD" appear in concert with statements of YHWH's singularity (see 45:5–6, 18). A further example:

Thus says the LORD, your Redeemer,
   who formed you in the womb:
I am the LORD, who made all things,
   who alone [*lĕbaddî*] stretched out the heavens,
   who by myself spread out the earth.
44:24

Another, even more direct way to rearticulate, "He is God," is, "I am He" (NJPS), which is exactly what YHWH does in a number of places in Second Isaiah, including our verses in chapter 43 (see also, e.g., 41:4).

The chapter begins by asserting YHWH's creation of Israel, a logical corollary of God's singularity, followed by an injunction not to fear because God has redeemed the people, called them by name, and claimed them (43:1; cf. 51:12). And so there is no place that YHWH will not accompany Israel (43:2) and no price that YHWH will not pay for them (vv. 3–4). Instead, "redeemed" is defined as God's accompanying presence (v. 5a) and the gathering up of exiles from all points of the compass (vv. 5b–7). As a result, all who see and hear of this redemption will "know and believe . . . that I am He" (v. 10; cf. 52:6). "I am He" means that there was no other god that preceded YHWH, nor will there be any after. Such a statement seems like an abstract or theoretical one, but it has an unmistakably pragmatic outcome as far as Israel is concerned: "Besides me there is no savior" (43:11). That statement, in turn, implies another one, surely meant for Israel's foes: there is no one who can deliver *out of* God's hand (v. 13). For Israel, God's aloneness is further defined as forgiveness, not due to contrition or some ritual, but solely for YHWH's own sake, accompanied by total divine amnesia about Israel's sins (v. 25). Only a bit later YHWH states, "I am He" who gave birth to remnant Israel, carrying them from the womb—a notable use of maternal language (see also 42:14; 49:15)—and YHWH will carry them to old age, making, bearing, carrying, and saving (46:3–4).

This assertion on the part of YHWH—that YHWH's sole Godness means goodness to Israel—must be seen in the context of two potential and powerful rivals for the title "Alone." The first, that of *political power*, is found throughout Isaiah but appears in a remarkable passage in Isaiah 47. There, wicked and haughty Babylon uses an "incomparable construction," not of YHWH, *but of itself*:

> You [Babylon] felt secure in your wickedness;
>   you said, "No one sees me."
> Your wisdom and your knowledge
>   led you astray,
> and you said in your heart,
>   "I am, and there is no one besides me."
>   47:10

But as the psalmist declares with reference to the wicked who say God does not see them,

> But you [God] do see! Indeed you note trouble and grief,
>   that you may take it into your hands;
> the helpless commit themselves to you;
>   you have been the helper of the orphan.
>   Psalm 10:14; see also Psalm 94:7–9

And given that divine ability to see and inclination to help, the prophet declares to Babylon:

> Evil shall come upon you,
>   which you cannot charm away;
> disaster shall fall upon you,
>   which you will not be able to ward off.
>   Isaiah 47:11

Once again, any and all superpowers like Babylon are put on notice. There is One that is still higher than they. Indeed, this One is the sole and only power that matters. There is only One who stands "Alone"!

The second and related rival to YHWH's aloneness is found in the *religious threat posed by idols*. Right after Isaiah 40:18, the prophet notes that one *could* compare the incomparable God to an idol, though Isaiah immediately satirizes such an option, noting that idols are fabricated things, made to look pretty on the outside but built of wood that will rot (40:19–20). Indeed, Isaiah 44:9–20 is famous for its satire on idol-making. The same piece of wood used to make an idol is used to make a fire for the idol-maker to stay warm and make his meal. The idiocy of thinking that the rest of the timber is somehow divine, and then bowing down and worshiping it, could not be clearer.

We would do well to realize that things were not so obvious on the ground, however, especially in Babylon, overrun as it was with a plethora of temples and the gods who inhabited them, many with divine images that were thought to be alive in some fashion. The prophetic parody may overstate the case precisely because these other gods were live options. But, the prophet says, not really: "All who make idols are nothing" (44:9) and their images "can do no good" (44:10); they are nothing but "a fraud" (44:20) that "cannot save" (45:20) so that all who trust in them are "turned back and utterly put to shame" (42:17). There is only one "Alone" who has the agency so often attributed to lesser gods, so much so that YHWH claims to do *everything*:

> I form light and create darkness,
> I make weal and create woe;
> I the LORD do all these things.
>   45:7

I Am He! (Isaiah 43:10–11)   147

When one considers the two threats to YHWH's uniqueness, *the political* and *the religious*, together, one sees how YHWH's aloneness is a clarion call to exclusive devotion. YHWH will brook no rivals. It is understandable, therefore, that many have found the origins of monotheism—or its first clear articulations—in Second Isaiah during the exile when Israel came face-to-face with unlimited imperial power in new, if not also exponentially more powerful, ways, accompanied by a marketplace of religious options undergirding that empire. Indeed, the good sense the exilic context makes for the "monotheizing" statements in Second Isaiah has led scholars to date similar sentiments in Deuteronomy to the same timeframe (see, e.g., Deuteronomy 4:35, 39).

The point of these assertions is not, however, an abstract theological axiom about the nonexistence of other supernatural powers. While that may seem to be the case, elsewhere the Bible is perfectly comfortable speaking of the existence of other such powers (see, e.g., Genesis 6:2, 4; Job 1:6; 2:1; Psalms 29:1; 58:1; 82:1; 89:6; 97:7; 138:1; 1 Corinthians 8:5–6). So while Second Isaiah may represent some new stage or development in Israel's theology, the far more important point about monotheism is not if one *believes it in theory* but if one *adheres to it in practice*. The only monotheism that matters is the practical variety: living as if there is no other rival to our lives, our hearts, our everything (cf. Deuteronomy 6:5; 10:12; 11:13).

In the New Testament, in addition to seconding the sole allegiance to YHWH (Matthew 22:37; Mark 12:30; Luke 10:27), we find Jesus using, "I am he!" in a number of passages. In the Synoptic Gospels, Jesus warns that many will come in the future and say, "I am he!" and, as a result, will lead numerous people astray (Mark 13:6; Luke 21:8). We may imagine that those "many" include the countless political and religious options that are, at the end of the day (and even to this day), as short-lived as fallen Babylon or as clueless as a woodcarving idol-maker. Jesus's own brand of practical monotheism draws the only appropriate conclusion: "Do not go after them" (Luke 21:8). In John's Gospel, Jesus uses, "I am he," repeatedly, where it identifies him as the Messiah (John 4:26), as one who can deliver from sin and death (8:24), and as united with the Father (8:28; see also 13:19). What the NRSV renders as "I am he" in these passages is, more woodenly, "I am" (Greek *ego eimi*). There can be no doubt that *ego eimi* harkens back to the "I am He" of Second Isaiah, but even further back to the divine name YHWH itself—a name that is initially defined as "I AM WHO I AM," then shortened to "I AM," then reuttered as "the LORD [YHWH]" (see Exodus 3:14–15). No wonder those who come to seize Christ in the garden of Gethsemane fall to the ground when they hear him say, "I am" (John 18:5–6, 8)!

Questions for Discussion

1. What is the difference between an abstract monotheism and a practical one? Why does a practical monotheism matter?

2. Beyond being the creator of all, what other "corollaries" can you think of that go along with an emphasis on the Lord alone? What other special qualities does the Lord alone have?

3. What political and religious rivals stand against the sole allegiance to God today?

Chapter 23

Cyrus, God's Messiah (Isaiah 45:1)

Thus says the LORD to his anointed, to Cyrus,
  whose right hand I have grasped
to subdue nations before him
  and strip kings of their robes,
to open doors before him—
  and the gates shall not be closed.

> **Scripture Passages for Reference**
>
> Isaiah 45:1–7
> Isaiah 44:24–28
> Ezekiel 34:15–16
> 2 Chronicles 36:23
> Ezra 1:2–5
> Luke 7:22

The tradition of Isaiah was silent after the "downer" of 39:1–8 concerning King Hezekiah. But then, after the long silence, the tradition sprang to life with new cadences of celebration and anticipation. We know that this new poetry in the Isaiah tradition was triggered by an abrupt turn in world history, a dramatic upheaval in international relations. The Babylonian regime of Nebuchadnezzar was despised in ancient Israel because of its brutality toward Jerusalem and its inhabitants. But by 540 BCE that despised regime had exhausted itself. In that year, the emerging Persian Empire (located in present-day Iran) moved west and conquered the capital city of Babylon. The Persians, led by Emperor Cyrus (550–530 BCE), reordered policies and administrative practices in a manner that was immensely beneficial to the exiles. Nebuchadnezzar had deported and held in deportation leading members of the Jerusalem community (see Jeremiah 52:28–30). With his new policy, Cyrus permitted those displaced Judeans to return home, albeit under Persian administration with continuing Persian supervision and taxation. That turn of policy by Cyrus is dramatically reiterated in 2 Chronicles 36:23 (see also Ezra 1:2–5):

> Thus says King Cyrus of Persia: "The LORD, the God of heaven, has given me all the kingdoms of the earth, and he has charged me to build him a house at Jerusalem, which is in Judah. Whoever is among you of all his people, may the LORD his God be with him! Let him go up."

This is the final verse of the final book of the Hebrew Bible. Thus, the Hebrew Bible ends on a note of keen anticipation for restoration of the displaced Jewish community. It is this radical turn of policy, with its practical political implications, that inspires the new poetry of the Isaiah tradition. "Second Isaiah" sees this moment of policy reversal as a decisive turn in Jewish historical possibility that is publicly certified by Persian power.

But of course, this Isaiah poetry does much more than mark the abrupt turn in imperial power and policy. Beyond that, it dares to articulate the conviction that this turn of policy reflects not only the shrewd calculations of Cyrus but also the will and intent of the God of Israel, who presides over human history and attends to the destiny of the chosen people, Israel. There is no doubt that the majestic governance of YHWH lives on the lips of such poets! It is of course important to recognize that in our verse we are reading poetry. In poetry, much can happen that overrides dry rational analysis. We are inclined to say in our careful retelling that *either* God willed emancipation *or* Cyrus the Persian undertook new policy, but for the poet there is no either/or. It is rather a *both/and*, because the God of the

Bible works in, with, and under historical processes. This is exactly Isaiah's point.

Isaiah mentions Cyrus only twice. Just before our verse, in 44:24–28, the poet offers a ringing doxology to YHWH placed in the mouth of YHWH. These verses articulate the identity of YHWH by a stunning inventory of God's decisive acts. One can notice, in a scan of these verses, that they are dominated by the pronoun "who" followed by active transformative verbs. This series of *who-verbs* moves from great cosmic claims (vv. 24–25), to prophetic anticipation of the restoration of Jerusalem (vv. 26–27), and finally to the specificity of Cyrus (v. 28). But it is all of a piece, all dominated by the resolve and the speech of YHWH, who by utterance causes newness. Thus YHWH,

- can say of Jerusalem, "It shall be inhabited";
- can say of the chaotic waters, "Be dry"; and
- can say of Cyrus, "He is my shepherd."

In this poetic scenario, Cyrus is caught up in a cosmic decision concerning rehabilitation, so that Cyrus carries out the divine resolve for a restored city and a rebuilt temple.

Given this dramatic presentation of the transformative speech of YHWH addressed to the city, to chaos, and to Cyrus, it is no surprise that, in our verse, YHWH has a specific word for the Persian ruler. In 44:28, Cyrus is designated as "my shepherd"—which is the same as saying "my king"—who must care for the people Israel.[1] Now in our verse, Cyrus is designated as "his anointed," the one who has been sacramentally marked to do the work of YHWH. The verse is interesting on two counts. First, the specific pronoun is somewhat uncertain. The Hebrew text has "his anointed," but elsewhere in other ancient translations of the Bible it is "my anointed"—thus direct speech of YHWH. In either articulation—and this is the second way this verse is interesting—what counts is that Cyrus is named to the role, office, and function of "messiah" (Hebrew *māśîaḥ*). That term has an elasticity of meanings. In the Christian tradition, it refers to "the Christ," the specific one designated by God. (The Greek translation of Hebrew *māśîaḥ* is *christos*). Prior to that Christian specificity, however, the biblical tradition allows that there may be many messiahs, many persons designated (that is, *anointed*) to do the particular work intended by God as God exercises sovereignty in the world (this included, especially, kings, priests, and the ancestors). None of this is specified in our verse, so we have some interpretive freedom. However, this verse receives great specification in the hymnic lines that follow (vv. 2–7). These verses are dominated by the divine "I." It is all the doing of YHWH. It is YHWH who "goes before," "breaks in pieces," and "gives you." Cyrus is on the receiving end of divine resolve; he is not permitted even to respond or assent to this calling. He simply will! He is unilaterally authorized by the resolve of YHWH. In verse 4, YHWH pauses to underscore that the summons to Cyrus (and the more general upheaval of international politics and power) is all because of YHWH's singular commitment to Israel:

> For the sake of my servant Jacob,
>   and Israel my chosen,
> I call you by your name,
>   I surname you, though you do not know me.

This is an awesome act of poetic imagination, to give Cyrus a last name: Cyrus Godson! But that is how particularity works in the Bible. God's persistent commitment to Israel in the Old Testament requires such daring administrative upheavals. In what follows in verses 5–7, there is nothing more about either Cyrus or Israel. It is all about YHWH, who is the creator of all that is, whether (and both!) good and evil. Given this sweeping doxological claim, we can see that 44:24–45:7 begins and ends in general celebration of the *grandeur of the creator God*, while at the center of the poem is the *historical particularity of Cyrus* upon whom the specific international newness now pivots.

The following may guide our interpretive work on our verse: First, we should not sugarcoat the imperial power of Cyrus the Persian. His was a power like any other dominating power, taking itself to be free to do whatever power requires. In a remarkable exposé, Bruce Lincoln details the brutality of torture, described in sickening detail, that was sponsored by Darius, Cyrus, and others of the Persian dynasty. Lincoln identifies three components of the maintenance of imperial power:

(1) a starkly dualistic ethics in which the opposition good/evil is aligned with that of self/other and correlated discriminatory binaries, (2) a theology of election that secures the ruler's legitimacy by constituting him as God's chosen agent, (3) and a sense of soteriological mission that represents imperial aggression as salvific action on behalf of divine principles, thereby recording the empire's victims as its beneficiaries.[2]

Lincoln's book has a postscript on the Abu Ghraib prison scandal and the shameless torture conducted in that Iraqi prison by US military forces. The analogue may help us not only to read Isaiah knowingly but to read our own US imperialism alertly. Lincoln concludes of Persia,

> Contradictions between sacred discourse and bestial practice, as well as the dialectical relation between moral confidence and moral depravity, are built into the deep structure of empire. . . . Staunch denial is always a favorite tactic, as are euphemism, blurring the issues, invoking the divine, flogging scapegoats, slandering critics, and reasserting one's devotion to traditional ideals.[3]

The interface of *Persian practice* and *US torture* summons us to read Isaiah on Cyrus with widely opened eyes. The Persian reality has an all too familiar ring! And yet, in the prophetic imagination, God uses Cyrus and Persia (!)—though given all that has come before in the Isaiah tradition, that "use" is surely limited in profound ways by God's own Torah and by God-given limitations on all power, hubris, arrogance, and overstepping.

Second, as we must not gloss over the ruthless realism of Cyrus, so we might also notice that the poetic claim made for "Israel my chosen" does not automatically or obviously pertain to the contemporary state of Israel, for the present secular, democratic state of Israel is something other than the covenantal community of ancient Israel that Isaiah has in purview. While many in the present state of Israel may want to appropriate these claims for themselves, the historical reality of Isaiah's time was otherwise.

Third and most important, we should notice how prophetic poetry (prophetic imagination!) attests to *worldly reality* and, at the same time, reads that reality with reference to the *sovereignty of YHWH*. Judged by any other norm, Cyrus would *not* be cast as the agent of

YHWH. Cyrus would not have recognized himself in that way, nor would any of his contemporaries. But then prophetic poetry is not contained in or domesticated by the "wisdom of this world." Rather, this poetry pushes beyond such sober rationality in order to bring listeners to the wonder of a world in which YHWH not only presides as creator but exercises sovereignty in particular ways for the sake of God's chosen, whom the rest of the world discounts (see Jeremiah 30:17).

Fourth, it is inescapable that Christians will link our text to our conviction of Jesus as the Messiah, the Christ. While the church has a long tradition of being preoccupied with the "person" of Jesus as Messiah and creedal confessions that he was "truly divine, truly human," we may notice that in this poetic rendering nothing is made of the "person" of Cyrus. Rather, the accent is on the "work" of Cyrus. His mandate from YHWH is (1) to subdue kings before him, (2) to strip kings of their robes, and (3) to open doors before him. In a word, the "work" assigned to Cyrus in this poetic charge is to subdue Babylon, to strip the royal regime of Babylon of its power, and so to provide an escape route for the exiles. That escape—the return of Israel—is not to be confused with cultural supremacy in Babylon or Persia.

When Christians think about Jesus as "Messiah," we tend to spend great energy pondering his "person." This text might draw us back to the "work" of the Messiah that Jesus himself summarized:

> The blind receive their sight, the lame walk, the lepers are cleansed, the deaf hear, the dead are raised, the poor have good news brought to them. (Luke 7:22)

Or to shift the imagery from "messiah" to "shepherd" (as in 44:28), the work of the shepherd is exactly a parallel to the list spoken by Jesus:

> I myself will be the shepherd of my sheep, and I will make them lie down, says the Lord GOD. I will seek the lost, and I will bring back the strayed, and I will bind up the injured, and I will strengthen the weak, but the fat and the strong I will destroy. I will feed them with justice. (Ezekiel 34:15–16)

In our opinion, Isaiah 45:1 might equip the community of faith to think poetically about the *both/and* of *divine initiative* and *human performance*. This requires a more resilient God of sovereignty than the one we often entertain. It requires as well the awareness that human power and agency can indeed take up the divine work of emancipation and restoration. Given these claims, we can then ask when and how and in what way we see the restorative, transformative work of the God of the gospel being performed by human agents. Such a wonderment will give the lie to imposters who make exalted claims for their authority but who do not do the work of the emancipatory God. It must have been a breathtaking moment in exilic Israel when the name of "Cyrus" was paired with the profoundly biblical designation "messiah." Biblical poetry permits such linkage upon which everything depends, even if that connection deeply disturbs our usual "enlightened" theology and confounds our political certainties.

Questions for Discussion

1. Can you identify other instances of God's both/and as opposed to our more flattened understanding of either-or?
2. What do you make of the fact that the Bible speaks of other "messiahs" who have played important roles in God's redemptive work?
3. How do divine initiative and human response go together?
4. How do we know that Cyrus's anointed work was severely limited?

Chapter 24

Short-Term Superpower(s) (Isaiah 47:6)

*I was angry with my people,
I profaned my heritage;
I gave them into your hand,
 you showed them no mercy;
on the aged you made your yoke
 exceedingly heavy.*

> ### Scripture Passages for Reference
>
> Isaiah 47:1–7
> Isaiah 14:18–19
> 1 Kings 8:12–13
> Jeremiah 24:1–10
> Jeremiah 25:9
> Jeremiah 27:6
> Jeremiah 50:2
> Jeremiah 52:17–27
> Psalm 46
> Revelation 18:21–24

The great kingdom of Babylon, led by Nebuchadnezzar, had a very short shelf life. It came to power after 605 BCE and was ended by Cyrus the Persian in 540 BCE. During that brief period, nonetheless, Babylon loomed large in the prophetic imagination of Israel. There was good reason for that, as Babylon assaulted the city of Jerusalem, took leading inhabitants of the city back to Babylon as captives (see Jeremiah 52:17–27), and, in a second attack, razed the city. It was the work of the prophets in Israel to articulate the significance of Nebuchadnezzar's attack with reference to the God who occupied the city (see 1 Kings 8:12–13) and was committed to its security and well-being (see Psalm 46).

Sometime before Isaiah 47 was written, the prophet Jeremiah faced a similar task: speaking of Babylon and Nebuchadnezzar within the context of Yahwistic faith. Because Jeremiah urged a policy of non-resistance in the face of the massive military power of Babylon, he read the Babylonian conquest of Jerusalem and the deportation of the Judeans as the work of YHWH. Thus, he identified Nebuchadnezzar as the "servant the Lord" who was doing the bidding of YHWH:

> I am going to send for all the tribes of the north, says the LORD, even for King Nebuchadrezzar of Babylon, *my servant*, and I will bring them against this land and its inhabitants. (Jeremiah 25:9)

> Now I have given all these lands into the hand of King Nebuchadnezzar of Babylon, *my servant*, and I have given him even the wild animals of the field to serve him. (27:6)

Indeed, Jeremiah would go so far as to claim that the deportees to Babylon were the "good figs," the faithful future of Israel (see Jeremiah 24:1–10).

However, later in the book of Jeremiah, in a section that could be contemporary with Isaiah 47, the prophet identifies Babylon as the *enemy* of YHWH (Jeremiah 50–51). Jeremiah's poem begins with the declaration of the defeat and destruction of Babylon and its gods:

> Declare among the nations and proclaim,
>   set up a banner and proclaim,
>   do not conceal it, say:
> *Babylon is taken,*
>   Bel is put to shame,
>   Merodach is dismayed.
> Her images are put to shame,
>   her idols are dismayed.
>   Jeremiah 50:2

The prophet does not show us how *the servant of YHWH* became *the enemy of YHWH*. That work has been left for Isaiah.

Babylon continues to occupy a prominent place in the book of Isaiah. In an earlier section of the book containing "Oracles against the Nations" (see chaps. 13–27, especially chaps. 13–21), Babylon is portrayed as an enemy of YHWH who must and will be destroyed. Pure and simple, Babylon is a brutal foe of YHWH, completely lacking in mercy. In these sections, the prophet imagines and anticipates the shame-filled demise of that mighty empire:

> All the kings of the nations lie in glory,
>   each in his own tomb;
> but you are cast out, away from your grave,
>   like loathsome carrion,
> clothed with the dead, those pierced by the sword,
>   who go down to the stones of the Pit,
>   like a corpse trampled underfoot.
>
> Isaiah 14:18–19

A possible analogue is the basement crypt in Vienna where the remains of the Hapsburg rulers are kept. The room feels crammed, disordered, and in disarray, reflecting the way the powerful so often end up in dishonor.

Isaiah 46–47 should be read together, as both of these chapters deal with the *theopolitical* end of Babylon. Chapter 46 is preoccupied with *theological* matters, that is, the struggle between the gods who contended for control. In the orbit of Isaiah, however, that struggle is no real contest. The Babylonian gods (Bel, Nebo) are impotent illusions. They have no power, strength, or energy. They have to be "carried" (46:1). Some have suggested here a reference to the great religious festivals of Babylon in which the images of the gods were carried in parade—not unlike the Rose Bowl parade. But these gods have no agency, because they are merely manufactured by the empire's artisans. They are "made-up" gods:

> Those who lavish gold from the purse,
>   and weigh out silver in the scales—
> they hire a goldsmith, who makes it into a god;
>   then they fall down and worship!
>
> 46:6

In Isaiah 44:9–20, the prophet offers an even more extended mocking dismissal of the manufactured gods of the empire who are crafted, sketched out, and carved by skilled workmen. These gods "do not know . . . do not comprehend . . . cannot see . . . cannot understand" (Isaiah 44:18; see also Psalms 115:4–8; 135:13–18). And yet the empire's citizens worship them: "Save me, for you are my god!" (Isaiah 44:17; see also 46:6).

But of course, the worship of such an idol is futile; Nebuchadnezzar was about to discover that theological reality.

> They lift it to their shoulders, they carry it,
>   they set it in its place, and it stands there;
>   it cannot move from its place.
> If one cries out to it, it does not answer
>   or save anyone from trouble.
>   46:7

Quite in contrast is YHWH. This is the God with energy, force, and intention who can and will "make, bear, carry, save" (v. 4):

> declaring the end from the beginning
>   and from ancient times things not yet done,
> saying, "My purpose shall stand
>   and I will fulfill my intention,"
> calling a bird of prey from the east,
>   the man for my purpose from a far country.
> I have spoken, and I will bring it to pass;
>   I have planned it, and I will do it.
>   46:10–11

The poet echoes an earlier cadence from the book of Isaiah:

> The LORD of hosts has sworn:
>
> As I have designed,
>   so shall it be;
> and as I have planned,
>   so shall it come to pass.
> . . . .
> For the LORD of hosts has planned,
>   and who will annul it?
> His hand is stretched out,

and who will turn it back?
14:24, 27

The "man for my purpose" is Cyrus, the Persian emancipator. But it is all the work of YHWH! While chapter 46 is concerned with *the theological background* of the crisis faced by the prophet and by Jerusalem, chapter 47 concerns *the foreground of historical political reality*. The prophet can imagine and anticipate the complete demise of the Babylonian Empire (47:1–3, note that the imagery used here reflects the misogynistic sentiments that were not uncommon at that time). Isaiah still has the legacy of Jeremiah that recognizes that Babylon is a tool for the purposes of YHWH. That much is still granted. Babylon could and would conquer Israel as the response of YHWH to its wholesale violation of Torah. Jerusalem, in a world governed by YHWH, needed to be punished, and the militarism of Babylon was an available, fitting vehicle for such punishment; that is the way of YHWH in worldly affairs. As our verse recounts:

I was angry with my people,
I profaned my heritage;
I gave them into your hand.
47:6

This strand of the poetry continues to regard Nebuchadnezzar as the useful *servant of YHWH*.

But the very next line of the poetry reverses field. There is no pause or punctuation mark, but simply the next clause that must follow! The invading army of Nebuchadnezzar, in its brutality, showed *no pity or mercy:* "You showed them no mercy!" (47:6; see Jeremiah 6:23). It is not in the style of any great military empire to show mercy. Not at Dresden, not at Hiroshima, not even at Gettysburg. Babylon was a characteristic military empire, neither better nor worse—ergo, *no mercy*. Babylon showed no compassion, not even with "the aged" or any other vulnerable part of the population. All were treated severely.

Of course, no one had informed Nebuchadnezzar that YHWH willed mercy toward Jerusalem. No such memo was sent to the Babylonian king. Nebuchadnezzar thought that he was free, as all military leaders think they are free, to exercise raw, unrestricted power. He thought he was as free as his power would permit. In the prophetic horizon, however, he should have known better. He should have known that he had authority against Jerusalem *only as granted by YHWH* who presides over Jerusalem (see Isaiah 31:9!). He should have known that YHWH wills mercy toward the holy city and its chosen people. He should have known that in the world of YHWH's fidelity there are limits to military power. He should have known to curb the extravagance of imperial violence. In the "real world" of politics, this is, of course, way too much to expect of Nebuchadnezzar. But in the world of prophetic calculus, this is a credible expectation. In the prophetic world, Nebuchadnezzar was penultimate; he had no warrant to pretend ultimacy. But he did so pretend—as also did Babylon, personified as a female—according to the prophet:

> You said, "I am forever—the eternal queen!"
> Isaiah 47:7 NIV

> [You] say in your heart,
> "I am, and there is no one besides me;
> I shall not sit as a widow
> or know the loss of children."
> v. 8

> You felt secure in your wickedness;
> you said, "No one sees me."
> v. 10a

> You said in your heart,
> "I am, and there is no one besides me."
> v. 10b

All of these statements assigned to Babylon (a metonymic stand-in for Nebuchadnezzar here) show that Nebuchadnezzar, in his arrogance, had acknowledged no limits to his power and no curb on his brutality. He thought himself autonomous in his great power.

Isaiah articulates worldly power in the context of the authority of YHWH, the creator, who makes all other power not only penultimate but answerable for mercy or its lack. Consequently, Babylon will suffer for its limitless brutality:

> Both these things shall come upon you
> > in a moment, in one day:
> > the loss of children and widowhood
> > shall come upon you in full measure.
> ....
> But evil shall come upon you,
> > which you cannot charm away;
> > disaster shall fall upon you,
> > which you will not be able to ward off;
> > and ruin shall come on you suddenly,
> > of which you know nothing.
> > > > 47:9, 11

The final verdict is unambiguous: "There is no one to save you" (47:15; see also 21:9).

It is not a surprise that in the book of Revelation the early church could take up the imagery of Babylon as a way to mark and mock the reality of the Roman Empire. That empire, not unlike Babylon, and not unlike many such empires, imagined that there was no limit to its capacity for control and greed. But the seer of the book of Revelation appeals to the imagery of Babylon to affirm that even Rome is answerable to the Lord of history who is the creator of the world and of all nations:

> With such violence Babylon the great city
> > will be thrown down,
> > and will be found *no more;*
> and the sound of harpists and minstrels and of flutists and trumpeters
> > will be heard in you *no more;*
> and an artisan of any trade
> > will be found in you *no more;*
> and the sound of the millstone
> > will be heard in you *no more;*
> and the light of a lamp
> > will shine in you *no more;*
> and the voice of bridegroom and bride
> > will be heard in you *no more;*
> for your merchants were the magnates of the earth,
> > and all nations were deceived by your sorcery.

> And in you was found the blood of prophets and of saints,
> and of all who have been slaughtered on earth.
>
> Revelation 18:21–24

The rhetorical pounding of *"no more, no more, no more, no more"* brings an end to the empire that took itself to be "Eternal." Rome, like Babylon, faced its penultimacy before the nonnegotiable reality of YHWH in the harshest of ways.

This imagery of Babylon has often been extended beyond Rome to the contemporary world. After the fall of the Soviet Union, and recent Russian resurgence, and before the abrupt rise of China, the United States stood briefly as sole superpower. It is easy enough to see that the United States, with its seemingly limitless capacity for expansion, could be readily cast in the role of Babylon, especially when its ventures of control were left unmarked by any show of mercy. This possible analogue presses upon us the deep question about the limits of worldly power and whether in any way divine mercy is stitched into the fabric of creation so that it must be shown . . . *or else*. In the end, so says the prophet, the God of mercy will not be mocked, not by all the power, all the wealth, and all the technology that any empire back then, now, or in the future can amass.

Questions for Discussion

1. What do you make of the way Isaiah (and other prophets) "articulates worldly power in the context of the authority" of God?

2. How does political power, whether ancient or contemporary, relate to the divine power of God?

3. What events or powers now are in need of articulation "within the context of faith"? How does one do that articulation responsibly and correctly?

4. In light of these reflections, what powers today seem penultimate in our world?

Chapter 25

A Man of Sorrows, Acquainted with Grief (Isaiah 53:4–6)

Surely he has borne our infirmities
  and carried our diseases;
yet we accounted him stricken,
  struck down by God, and afflicted.
But he was wounded for our transgressions,
  crushed for our iniquities;
upon him was the punishment that made us whole,
  and by his bruises we are healed.
All we like sheep have gone astray;
  we have all turned to our own way,
and the LORD *has laid on him*
  the iniquity of us all.

Scripture Passages for Reference

Isaiah 52:13–53:12
Isaiah 41:8–9
Isaiah 42:1–4
Isaiah 49:1–6
Isaiah 50:4–9
Acts 8:26–40

The title of this chapter comes from the King James Version's translation of Isaiah 53:3 (which is the same in the New King

James Version). The NRSV's rendition has "a man of suffering and acquainted with infirmity," though an accompanying note in the NRSV offers "a man of sorrows" as a possible translation for the first part. More recent translations, like the CEB, line up with the NRSV on the second descriptor: "who knew sickness well." Whatever the inclination of more recent versions, the KJV's translation is well known, not least because it is often applied homiletically to Jesus. Indeed, this passage about a suffering servant in Isaiah 52:13–53:12—called here, for simplicity, chapter 53—has the feel of holy ground. For the reader who is otherwise unfamiliar with Isaiah, this passage may be second in fame only to the passage about Immanuel in chapter 7. If such a reader knows any specific part of Isaiah 53, it is likely verses 4–6 or some part of them. In fact, one clause from verse 5, "with his stripes we are healed" (KJV), proved so popular in the mid-1980s that it lent a Christian heavy metal rock band its name. The band in question, *Stryper*, included "Isaiah 53:5" in its logo, making clear which "strypes" they were talking about, further underscoring the point by striping their name with yellow and black bands.

A connection between Isaiah 53 and the New Testament does indeed seem obvious. Even a cursory reading—albeit one with Christian eyes—is hard-pressed *not* to find allusions to Christ's passion and the idea of vicarious suffering. Of course, the qualifier "with Christian eyes" is telling, because one can read the chapter differently—for instance, and most obviously, when reading with Jewish eyes. Jewish interpreters have long read the passage as having a number of possible referents, none of whom are Jesus.[1] Modern biblical scholars of various faith persuasions have done the same with a large cast of characters now considered as candidates for the job of "suffering servant." A partial listing includes the prophets Isaiah, Jeremiah, or Ezekiel; the kings Uzziah, Hezekiah, Josiah, or Jehoiachin; Moses or the pathos-ridden Job; even Cyrus or Zerubbabel or Nehemiah—among others. To quote Old Testament scholar Tryggve Mettinger, this list "resembles the contents of a successful big-game hunt on the exegetical savannah," though, since none of these suggestions have carried the day, it would be more accurate to say the hunt has been *un*successful![2]

Several important issues should be mentioned. First, it was Bernard Duhm in the late nineteenth century who first posited that the book of Isaiah was a composite, separable into "First," "Second," and "Third." Duhm was also the first to identify four "servant songs" in Second Isaiah (42:1–4; 49:1–6; 50:4–9; 52:13–53:12), arguing that these four texts belonged together and were unrelated to their surrounding contexts. This judgment allowed him and those who followed him to excise these four texts from the larger context and treat them together. While Duhm's position captured the scholarly imagination for a long time, more recent work has argued that these four texts *cannot* be removed from their contexts; rather, they make perfect sense within the larger context of Second Isaiah. "Perfect sense" must be qualified, however, since it is quite clear that much in the "servant songs" (if we may continue to speak of them this way)—and especially much in Isaiah 53—is quite *un*clear. As David Clines has argued, this unclarity is inherent to the poetry of this passage, which frustrates any attempt to "crack the code" or "solve the puzzle" of Isaiah 53. This is to say that the poetry may, by definition if not also by design, resist and refuse all attempts to identify the suffering servant. As Clines says of this poetry, specifically its ambiguity, "it is of its essence that unequivocal identifications are not made and that the poem in this respect also is open-ended and allows for multiple interpretations."[3]

Of course, it is not only critical scholarship that wants answers, and precise ones at that; it is also the community of faith that often desires the same, sometimes at all costs: according to many Christians, Isaiah 53 *simply must* refer to Jesus!

Thus far then, the following items seem clear:

- A number of texts in Second Isaiah speak of YHWH's servant (or servants).
- These passages are best interpreted within the larger context of Isaiah, not separated out as if they were a foreign body referable only to themselves; the larger context includes several other texts that also speak of the servant(s).
- The poetic form greatly complicates the identification of the suffering servant.

The last point in particular explains how and why so many options have been offered for the servant's identity in chapter 53. It also explains why none of those candidates have yet secured the job.

According to Clines, the only truly clear thing about Isaiah 53 is its division of time into "before" and "after." *Before* refers to everything prior to Isaiah 53:4. That is the pivotal turning point for all that follows. Prior to that, we read of "my servant" who "shall prosper . . . be exalted and lifted up" (52:13), but then we hear immediately of this servant's severely marred appearance (v. 14). Despite that, he will "startle many nations" and cause kings to "shut their mouths" (v. 15). How this happens we are not told, but the text goes on to describe the servant's unremarkable appearance and stature (53:2), culminating in the lines about being "a man of suffering, acquainted with grief"—so much so that he was despised "and we held him of no account" (v. 3).

That was all *before*. But something takes place between 53:3 and 53:4 such that everything that follows verse 4 is *after*. This *after* is characterized by a realization that this servant's affliction and woundedness, his being struck and crushed, was vicarious: all of that was due to "our infirmities," "our diseases," "our transgressions," "our iniquities" (vv. 5–6). This is an impressive, if not comprehensive, list of wrongdoings confessed by an unspecified "we" that somehow also includes "us" now. It is capped off by a metaphor: "we" are like wandered-off sheep, all turned "to our own way," but somehow, someway "the Lord has laid on him the iniquity of us all."

Readers may be excused if they are confused. What is happening to whom and how? What made this particular individual's suffering vicarious for us? How is it the result of God's agency (v. 4) and the Lord's will (v. 10) and at the same time a perversion of justice (v. 8)? Did the servant die, and if so, how (vv. 8–9, 12)? If the servant died, how then does he "see his offspring, and prolong his days" (v. 10)? How will this possibly dead and yet (subsequently?) alive servant "prosper" (v. 10; see 52:13), "see light," and "make many righteous" (53:11), receiving "a portion with the great" (v. 12)?

Clines and others who have followed him seem right: these many questions (and others) are raised by the poetic presentation, which at the same time does not seem much interested in answering them. There is something inescapably ambivalent about this servant figure in our chapter and in other passages as well.⁴ Those other passages—best read in their larger contexts, to be sure—can nevertheless be considered together with regard to the identity of the servant. The very first instance of *servant language* in Second Isaiah seems clear enough:

> But you, Israel, my servant,
>   Jacob, whom I have chosen,
>   the offspring of Abraham, my friend;
> you whom I took from the ends of the earth,
>   and called from its farthest corners,
> saying to you, "You are my servant,
>   I have chosen you and not cast you off."
>   41:8–9

Nothing in the first *servant song* (42:1–4) would lead us to doubt the equation chapter 41 draws quite simply here—namely, that the servant is Israel. This is seconded in the second servant song (49:1–6), which is uttered by the servant proper. Here God's identification of the servant as Israel in 41:8–9 is repeated:

> And he [YHWH] said to me, "You are my servant,
>   Israel, in whom I will be glorified."
>   49:3

But we then learn in the following verses that the servant is somehow *not* identical or coterminous with Israel because the servant's mission is *to Israel*. There is, therefore, some sort of "conceptual distinction between the servant and Israel as such."⁵

> And now the LORD says,
>   who formed *me* in the womb to be his servant,
> to bring *Jacob* back to him,
>   and that *Israel* might be gathered to him. . . .
>   49:5

Here too we read that the servant's task goes *beyond Israel*:

> He [YHWH] says,
> "It is too light a thing that you should be my servant
>   to raise up the tribes of Jacob

> and to restore the survivors of Israel;
> I will give you as a light to the nations,
>   that my salvation may reach to the end of the earth."
>
> 49:6

In the third servant song (50:4–9) we see that the servant is willing to suffer on account of his mission, even as he is confident of his ultimate vindication:

> I gave my back to those who struck me,
>   and my cheeks to those who pulled out the beard;
> I did not hide my face
>   from insult and spitting.
> The Lord GOD helps me;
>   therefore I have not been disgraced;
> therefore I have set my face like flint,
>   and I know that I shall not be put to shame.
>
> 50:6–7

When considering the prior servant songs within their larger contexts, it seems patently clear that the servant is, at least at first, the nation of Israel in its entirety, then, later, a selected segment therein. Here we have come back to the most common Jewish interpretation of Isaiah 53: the servant is Israel itself, suffering vicariously for others. That said, much remains uncertain and enigmatic, with the distinction drawn between the servant and Jacob/Israel, present in 49:1–6, looming large. The notion of a faithful remnant is nothing new in Isaiah, however, and thus is fully possible within a servant-as-Israel interpretation. The servant as "selected segment" can be seen as "the steadfastly righteous minority."[6]

But the presentation of the servant as an individual—if it isn't solely a literary conceit—is a lingering question. Here we have to return to and reckon with the enigmatic nature of poetry. When confronted with the elusiveness of the poetry, Christian readers who have identified the servant too quickly with Jesus might find themselves despairing. But it is precisely the openness of the poetry that also makes it capable of more than one meaning. If poetry—all poetry, to be sure, but certainly also this poetry—is not about information, then poems are never about one thing only, one singular meaning or referent, but are open to many meanings and a multiplicity of readings. Not all of these readings are equally compelling. But to return to Clines:

> The poem's very lack of specificity refuses to let it be tied down to one spot on the globe, or frozen at one point in history: it opens up the possibility that the poem can become true in a variety of circumstances—that is its work.[7]

This rings true, of course, for a Christian interpretation of Isaiah 53 as referring "in the fullness of time" to Jesus and his passion. We should tread carefully, however, and not only because of the nature of the poetry. Donald Juel has observed that the New Testament does not cite Isaiah 53 nearly as much as one might imagine and almost never on the most obvious point of vicarious suffering (see only 1 Peter 2:24–25; contrast Matthew 8:17; 12:18–21; Luke 22:37; Acts 8:32–33).[8] The connections between Jesus and Isaiah 53 that seem so obvious to Christians today, that is, were apparently not quite so obvious to the New Testament writers. That said, one thing is abundantly clear, and that is "that the servant of Yahweh in Isaiah 53 *does nothing and says nothing but lets everything happen to him.*"[9] Here, if nowhere else, those of us who read with Christian eyes may find the closest point of connection between this chapter and the Gospels, which repeatedly emphasize how, even if Jesus *could* have done something (e.g., Matthew 26:53; John 18:36), he most decidedly did *not* (see, e.g., Matthew 26:64; 27:12–14; Mark 14:61). Small wonder, then, that much later when an Ethiopian eunuch sat puzzled by Isaiah 53:7–8 and asked Philip about whom the prophet was speaking, the disciple "began to speak, and starting with this scripture, he proclaimed to him the good news about Jesus" (Acts 8:35).

Questions for Discussion

1. Do you think it makes good sense to read the suffering servant of Isaiah 53 as referring to Israel? Is it possible to think this chapter refers to *both* Israel *and* Jesus?
2. Does the ambiguity of poetry excite you or bother you?

3. How do you see the interpretive dynamics of Isaiah 7's sign of Immanuel and Isaiah 53's suffering servant—both applied to Jesus in Christian readings—as similar or different?

4. In your opinion, how can suffering be vicarious?

Chapter 26

Wrath for a Second—Love Everlasting (Isaiah 54:7–8)

For a brief moment I abandoned you,
  but with great compassion I will gather you.
In overflowing wrath for a moment
  I hid my face from you,
but with everlasting love I will have compassion on you,
  says the LORD, *your Redeemer.*

> ***Scripture Passages for Reference***
>
> Isaiah 54:1–10
> 2 Samuel 7:5–7
> Job 23:3, 8–9
> Psalm 38:21
> Psalm 94:14
> Psalm 139:7–12

In our culture we habitually embrace, quite uncritically, a notion of God derived from Greek philosophy, that God is *omnipresent* (present always everywhere), *omnipotent* (all-powerful), and *omniscient* (all-knowing). The *omnipresent* part of this formulation is understood for the most part as an assurance that God's good governance is everywhere and always guaranteed and trustworthy. The Bible largely attests otherwise. In place of these *universal categories* that

173

yield *certitude*, the Bible regularly opts for the *relational language* of justice, righteousness, steadfast love, faithfulness, and compassion (*tzedeqah, mishpat, ḥesed, emunah*, and *raḥam*; see Exodus 34:6–7; Hosea 2:19–20; Lamentations 3:22–23). These latter categories never allow for *certitude* but instead voice the prospect of *fidelity*. We then discover that this relational language aimed at fidelity allows for freedom, risk, and fierce contestation. It is the latter rhetoric that dominates the Bible and that shows up in Isaiah 54:7–8. Thus an entry point into our text is the recognition that in biblical rendering we are not concerned with the God of the three big "omnis."

To be sure, the psalmist can readily affirm the inescapability of God:

> Where can I go from your spirit?
>> Or where can I flee from your presence?
> If I ascend to heaven, you are there;
>> if I make my bed in Sheol, you are there.
> If I take the wings of the morning
>> and settle at the farthest limits of the sea,
> even there your hand shall lead me,
>> and your right hand shall hold me fast.
> If I say, "Surely the darkness shall cover me,
>> and the light around me become night,"
> even the darkness is not dark to you;
>> the night is as bright as the day,
>> for darkness is as light to you.
>>> Psalm 139:7–12

The psalmist attests that this God will indeed "lead" and "hold fast" in every circumstance.

To the contrary, however, Job eagerly wants to get a hearing with God but articulates that he cannot find God:

> Oh, that I knew where I might find him,
>> that I might come even to his dwelling!
>>> Job 23:3

Job has sought God everywhere, but he cannot *perceive, behold*, or *see* God:

Wrath for a Second—Love Everlasting (Isaiah 54:7–8)

> If I go forward, he is not there;
> or backward, I cannot perceive him;
> on the left he hides, and I cannot behold him;
> I turn to the right, but I cannot see him.
>
> 23:8–9

"He is not there"! Job's deep reality is the absence of God, whom he cannot locate or contact. The Bible is a long, perhaps unfinalizable adjudication concerning these *relational realities* that are critical for *fidelity* but that eschew any possibility of *certitude*. *Present*, yes, but *not always*; sometimes *absent*.

We might fairly judge that the core reality of this relational God is God's freedom to "move about" according to God's own will (see 2 Samuel 7:5–7). This God will not be domesticated or caged, not by Solomon's temple, nor by our best orthodoxies, nor by any of our best ideologies. All such gods are "too small." We may best understand biblical testimony concerning God as an undecipherable contest between *God's freedom* to come and go and *God's faithfulness and responsiveness* to the needs and requirements of God's covenant partners. Furthermore, even as the church confesses the *full presence of God*, we note that much of the church's missional energy and pastoral attentiveness are preoccupied with the *absence of God*. Given such experienced reality, it is perhaps unhelpful and eventually unpersuasive to say (as is often said), "God is most present even when it feels that God is most absent." The abrasive testimony of Job about divine absence in his experience runs well beyond emotive complaint to the very bottom of his lived reality.

Our verses are situated in the book of Isaiah as the poet, living in the exile, is about to conclude with a ringing, dramatic scenario of the wondrous return of exiles from Babylon (55:12–13). But before the poet arrives at this victorious crescendo, he lingers in chapter 54 to ponder the interaction God has had with Israel. In the rhetoric of relationality, the Bible most often appeals to two images, that of husband-wife and that of parent-child, both of which aim at fidelity and both of which involve freedom, risk, and fierce contestation.

Chapter 54 begins with an appeal to marital imagery that was well established before Isaiah in the poetry of Hosea and Jeremiah. Isaiah 54:1 begins with "barren" Israel, an image that reaches back to barren mother Sarah in the book of Genesis (see Genesis 11:30; also Galatians 4:21–31). Sarah is remembered as being without child, understood as without a future and without hope. And now in Isaiah, Israel in exile is "barren," without a future or a hope. But here it is promised that the "barren one" will prosper and flourish *beyond* the one already "married," that is, Babylon! The poet dares to anticipate that Israel will have a glorious future that is not on offer to mighty Babylon. The inversion of historical reality is scripted according to the belated but altogether wondrous birth of a son to Sarah (Genesis 21:1–7).

But then, in Isaiah 54:4, the imagery shifts from birth to a difficult marriage. The barren mother now becomes the abandoned wife. YHWH, the creator, is named as "your husband" (Hebrew *bāʿal*, v. 5), the one who fructifies, makes pregnant, and creates futures. This is the God who has the whole world in his hands, who can do all things, and who will create a future for his wife, Israel. But then in verse 6, the poet must recognize a marital reality that contradicts the good assurance of verse 5. In reality, according to the imagery, the wife-Israel has been forsaken (*ʿāzab*) and made very, very sad. Indeed, in the poetic parallel, she is "cast off" (*māʾas*). The marriage has failed; the abandoned woman is left to grieve in her abandonment.

It is important to recognize that this marital imagery takes place within a patriarchal culture. In such a culture, the husband has most of the power and holds most of the options in the relationship. Already in the Torah provision of Deuteronomy 24:1–4, two husbands, sequentially married to the same woman, have the right to divorce and send a rejected wife away. In the poetry of Hosea, an unfaithful wife will receive no pity (Hosea 2:2–13). And in the long poetic development of the imagery in Jeremiah 3:1–4:4, it is expected that a disloyal wife must repent of her adultery. This trajectory of the image in Torah, Hosea, and Jeremiah was available to Isaiah and further developed after him in the disconcerting texts found in Ezekiel 16, 20, and 23.

This brings us back to our verses, Isaiah 54:7–8. The subject is the abandonment of the wife by the husband, but we have had nothing like this before in the poetry of Israel. There are, to be sure, *petitions* not to be abandoned, suggesting at least that there is some fear and some possibility of divine abandonment:

> Do not forsake me, O LORD;
> O my God, do not be far from me.
>> Psalm 38:21; see also
>> Psalms 27:9; 71:9, 18

There are also *assurances* from God that God will not forsake:

> For the LORD will not forsake his people;
> he will not abandon his heritage.
>> Psalm 94:14; see also
>> Psalms 27:1; 37:28

But the petitions to not forsake and the assurances to not abandon together suggest that in the relational rhetoric of Israel such a possibility was in fact always present. It is in the nature of a relationship (and thus also in relational language) that such an option exists. The husband may leave the wife! And finally, of course, we must come to the cry of abandonment in Psalm 22:1:

> My God, my God, why have you forsaken me?
> Why are you so far from helping me, from the words of
> my groaning?

This cry is without parallel in the tradition, but it is enough to see that God, in God's freedom, can abandon. It is important for Christians that this cry of the psalmist became the cry of Jesus on the cross (Matthew 27:46; Mark 15:34). Abandonment swirls all around the execution of Jesus—even around Jesus! Indeed, Jürgen Moltmann goes so far as to declare of this cry of abandonment, "The Fatherlessness of the Son is matched by the Sonlessness of the Father."[1] There is abandonment all around! The cry of Psalm 22:1–2 permits the reality of God to sink to the depth of abandonment. And now, in our verses, all of the possibility of divine abandonment comes to speech on the lips of God, who admits its truth. The cry of abandonment has been on the lips of a desperate petitioner, but here the words are God's own confession. Two lines are uttered in due humility by God:

> For a brief moment I abandoned you.
> ....
> In overflowing wrath for a moment
> I hid my face from you.
>> Isaiah 54:7–8

It is as though God says, "Okay, I admit it. I did indeed abandon you. But I did it only for a second—an instant—a moment!" This is a striking divine admission on two accounts. First, in these verses no punishment toward Israel is expressed, no motivation given based on Israel's guilt or failure. The divine abandonment here is not in response to Israel's disloyalty. Indeed, there is no suggestion here that divine abandonment was evoked by Israel. Rather, YHWH just did it! YHWH exercised freedom. To be sure, this is no "confession of sin" on God's part. But, in the most *immediate literary context*, it recognizes that the departure of the husband was due to his agency, not the fault of the wife—at least none of the latter is expressed.[2] That said, these verses surely cannot be read outside of the *larger context of Isaiah* that is overfull with candid details about wife-Israel's infidelity, all the way back to Isaiah 1:2. Of course, that only makes the absence of Israel's guilt in this particular poem even more noticeable and noteworthy.

The second matter to observe is that what God calls "a second" (NRSV: "a brief moment"; Hebrew *regʿa qātōn*) was for Israel *seventy years* of deportation and displacement. Perhaps such a passage of time is not unlike the psalmist's assertion:

> For a thousand years in your sight
> are like yesterday, when it is past,
> or like a watch in the night.
> Psalm 90:4

Or like the hymnist's:

> A thousand ages in thy sight are like an evening gone,
> short as the watch that ends the night before the rising sun.
> . . . .
> They fly forgotten, as a dream dies at the opening day.[3]

Perhaps for the "Omni-God," but the long years of exile did not "fly forgotten" for Israel. They were vigorously remembered as Israel continued to be marked and scarred by the desertion and displacement. These two lines in the divine utterance constitute an astonishing recognition of God's desertion and God's coming to a new sense about this relationship.

These two lines of divine utterance are promptly countered by the two lines that follow, each of which is introduced by an adversative pronoun, "but." God now marks a contrast and contradiction to the *dreadful-but-brief moment of abandonment* by bearing witness to *a long, durable-even-eternal fidelity* that follows. YHWH twice utters the word that may initiate a restored relationship: compassion! The term conveys an attentive solidarity with the other that takes into serious account and pays attention to the needs and hopes of the other. Isaiah in exile will use the term twice more before the victorious climax in chapter 55. In 54:9–10, YHWH declares that there will never again be a devastating flood as beset Noah in Genesis. God's promise, it is affirmed, is more reliable than creation itself:

> But my steadfast love shall not depart from you,
> and my covenant of peace shall not be removed,
> says the LORD, who has *compassion* on you.
>
> 54:10

The two verbs "depart" (*mûš*) and "remove" (*mûṭ*) are used for the destabilization of creation (see Psalm 46:5–6; Jeremiah 31:36). But YHWH's fidelity is in contrast to that destabilization. These lines feature the clustered triad of God's *steadfast love*, God's *covenant of shalom*, and, as a final accent, God's *compassion*. In 55:6–7, the poet issues a summons to Israel to "return to YHWH" in order that YHWH may pardon and show mercy:

> Let them return to the LORD, that he may have mercy on them,
> and to our God, for he will abundantly pardon.
>
> 55:6

Thus the poet appeals to the memory of the flood (54:9–10) and David (55:3) in order to affirm that God as creator and as Lord of Israel has a history of compassion that now yet again receives emphasis. Moreover, in our verses, 54:7–8, divine compassion is contrasted with divine anger and divine wrath. The anger and wrath are momentary; the compassion is long-term and abiding. God's long-term goodness trumps God's momentary lapse. As a result, Israel may be on its way from exile rejoicing (55:12–13). All is well that ends well! If, however, we stay inside the imagery of marriage, abandonment, and restoration, we may need to be careful with this divine assurance. All one has to do is observe this reversal from the perspective of the abandoned wife. The husband (YHWH) may indeed speak in good faith with genuine intentionality. The wife, nevertheless, hears these words of assurance through the lingering hurt of abandonment. She may be so needy that she readily accepts the assurance. She may be so lonely that she embraces the reversal. But in her pain she may be cautious, or reticent, perhaps even unmoved. In any case, the memory of abandonment lingers. And in the text of Israel it was remembered without any ambiguity that the seventy years of displacement was not the work of Nebuchadnezzar, but exactly the work and will of YHWH. No wonder husband-YHWH is at pains to reassure wife-Israel—not only here but throughout Second Isaiah.

When interpreting this text, we have to weigh how long and how deeply to remain inside the metaphor of marriage. Said differently, how soon can we move beyond the metaphor itself to think theologically with these fraught terms about fidelity? We must not be so innocent that we permit good-sounding theology to override the lingering alienation that the imagery also communicates. And we may be sure that Israel—the abandoned wife—will not have her hurt resolved by any appeal to the antiseptic categories of "omni." The wife-Israel does not wait for or want omnipresence or omnipotence or omniscience. What she wants is steadfast fidelity and compassion—nothing less than divine presence.[4] She now gets it—or at least hears of it—but she will have to wait and see to learn how serious the divine reversal is, how quickly restoration occurs. It is likely fair to say that as heirs of this text, both Jews and Christians are waiting and watching together to see about the reliability of this divine resilience. If—or rather *when*—we too have felt abandoned and are promised presence, we wonder how long we must wait. The poet shows that he trusts the divine declaration. Isaiah invites us to embrace a proper homecoming and restoration, offering us that in the words of God's own poetry. And we who appeal to this text may also do so. We do so, however, with the lingering scars left on the body and in the memory of wife-Israel and, belatedly, son-Jesus. Covenantal fidelity does not ever yield certitude, and it surely does not arrive at certitude from the words of the one who has, even if only for a "second," been abandoned. It invites trust, and so we, like the wife, trust as we are able, forgiving (if that is the proper term) even if we are never able to forget completely.

Questions for Discussion

1. How do you think about the difference between God's "momentary" abandonments versus God's "everlasting" love?
2. Do you like divine "omnis," or do you prefer God's relationality? How do (or can) these go together? Beyond your own sense of how these terms do or do not relate to each other, how does the Scripture relate to them?
3. What do we do with the things we seem unable to forget?

Chapter 27

A House of Prayer for All People (Isaiah 56:7)

*These I will bring to my holy mountain,
and make them joyful in my house of prayer;
their burnt offerings and their sacrifices
will be accepted on my altar;
for my house shall be called a house of prayer
for all peoples.*

> ***Scripture Passages for Reference***
>
> Isaiah 56:1–8
> Isaiah 58:1–9
> Amos 5:21–24
> Zechariah 4:10
> Psalm 1
> John 10:1–18

Isaiah in exile (chaps. 40–55) had anticipated a victorious homecoming to Jerusalem for the deported exiles. That return was facilitated by Cyrus but authorized and generated by YHWH. This wondrous return would reflect the sovereign rule of YHWH and ensure a restored Jerusalem of well-being. But as things happened, the return proved to be more modest—perhaps even disappointing—than the high poetry of Second Isaiah had suggested.

In the biblical account, the return home stretches all the way from the mention of Cyrus by name in Isaiah 44:28; 45:1, 13—not to mention his decree in 2 Chronicles 36:22–23 and Ezra 1:1–4—to the books of Haggai and Zechariah (both figures dating to the reign of Darius the Persian; ca. 520 BCE) to the new administrative arrangement under Nehemiah authorized by Artaxerxes (444 BCE). The view from these texts is that the return from exile amounted to nothing as grand or spectacular as Second Isaiah's vision. Zechariah characterizes the time as "the day of small things" in which hopes for Jerusalem had to be modest (Zechariah 4:10). We also know that the new governance under Nehemiah and the leadership of Ezra had to cope with vexing problems including harassment by those who stood opposed to Jerusalem's restoration (see Nehemiah 4:1–5; 6:10–14). It was a time that demanded tenacious faith by Israel's leaders; often, however, there seemed little to celebrate.

It is in this period that we encounter a new voice in the Isaiah tradition, chapters 56–66, commonly called "Third Isaiah." These chapters add further support to other postexilic texts that reflect disappointment over the failure of the great promises of return to materialize. But as is characteristic of the Bible, circumstances of failure and disappointment did not lead to cynical resignation or full abdication. Rather, the Isaiah tradition once again rallies to counter despair with a new wave of hope and expectation that is grounded not in the circumstances on the ground but in the uncompromising resolve of YHWH as articulated by the poetry.

Chapter 56 is the first one assigned to Third Isaiah. Unlike the marked shift from prose to poetry found at the start of Second Isaiah, coupled with its unexpected message of consolation (40:1), this new moment in the Isaiah tradition begins with a simple—yet staple—divine utterance:

> Thus says the LORD:
> Maintain justice, and do what is right,
> for soon my salvation will come,
> and my deliverance be revealed.
>   56:1

The combination of *justice* and *right* is common in the prophets, not least in Isaiah, as a stereotypical word pair. These two words

A House of Prayer for All People (Isaiah 56:7) 185

and concepts go together, so much so that they are commonly conjoined as parallel terms in Hebrew poetry (cf. Amos 5:24). Notably, this opening line in Isaiah 56 calls back to the very beginning of Isaiah's vision:

> Zion shall be redeemed by *justice*,
> and those in her who repent, by *righteousness*.
> 1:27

For those who, much later, lament the sad circumstances of "returned life," Isaiah 56 reminds them of the divine blueprint to salvation, deliverance, and repentance: it is via justice and righteousness, something that an earlier people failed to do:

> For the vineyard of the LORD of hosts
> is the house of Israel,
> and the people of Judah
> are his pleasant planting;
> he expected *justice*,
> but saw bloodshed;
> *righteousness*,
> but heard a cry!
> 5:7

The returnees of Isaiah 56 thus receive commands about justice and righteousness: *maintain* and *do*! As a result, another result will follow "soon": YHWH's salvation will draw near and YHWH's deliverance will be revealed. Although obscured in the NRSV's translation, "deliverance" in v. 1 is the same Hebrew word as "right" earlier (both *ṣĕdāqāh*). There is something comparable and commensurate between human righteousness and divine rescue. What an amazing claim accomplished by just one simple line of Hebrew poetry!

The mandates of v. 1 are motivated and clarified in the next verse. Those who do what YHWH says are "happy." "Blessed" is another common translation for the Hebrew term used here (*'ašrê*), which connotes a fortunate or enviable position (cf. Psalm 1). That is good motivation for obedience to be sure, but the obedience is further specified. Those who do what YHWH wants do so carefully, perhaps even extremely: they "hold it fast" (*ḥāzaq*). Further details concern the keeping of the Sabbath, one of the great commandments from the Decalogue (Exodus 20:8; Deuteronomy 5:12), and refraining "from doing any evil" (Isaiah 56:2).

The poetry shifts in 56:3–8, suggesting that verses 1–2 compose a kind of introduction and motto for chapters 56–66. Be that as it may, the mention of keeping the Sabbath without polluting it in verse 2 may be what prompted the placement of verses 3–8, which consider the status of people who have traditionally been barred from certain ritual practices. Foreigners are mentioned first, followed by eunuchs. Both types of individuals would have encountered barriers to participating in the worship life of the community.

The status of foreigners in ancient Israelite society and worship is a complicated question and no doubt varied in different periods. It must suffice to say that in some instances their involvement in Israel's worship practices was required, but in others it may have been optional; in still others it was forbidden. We may note, for instance, restrictions on the later, Second Temple precincts that allowed non-Jews entrance only so far. That Second Temple, greatly expanded by Herod in New Testament times, was first built in the postexilic period, precisely the time from which Third Isaiah dates. We know, furthermore, from other texts dating to this period that genetics and lineage—specifically foreignness versus native-born status—loomed large in debates over the community's composition and future existence. It is understandable, therefore, that the foreigner quoted in verse 3 says, despairingly, "The LORD will surely separate [*bādal*] me from his people." It was indeed a requirement of "Aaron and sons" to "distinguish [*bādal*] between the holy and the common, and between the unclean and the clean" (Leviticus 10:10; see also 11:47; 20:25). The foreigner in the time of Isaiah 56 therefore knew that when it came to things like *Sabbath* and *profanation*, let alone *God's people*, they would most certainly find themselves outside looking in. But, Isaiah says, let not the foreigner say that—which means, of course, "No such separation will take place! Don't believe that! That is not accurate!"

The statement attributed to the eunuch, "I am just a dry tree," is also judged inaccurate and deemed inadmissible. Eunuchs are, of course, men who have been castrated. Reasons for such castration no doubt varied, but it was common in antiquity for high palace officials to be eunuchs, likely to prevent illicit acts of procreation with royal women. This was a way to ensure that the royal bloodline was pure. It is possible that the Hebrew word for eunuch used in Isaiah 56:3, *sārîs*, refers generically to "high officials" in some passages, but it is just as likely that such high officials were, as a matter of course, also castrated eunuchs.

Several points are important about the use of *sārîs* in Isaiah 56. First, *sārîs* is found quite frequently in late Old Testament literature, where it occurs numerous times in Daniel (e.g., 1:3, 7, 8, 9, 10, 11, 18; NRSV's "palace master" is more woodenly translated "chief of the eunuchs") and Esther (1:10, 12, 15; 2:3, 14, 15, 21; 4:4, 5; 6:2, 14; 7:9), and where it typically refers to officials in the Babylonian and Persian courts, respectively. It is possible that such individuals chose castration *willingly*, as part of their service; it is equally possible, however, if not far more likely, that such castration was a *requirement* for this particular kind of work. The eunuch in Isaiah 56, therefore, may be one *by choice* or *by compulsion*. The former could reflect a kind of *assimilation to imperial domination*—choosing to work for the empire, as it were. The latter would reflect *the extent of imperial domination*—the lengths an empire can go to impose its will on the human body, even those parts we treat with special honor (1 Corinthians 12:23).

Either option explains the eunuch's despairing remark, "I am just a dry tree" (Isaiah 56:3). The sense of the verb suggests, of course, lack of virility, which makes good sense in light of the eunuch's condition, but the image of the withered tree as a whole evokes Psalm 1's comparison of the righteous tree that flourishes with not a single leaf withering (Psalm 1:3). This connection suggests the eunuch is not (only) lamenting his reproductive status but (also) his unrighteous standing (whether by choice or compulsion), a point that makes good sense in light of the parallel sentiment uttered by the foreigner. This interpretation gains further strength by noting Leviticus 21:20, which prohibits priests from having "crushed testicles" (see also Leviticus 22:24), and Deuteronomy 23:1, which expands the prohibition such that no one in such a status—and the eunuch would certainly qualify—"can belong to the LORD's assembly." (Deuteronomy 23:3 contains a similar prohibition regarding foreigners, specifically Ammonites and Moabites, who are inadmissible to the assembly "even to the tenth generation.") These are weighty laws, but the poet overturns them. Let not the eunuch utter such a thing, which is to say, "Don't *believe* such a thing!" Once again, the briefest of poetic lines has massive ramifications.

Instead, the poet says, to those eunuchs who keep the Sabbath and hold fast (*ḥāzaq*) to the covenant (v. 4), YHWH will give a shower of blessings:

- *a monument and a name*—a legacy better even than progeny, not least because it is
- *an everlasting name that shall not be cut off*, with the verb here used elsewhere to describe both castration proper and "cutting" (that is, establishing) a covenant—a remarkable double entendre!

Even more remarkably, all of this will be given, YHWH says, "in my house and within my walls" (v. 5), which is to say that the eunuch will no longer be kept away from YHWH's assembly or prohibited from serving YHWH as priest.

This is a remarkable change of circumstance, and the following verses establish the same for foreigners. God will bring them to "my holy mountain" and "make them joyful in my house of prayer." If there is any confusion about the specific location, it is clarified immediately: "Their burnt offerings and their sacrifices will be accepted on my altar" (v. 7). There will be no keeping foreigners outside the sacred precincts anymore!

Here is where our verse occurs, particularly the latter part of verse 7b, which provides the motivation for this stunning turn of events for eunuch and foreigner: it is *because* "my house shall be called a house of prayer for all peoples." The vision is remarkably inclusive and apparently knows no limits. YHWH's temple is for *all peoples*. Verse 8 adds further support, stating that YHWH, who is in the habit of gathering "the outcasts of Israel," is in the gathering business more generally:

> I will gather others to them
>   besides those already gathered.
>   v. 8b

A House of Prayer for All People (Isaiah 56:7) 189

In its historical context, our poem must have sounded nothing short of radical. Emotions ran hot over who constituted "the true Israel" in postexilic times. Our own, present-day debates over immigration and deportation are not unrelated and quite comparable. Into such a contested situation, where not only proper genes matter but also religious "purity," Isaiah 56 offers a stunningly inclusive vision. Those who do *not* qualify by ethnicity or by religious standards—such disqualifications having more than ample legal support—are suddenly qualified. They now have a place and a legacy inside God's walls, in YHWH's own house, in the very temple which turns out to be place of prayer *for all*.

This inclusivity is not devoid of ethics, however. It must not be missed or downplayed that the foreigners who are included and gathered up are those

> who join themselves[1] to the LORD,
> to minister to him, to love the name of the LORD,
> and to be his servants.
>   v. 6a

This involves, once again, keeping the Sabbath, not profaning it, and holding fast (*ḥāzaq*) to God's covenant (v. 6b). These requirements come as no surprise. They were present in the opening of Isaiah 56 (see v. 2) and are the same requirements placed on the eunuchs. Religious, even ritual matters, *matter*; obedience to the covenant *continues to matter*. This is not an "anything and everything goes" kind of scenario. This is a scenario marked, at the end of the day, by obedience to God and God's covenant, which must include the Lord's good law given the importance of Sabbath (among other things). But if that obedience is there—an obedience that can be defined as loving YHWH's name—then there is nothing that can separate anyone from God's own love in return (see Romans 8:39). In the absence of such obedience, however, any and all acts of religiosity, no matter how pious, are void and divinely rejected (see 58:1–9; Amos 5:21–24).

Two points of connection with the New Testament are noteworthy here. First, when Jesus cleanses the temple, he cites our verse as the motivation for his actions (Matthew 21:13; Mark 11:17; Luke 19:46). The Gospel accounts make no mention of foreigners or eunuchs but add a further important detail marking the house of prayer for all peoples: it is exactly *not* a house of commerce. Read alongside Isaiah 56, the Gospel accounts suggest another way people are kept out of God's assembly—namely, via economic barriers of one sort or another that easily become *socio*economic considerations that often trace back to matters of ethnicity and status.

Second, in John 10:16, in the midst of his self-description as a shepherd, Jesus candidly states, "I have other sheep that do not belong to this fold. I must bring them also." Surely this resonates with Isaiah 56:8 and the "others" who must be gathered "besides those already gathered." Jesus continues, "And they will listen to my voice. So there will be one flock, one shepherd." This surely resonates with the obedience manifested by those who "join themselves to the LORD" and keep God's covenant in Isaiah 56. The result is one flock, one house of prayer, one Good Shepherd and Lord.

Questions for Discussion

1. Can you identify ways that people have been kept outside God's assembly? How might they be included?
2. Do you agree there are limits on divine inclusivity here in Isaiah 56? What does that mean in your estimation?
3. What permits the overturning of the prior legal statements about foreigners and eunuchs? Where do you find contemporary parallels?

Chapter 28

Wealth Brought and Transformed (Isaiah 60:6)

*A multitude of camels shall cover you,
the young camels of Midian and Ephah;
all those from Sheba shall come.
They shall bring gold and frankincense,
and shall proclaim the praise of the* LORD.

> ***Scripture Passages for Reference***
>
> Isaiah 60:1–7
> Matthew 2:1–12
> Luke 4:18–19
> Acts 17:22–31

As noted in the previous chapter, the great vision about the exiles' homecoming found in Isaiah 40–55 (see also Ezekiel 40–48) did not pan out as hoped. "Reentry" proved difficult. We know from various texts scattered throughout the Bible that date to this time—bits from Chronicles, Ezra, Nehemiah, Haggai, Zechariah, Ezekiel, and Isaiah itself—that life "back home" was much harder than anticipated. It often seemed like there were more problems than solutions, with the community left with little to celebrate. The material from Isaiah 56–66, "Third Isaiah," is dated by scholars to this time and reflects the ups and downs of life back home even as it speaks into the hard circumstances facing the postexilic community.

It must be admitted that biblical scholars are less clear about the coherence of Third Isaiah than they are of Second Isaiah. In this way, Third Isaiah is more similar to First Isaiah. As we have had occasion to note, not all of Isaiah 1–39 is of a piece: it is a mixture of poetry and prose (especially in chaps. 36–39), and there is evidence that some of these chapters likely date to periods long after the career of Isaiah, Amoz's son, who lived and prophesied in Jerusalem in the eighth century BCE. Indeed, as noted earlier, some see chapters 34–35 as a kind of "anticipation" of Second Isaiah within the bounds of First Isaiah. For its part, Second Isaiah seems more unified, especially around the theme of homecoming, but Third Isaiah feels far more disparate. It might be that it stems from several different poets such that we have, in the end, far more than just three Isaiahs! Be that as it may, the book of Isaiah manifests plenty of coherence across all of its sixty-six chapters, and so themes and motifs, language and terminology are found in Third Isaiah that are also found in the previous fifty-five chapters. There is, in the end, just one book of Isaiah.

This helps to explain a particular cluster found midway through Third Isaiah that seems to hold together as a piece: chapters 60–62. There is much here that resonates closely with Second Isaiah; some scholars have gone so far as to posit that the poet responsible for these chapters was a disciple of Second Isaiah in one way or another. Whatever the case, this particular unit gives voice to the deep resolve of God that is in no way detracted by or toned down by the problematic circumstances of postexilic life. This is faith that will not surrender to circumstance!

In these three chapters, which can be read as one large poetic unit, it is anticipated that Jerusalem will emerge as a prosperous, dominant economic power that will receive and benefit from the resources of others. Within these chapters, the summons of 61:1–4 is most familiar to us, as these verses anticipate a new Jubilee-based economic restoration—a restoration that is reiterated and performed, in Christian tradition, by Jesus (see Luke 4:18–19). It is anticipated that

> strangers shall stand and feed your flocks,
> foreigners shall till your land and dress your vines.
> Isaiah 61:5

Israel will be on top, and others will do the hard work. Other nations will serve and assist Israel; Israel will be known as "a people whom the LORD has blessed" (61:9). In chapter 62, it is anticipated that the Lord will give Israel a set of new names that properly characterize its restored status. These new names will be "My Delight Is in Her," "Married," "The Holy People, The Redeemed of the Lord," and "Sought Out, A City Not Forsaken" (62:4, 12). This people will no longer be known by derogatory names like "Forsaken" or "Desolate" (62:4). The new status, affirmed by these new names, will be a public manifestation, evident to all other nations and peoples. Everyone will know that this spectacular restoration is the good and faithful work of the God of Israel.

Chapter 60 introduces this triad of wondrously promissory chapters. The basis for the new prospect for Jerusalem is nothing other than the return of "the glory of the LORD" (60:1). We are dealing with poetic imagery, so these lines do not specify how or in what way or by what means the transformative glory of YHWH will be performed. The rhetoric sounds like a new temple epiphany that is reminiscent of the new tabernacle of Moses in Exodus 40:34 (see also Ezekiel 43:1–5; 44:1–2). But the impact of God's coming glory is not contained in the sanctuary; it has an immediate impact on the daily life and well-being of the inhabitants of Jerusalem. On the one hand, this promissory vision imagines the enhancement of the temple:

> The glory of Lebanon shall come to you,
>   the cypress, the plane, and the pine,
> to beautify the place of my sanctuary;
>   and I will glorify where my feet rest.
>   60:13

On the other hand, the vision foresees that the other nations will be in subservience and deference to Israel:

> Foreigners shall build up your walls,
>   and their kings shall minister to you.
> . . . .
> For the nation and kingdom
>   that will not serve you shall perish;
>   those nations shall be utterly laid waste.
> . . . .

> The descendants of those who oppressed you
> > shall come bending low to you,
> and all who despised you
> > shall bow down at your feet.
> ....
> You shall suck the milk of nations,
> > you shall suck the breasts of kings.
> > > 60:10, 12, 14, 16

The measure of this reversal of fortune is that Jerusalem will be a site of immense wealth:

> The abundance of the sea shall be brought to you,
> > the wealth of the nations shall come to you.
> ....
> For the coastlands shall wait for me,
> > the ships of Tarshish first,
> to bring your children from far away,
> > their silver and gold with them.
> ....
> Your gates shall always be open;
> > day and night they shall not be shut,
> so that nations shall bring you their wealth,
> > with their kings led in procession.
> > > 60:5, 9, 11

The latter is an image not unlike that of King Solomon in 1 Kings 10:14–23.

It is in the midst of and as a part of this wondrous flow of wealth to Jerusalem that our verse, Isaiah 60:6, appears. The poet offers a vision of caravans of camels that are heavy-laden with wealth and tribute, all of which will be offered to Israel. Of all of this wealth, the poet identifies two particular commodities. Of course he will mention gold, always the measure of royal plunder, to which he adds frankincense. The latter is a valuable incense used for sacrificial offerings in order to raise up to God a pleasant aroma (see Jeremiah 17:26; 41:5; Isaiah 43:23; 66:3). While frankincense belongs most often to the sphere of worship, in our text it bespeaks a great luxury. Israel will enjoy a good supply of such perfume.

Wealth Brought and Transformed (Isaiah 60:6)   195

Thus the poet anticipates a great reversal of fortunes that is summarized with a recital of verses that repeat the word "instead":

> *Instead* of bronze . . . gold,
> *Instead* of iron . . . silver,
> *Instead* of wood, bronze,
> *Instead* of stones, iron.
> 60:17

Everything will be upgraded to a better material. It is likely that this reiteration of the word "instead" is intended as a counterpoint to the negative repetition of "instead" in early Isaiah:

> *Instead* of perfume . . . a stench,
>   and *instead* of a sash, a rope;
> and *instead* of well-set hair, baldness;
>   and *instead* of a rich robe, . . . sackcloth;
> *instead* of beauty, shame.
> 3:24

This repetition of "instead" anticipates degradation, humiliation, and slavery. Now in chapter 60, all of that is reversed. Now the one humiliated will be *exalted*, the one depleted will be *enriched*, the one enslaved will be *elevated to dominance*.

This declaration is vigorously materialistic. The new prospect for Israel is unreservedly this-worldly in ways that matter to political economic reality and leverage. But the Bible refuses any dualism; the imagery is not *simply* materialistic. It is, rather, a vision that attests to the faithful rule of YHWH:

> You shall know that I, the LORD, am your Savior
>   and your Redeemer, the Mighty One of Jacob.
> 60:16

Jerusalem is glorified; but the glory belongs to YHWH:

> I will glorify my glorious house. . . .
> They are the shoot that I planted, the work of my hands,
>   so that I might be glorified.
> 60:7b, 21

Thus it turns out that the dazzling imagery of camel caravans in Isaiah 60:6 is one vehicle among several utilized by the poet to articulate the new luxurious abundance that will be delivered to Jerusalem. The culmination of the chapter is the mighty affirmation of this historical reversal:

> The least of them shall become a clan,
>   and the smallest one a mighty nation;
> I am the LORD;
>   in its time I will accomplish it quickly.
>   60:22

The final words are terse and a bit enigmatic:

> I am the LORD; in its time, I will hasten it.
>   60:22b; our translation

This reversal will be abrupt, but only when the time is right. Israel must wait for that time. This interface of "quick" and "time" (that cannot be hurried) is wise counsel to a community that might be in despair or that might be impatient as it lacks power for domination or resources for affluence. All good things are promised, but all in God's good time.

This breathtaking vision of restored well-being lingers for Israel. Israel awaits delivery and implementation of it. Israel must wait. There is no doubt that these poetic chapters have future relevance for the community of faith. On the one hand, the uncompromisingly materialistic imagery is something of a seduction, because it imagines that God's processes of fortune reversal are worldly processes. Indeed, they could not be otherwise. But that in turn has sometimes led to a "pie in the sky" eschatology that offers false expectations to those denied well-being in this world by a bet on a future chance.[1] Such a seductive vision has sometimes been used to sedate the vulnerable into anticipating otherworldly abundance (while giving up hope for a better here and now), or, alternatively (and illogically), it has given supposed sanction to greedy and covetous accumulation of wealth by pretend believers. Such promises may undergird a grasping kind of "Zionism" in which contemporary people lay claim and entitlement to this-worldly wealth and real estate. The poet does not and cannot control the future use of his poetic words. The poetry is remarkably supple, of course, and can be taken in many different directions. But this much is clear: the God attested in Isaiah 60 is the God of transformative power, who traffics in this-worldly well-being, the one who has not forgotten God's own beloved people, not even in their most desolate and humiliating circumstance.

In Christian tradition, our verse seems to be a source of the narrative in the Gospel of Matthew concerning the "visit of the wise men" to the Christ child in Bethlehem (Matthew 2:1–12). This rendering by Matthew (and the subsequent rendering in many church Christmas pageants) accents the mysterious quality of the magi, made more inscrutable and awesome by our crèches that have the kings riding on camels—something that Matthew does *not* report. In the narrative we are not told all we'd like to know about why or how the wise men had come to the child, though it is intimated that, as learned scholars of that day, they had discerned some sort of clue via astronomical investigation. In any case, the presenting issue in the narrative is the presence of Herod, a Jewish king who represents the authority of Rome. In their quest, the magi turn from the manifest rule of Herod to the alternative rule of a newborn child. And they worship! They bring their luxurious offerings to worship the child. The poor baby born in a barn is exalted. To the "gold and frankincense" of Isaiah, the magi add "myrrh," yet another luxurious incense used in worship. When we read this narrative in the wake of Isaiah 60:6, we can see that in place of *soon-to-be exalted* Israel is the *soon-to-be-crucified* Christ child who represents the edge of restored Israel no longer under Rome. As Isaiah has the nations submit to Israel, so Matthew has the learning and wealth of the Gentiles offered in worship to the lordship of the Christ child. It is as though all the learning and wealth of the nations must be transposed through the rule of Christ.

As we think about the interface of *Israel and the nations* and *the world and Christ,* two texts speak to "understanding seeking faith." First, in 1 Corinthians 1:23, Paul asserts that "Christ crucified" is "foolishness" to the Gentiles. Perhaps the newborn child in Bethlehem appeared to these wise Gentiles as "foolishness" that contradicted all that they knew. But they submitted to this new reality nevertheless! They accepted the foolishness that must have struck them as ludicrous and worshiped Christ anyway. Second, in Acts 17, Paul does not flinch from summoning his *Gentile* listeners to faith.

Paul asserts that the community of Christ knows what wise Gentiles do not—namely, the name of their unnamed God:

> Athenians, I see how extremely religious you are in every way. For as I went through the city and looked carefully at the objects of your worship, I found among them an altar with the inscription, "To an unknown god." What therefore you worship as unknown, this I proclaim to you. The God who made the world and everything in it, he who is Lord of heaven and earth, does not live in shrines made by human hands, nor is he served by human hands, as though he needed anything, since he himself gives to all mortals life and breath and all things. From one ancestor he made all nations to inhabit the whole earth, and he allotted the times of their existence and the boundaries of the places where they would live, so that they would search for God and perhaps grope for him and find him—though indeed he is not far from each one of us. . . . While God has overlooked the times of human ignorance, now he commands all people everywhere to repent, because he has fixed a day on which he will have the world judged in righteousness by a man whom he has appointed, and of this he has given assurance to all by raising him from the dead. (Acts 17:22–31)

Paul summons these bewildered Gentiles to seek for God and then bears witness to "a man whom he has appointed" (v. 31). As Matthew can imagine that the magi submitted to the Christ, so the prophets can anticipate the nations submitting to the Torah in Jerusalem (see Isaiah 2:2–4; Micah 4:1–4). In both traditions, the claim by the prophets and the evangelists is that wealth and learning *submit* and are thereby *transposed*.

Our verse in Isaiah 60 concerning camels, gold, and frankincense invites a demanding interface between the *claim of faith* and the *reality of wealth and learning in the world*. The Isaiah imagery traces the way in which the wealth and learning of the world are submitted to the claim of Israel. In Christian confession, embodied in Jesus, the same submission of wealth and power is narrated. One may indeed enjoy the romanticism of "We Three Kings of Orient Are." But we should not miss the deep claim of the poetry that puts a quite odd claim on the wealth and learning of the world. The promise made to Israel indicates that such worldly wealth and learning are *perforce* penultimate, and that they will quickly—"in time"—be submitted to the truth of Israel's God. It is this submission that evokes the recital of "instead" in verse 17. The wealth and learning of the world are measured by a deeper, more elemental truth. Even the camels know this, and so in Isaiah they bring their cargo to Jerusalem. And then in Christian imaginative rendering they carry the treasures of the wise to Bethlehem. The magi kneel; they worship. They go home another way, still with their learning (if not also some wealth) that is no doubt *transformed*. All of this, perhaps, is in purview already when Isaiah writes,

> Nations shall come to your light
> and kings to the brightness of your dawn.
>   60:3

Questions for Discussion

1. What have you had to wait for in God's good time?

2. Does the promise of reversal, even riches, after waiting appeal to you? Does it help you to wait?

3. Do you see further connections between Isaiah 60 and Matthew 2 or Acts 17?

4. What kinds of wealth and learning do you think need to be submitted to and transformed by Christ?

Chapter 29

Parent and Potter
(Isaiah 64:8–9)

> *Yet, O LORD, you are our Father;*
> *we are the clay, and you are our potter;*
> *we are all the work of your hand.*
> *Do not be exceedingly angry, O LORD,*
> *and do not remember iniquity forever.*
> *Now consider, we are all your people.*

Scripture Passages for Reference

Isaiah 64:1–12
Jeremiah 18:1–11
Jeremiah 19:1–13
Psalm 103
Psalm 106
Lamentations 5:22
Ezra 9
Nehemiah 9

Once again it seems that the prophetic promises did not pan out as expected in the time of Third Isaiah. After the glorious expectations of chapters 60–62, Israel was still left in disappointment, bereft of power, short on resources, reliant on the tricky support of Persia. Thus chapters 63–64 exhibit a stark contrast to chapters 60–62.

Chapters 60–62 are laden with glorious expectation; chapters 63–64 give voice to life in Jerusalem where lived reality fell far short of the promises.

Much of the material in chapters 63–64 consists in lament and complaint not unlike that of the Psalter. In its deep disappointment, Israel did not give up on YHWH. Rather, it intensified its hope and expectation, for it had nowhere else to turn. This extended lament material resonates with themes found in Psalm 106 and in the extended prayers of Ezra and Nehemiah, all likely dated to approximately the same period. The recurring themes include the following.

1. The acknowledgment of *YHWH's good generosity* that has marked the life of Israel in every season. Thus Israel can remember "deeds of fidelity" that YHWH has worked on their behalf (63:7–9). It was indeed YHWH who "saved them," who "lifted them up," and "carried" them. Every element of Israel's past well-being is a gift to YHWH's faithfulness. And that faithfulness has been grounded in YHWH's confidence that Israel would not "deal falsely" but would respond to YHWH in mutual fidelity.

2. But this mutual trust and loyalty was disrupted by *Israel's rebellion* (63:10). That rebellion is the oft-reiterated refusal of God's goodness:

> But you were angry, and we sinned;
>   because you hid yourself we transgressed.
> We have all become like one who is unclean,
>   and all our righteous deeds are like a filthy cloth.
> We all fade like a leaf,
>   and our iniquities, like the wind, take us away.
> There is no one who calls on your name,
>   or attempts to take hold of you;
> for you have hidden your face from us,
>   and have delivered us into the hand of our iniquity.
>   64:5–7

A closer look reveals that Israel's confession is subtle. One might assume that the sin of Israel evokes the anger of YHWH. But in the NRSV's rendering, Israel's sin *follows* YHWH's anger; the faithlessness of Israel follows the "because" of divine hiding. Israel sinned, in other words, because YHWH hid from them (v. 5; perhaps reiterated in v. 7). Of course, in this unit we do not hear anything more about divine hiding and whether Israel's confession is not thus somehow a cop-out.

In any case, the foundation of Israel's covenant tradition is that *God's goodness* and *Israel's recalcitrance* go together. This is the capstone of how Deuteronomy understands covenant. It is, moreover, reflected in Psalm 106, wherein the goodness of God (vv. 1–5, 8–12, 44–46) collides with the waywardness of Israel (vv. 6–7, 12–43). Unsurprisingly, Psalm 106 ends with a petition for rescue (v. 47). The same general pattern recurs in the prayers of Ezra 9 and Nehemiah 9. Thus Israel in Isaiah 63–64 participates in the common covenant theology of Israelite tradition, exhibiting the tension between God's generosity and Israel's refusal of that goodness.

The problem with this twofold recital is that it is all past tense. It is all in memory. When the poet calls us back to the moment of contemporary crisis, there is an absence of God's goodness. In the present, the poet, on behalf of Israel, can ask,

> Where is the one who brought them up out of the sea
>   with the shepherds of his flock?
> Where is the one who put within them
>   his holy spirit,
> who caused his glorious arm
>   to march at the right hand of Moses,
> who divided the waters before them
>   to make for himself an everlasting name,
> who led them through the depths?
>   63:11–13

The twice repeated question of "Where?" is left unanswered. And Israel, in its moment of crisis, is left undelivered and with questions unresolved.

3. With that background of divine goodness and Israel's rebellion, it is inescapable that the text will next move to *petition*. Israel dares to bid, yet again, for the goodness of God in their present circumstance of need:

> Turn back for the sake of your servants,
>   for the sake of the tribes that are your heritage.
>   63:17

The imperative "turn back" is framed, characteristically, by motivations that give God reason to act. In verse 17, Israel accuses God of causing their hardness of heart. The trouble is caused by God! Verses 18–19 describe Israel's sorry state, a condition that contradicts their special status as "your holy people" who now are treated like a people over whom YHWH does not rule. They are abandoned in spite of their special status. This bid for divine action is based on the fact that Israel suffers as if YHWH did not govern. The intent is to move YHWH to new saving action.

The petition for divine help continues with the powerful imperative of 64:1: "tear open, come down."

> O that you would tear open the heavens and come down,
>   so that the mountains would quake at your presence—
> as when fire kindles brushwood
>   and the fire causes water to boil.

It is as though God were remote from Israel, as though God were cut off by a barrier from the earth. The prayer is that YHWH, from the throne of heaven, would manifest majesty in the earth. Israel hopes for nothing less than a new theophanic eruption of divine presence in the earth for the sake of Israel that is, on its own, bereft of hope or possibility.

The confession of sin and helplessness in 64:5–7 prepares the way for our verses that are a follow-up of the previous petition. Verses 8–9 nicely summarize and give poignant voice to the great emergency of Israel after the promises of Second Isaiah have failed to come to pass as expected, after restored Israel in Jerusalem finds its life shabby and without adequate resources to maintain or protect itself.

In these two verses the poet expresses, in turn, *motivation* and *petition*. The motivation of verse 8 intends to move God to act for Israel. The NRSV nicely translates the introductory preposition as "yet"—that is, "all the foregoing notwithstanding." In spite of all that has been said thus far, God, about your hiding and our failure, in spite of all of that, pay attention to this petition! Two motivations are offered. The first is a terse but compelling statement of theological reality: "You are our father." You, God, cannot avoid that role! It is a given of our existence. It has been so since the exodus when you yourself declared, "Israel is my firstborn son" (Exodus 4:22). Every firstborn son in that patriarchal society is entitled to protection, property, and well-being. This relation of father-son is explicated in the familiar words of the psalmist:

> As a father has compassion for his children,
> so the LORD has compassion for those who fear him.
> Psalm 103:13

It is the burden of the father to have compassion for the son. It belongs intrinsically to the relationship and is not an option. The imagery shifts in the less well-known protest of Moses in Numbers 11, wherein Moses reminds God that it is God who has borne and begotten Israel:

> Did I conceive all this people? Did I give birth to them, that you should say to me, "Carry them in your bosom, as a nurse carries a sucking child," to the land that you promised on oath to their ancestors? (Numbers 11:12)

In Moses's rhetoric, YHWH seems painted as the mother of Israel, the one who conceived Israel. Either way, as father or as mother, God has responsibility for the desperate, vulnerable, needy child, Israel. How could this compassionate parent be so indifferent or hard-hearted as not to care (see Hosea 11:1–9; cf. Isaiah 49:16; Psalm 27:10)? This terse motivation in our verse poses a direct challenge to the indifference of YHWH, a call to take responsibility for the plight of Israel.

In the same verse, a second image is mobilized as motivation, namely, that of *potter and clay*: Israel is the clay, YHWH is the potter. It is the potter who shapes and governs the clay. The clay depends completely on the artistic capacity and attentiveness of the potter to evoke something that is beautiful and/or useful. Behind this poetic usage in Isaiah is the dual use of the imagery by Jeremiah. In Jeremiah 19:1–13 the prophet compares failed Israel to a broken pot that is beyond repair. Israel cannot be restored! But in Jeremiah 18:1–11, the imagery of potter and clay is more supple and perhaps suggests that the potter has freedom to decide either to break or restore the pot. The prophet's imagery more likely means to convey the idea that God has the freedom to restore broken Israel. Beyond this imagery by Jeremiah, our poet recalls the old tradition, which affirms that human creatures are "from dust" (Genesis 2:7). Psalm 103:14 references this tradition:

> For he knows how we were made;
> he remembers that we are dust.

Here, God remembers all the way back to the book of Genesis. God remembers that God's creatures are dust. So Israel has no life of its own. Israel is not and cannot be a self-starter. Everything depends on the potter; everything depends on the father. Everything depends on the willingness and readiness of God to act restoratively; otherwise, Israel is lost.

On these bases, our verses turn to petition. It seems important that the petition does not even ask explicitly for something positive. It voices two imperatives:

- Don't be angry.
- Don't remember our iniquity.

Perhaps the anger of YHWH is appropriately directed at Israel, but Israel nonetheless appeals to YHWH's "better self." Or perhaps YHWH's anger is disproportionate, beyond what Israel justifiably deserved. Either way, Israel has no future as long as it is the recipient of divine anger. But surely no father remains angry forever! Surely a potter does not destroy the clay! In the end, such anger is out of character for YHWH—as father, as potter. As father and potter, YHWH should not be defined and consumed by anger. The final line of our verses is introduced by the particle "behold": Look here! Look at us! We are your people; all of us are our people! We rely on you! We depend on you!

> Our hope is in no other save in thee;
> Our faith is built upon thy promise free;
> Lord, give us peace, and make us calm and sure,
> that in thy strength we evermore endure.[1]

The prayer of Israel in an unbearable circumstance appeals to the most elemental reality of its life and the life of YHWH. There is nothing more basic to God than that God has formed this people to be a "holy people" in the midst of the nations. There is nothing more basic to the life of Israel than the awareness that its life proceeds—day by day—as the gift given by the God of creation and exodus. It is difficult to imagine a prayer that could more effectively impact the life and inclination of God.

As though to underscore Israel's desperate need, verses 10–11 continue spurring God into action, here in response to the devastation wrought on Israel:

> *Your holy cities* have become a wilderness,
>   Zion has become a wilderness,
>   Jerusalem a desolation.
> *Our holy and beautiful house*,
>   where our ancestors praised you,
> has been burned by fire,
>   and all our pleasant places have become ruins.
>   64:10–11

This description pertains to "your holy cities" and to "our holy and beautiful house," the temple. The description aims to evoke retaliation from God upon those who have violated that holiness. This description of the ruins is not unlike the great lament of Psalm 74:6–11, which describes "your holy place" as having been grossly violated. Indeed, if YHWH did not care about YHWH's own "holy people," YHWH still might and should care about YHWH's "holy place." Thus, in our verses 10–11, Israel ups the ante for YHWH. YHWH should act in YHWH's own best interest!

By the time we reach the end of chapter 64, Israel has prayed its most moving, most desperate, and neediest prayer. But like much prayer, this prayer earns no immediate, ringing answer. Israel gets back only silence. For that reason, the chapter ends with two questions of anxious wonderment:

> After all this, will you restrain yourself, O LORD?
> Will you keep silent, and punish us so severely?
>   v. 12

Israel hopes for divine restraint from anger. Israel hopes that YHWH will break the silence and answer. But Israel can only wait. So the question lingers into Israel's future. Perhaps these questions echoed in the councils of the angels around the heavenly throne. But the Holy One would not be rushed or compelled. Prayer is not automatic; God is not an automaton. These unanswered questions are not unlike the final verses of the book of Lamentations that also pose unanswered questions:

> . . . unless you have utterly rejected us,
> and are angry with us beyond measure.
> Lamentations 5:22

This is an ending that requires Israel to continue to do the work of completing the transaction. As Tod Linafelt suggests, Israel is always at work formulating an answer to these questions.[2] The God to whom these questions are posed is elusive. The historical processes through which this God works are maddeningly undecipherable. It is, nevertheless, an act of serious faith to continue to *pose the questions* and to continue to *anticipate an answer*. Indeed, Israel has no alternative but to continue this work and to continue to ponder possible divine answers. Israel has no alternative precisely because YHWH is the father without whom the son, Israel, has no future. YHWH is the potter without whom the clay remains formless and lifeless.

We might ponder for a long time the terse declaration "You are our father." This statement in 64:8 is a reiteration of 63:16. It is YHWH, not Abraham, who is the father of Israel. The defining importance of God as father is carried into the New Testament. The motif of God as "father" is prominent in Jesus's teaching. For example, in his instruction on how to pray, Jesus begins with "Our Father," identifying the one in whom we have ultimate grounding and identity (Matthew 6:9). In his Sermon on the Mount, Jesus witnesses to the attentive generosity of the Father God:

> Is there anyone among you who, if your child asks for bread, will give a stone? Or if the child asks for a fish, will give a snake? If you then, who are evil, know how to give good gifts to your children, how much more will your Father in heaven give good things to those who ask him! (Matthew 7:9–11)[3]

The father is the one who "gives good things," because the father is greatly committed to the well-being of the child. On the cross, among his final utterances, Jesus addresses God as father and bids forgiveness for his executioners (Luke 23:34). It is this same fatherly forgiveness that is requested in Isaiah 64:9 and is in turn cited in the liturgical formulation of the psalm:

> He does not deal with us according to our sins,
> nor repay us according to our iniquities.
> Psalm 103:10

Still, at the end of Isaiah 64, Israel must wait for such fatherly mercies. Perhaps an answer comes in Isaiah 65 where we hear these two divine utterances:

> Here I am, here I am.
> . . . .
> I will not keep silent, but I will repay.
> Isaiah 65:1, 6

These divine utterances, however, do not fully respond to the prayers of Isaiah 64. As a result, Israel's desperate petitions linger. They linger as Israel, in the time of later Isaiah, must repeatedly face disappointment and vulnerability. So it is with this holy people defined by this holy God who is known in faithfulness and in freedom, in presence and speaking, and in absence and silence. Israel at its best will wait. Sometimes, as in the old text about Aaron and the people in their impatience, the wait is too hard and too long, and poor "divine" substitutes are devised (Exodus 32:1–6). But Israel, at its most faithful, waits and hopes, obeys and petitions. It is the work of faith, in such seasons of desperation and vulnerability, always again to remember what this community is, where its life is grounded, and where its best hope lies.

Questions for Discussion

1. How do we pose the questions of divine presence (and absence) now, in our lives and in our world?
2. How do we anticipate answers to those questions?
3. How do you see God as a parent and potter in your life, or in the life of the church, or in the world?
4. How do you personally wait for God?

Chapter 30

God's Newness
(Isaiah 65:18–19)

*Be glad and rejoice forever
    in what I am creating;
for I am about to create Jerusalem as a joy,
    and its people as a delight.
I will rejoice in Jerusalem,
    and delight in my people;
no more shall the sound of weeping be heard in it,
    or the cry of distress.*

> **Scripture Passages for Reference**
>
> Isaiah 65:16–25
> Isaiah 11:1–9
> 1 Kings 21
> 2 Chronicles 36:23
> Jeremiah 31:33–34
> Psalm 131
> Revelation 21:3–4

At the very outset of the book of Isaiah, we are given a glimpse into the large dramatic movement of the book. Isaiah 1:25–26 states that the book will move from *punishment and purification* to a future of *righteousness and faithfulness*:

211

I will turn my hand against you;
>   I will smelt away your dross as with lye
>   and remove all your alloy.
> And I will restore your judges as at the first,
>   and your counselors as at the beginning.
> *Afterward* you shall be called the city of righteousness,
>   the faithful city.

Thus chapters 1–39 of Isaiah concern *divine judgment and punishment for Israel and for Jerusalem.* The imagery of smelting the dross suggests the reduction of the community to the righteous remnant, the ones left after the disposal of the unworthy (see Jeremiah 6:27–30). But then, says the poetry, there will be an *afterward*, which is voiced in Isaiah 40–66. That afterward is what comes after desolation, deportation, and displacement. The afterward for Israel began, historically, in the decree of Cyrus the Persian that permitted the homecoming of the exiles:

> Thus says King Cyrus of Persia: The LORD, the God of heaven, has given me all the kingdoms of the earth, and he has charged me to build him a house at Jerusalem, which is in Judah. Whoever is among you of all his people, may the LORD his God be with him! Let him go up. (2 Chronicles 36:23)

The "afterward" was embodied in the "time of small things" of Haggai and Zechariah and enacted in the harassed restoration under Ezra and Nehemiah. None of these efforts at newness, however, met or fulfilled prophetic expectation. Each was a historical effort that turned out to be modest and fell far short of the prophetic hope. As we noted earlier, Third Isaiah (chaps. 56–66) contains grand expectations in chapters 60–62 that are followed by the sad and bewildered lamentations of chapters 63–64. And now, in chapter 65, we arrive at *the ultimate afterward* of the book of Isaiah, which we may even take as the ultimate afterward of the entire Old Testament—a most grand voicing of divine newness that has propelled Jews (and belatedly Christians) into deep hope and fierce expectation.

By way of introduction to our lyrical poem in 65:17–25, we may mention the promise of blessing in verse 16:

> Then whoever invokes a blessing in the land
>   shall bless by the *God of faithfulness,*

and whoever takes an oath in the land
    shall swear by the *God of faithfulness;*
because the former troubles are forgotten
    and are hidden from my sight.

Twice reference is made to "the God of faithfulness" who will bless. This is the God who will not relent being the God of Israel. Further, the phrase "former [*ri'šōnôt*] troubles" sounds like an echo of "our judges at the first [*ri'šōnāh*]" (Isaiah 1:26). All that remains from former vexed times when Israel was alienated from YHWH will be forgotten amid the rush of God's generous newness.

And then, in 65:17, the poet has YHWH break out in wondrous, surging new possibility. The one who speaks is the creator God. This is the God who can actually evoke a radical newness, something not derived from what is old, alienated, or failed. This doxological formulation does not pause to quibble over *ex nihilo*, that is, whether the newness from God is "out of nothing" or by a reconfiguration of what had previously been. The rhetoric suggests an utterly new beginning in which "former troubles" are forgotten (v. 16), and "former things" are not remembered (v. 17). The poet plays upon the imagery from Isaiah 43:18–19:

> Do not remember the former things [*ri'šōnôt*],
>   or consider the things of old.
> I am about to do a new thing;
>   now it springs forth, do you not perceive it?

In that passage, we are led to expect a new exodus of emancipation. But now in our text, the poet goes "cosmic." Here there is no worry about or calculation concerning "science and religion" or how a new world might come into existence. Now we are in the realm of faithful imagination, wherein lyrical utterance invites relinquishment of all that is old in order to begin afresh. The poet intends that we should be shocked into awe and wonder. Imagine: a new heaven—a new gloriously outfitted habitat for the gods, angels, and messengers who surround the holy throne! Imagine: a new earth, an environment not vexed by war, hunger, pollution, violence, poverty, or predation! Taken together "a new heaven" and "a new earth" bespeak an utterly new realm over which the creator God presides in generous fidelity.

Recipients of this poetry are no longer permitted to grovel in old guilt, or to remain vexed about old failures, or to remember old hurts. All is new from top to bottom! The God who speaks (and so enacts) newness is the one who generated the first heaven and first earth, but who was then "sorry" that the world came to evil—the God whom humanity "grieved . . . to his heart" (Genesis 6:6). But not now! Now the creator streams out newness that is beyond explanation.

In Isaiah 65:17, the newness of God comes into sharper focus. To be sure, the cosmic backdrop lingers. But now it is Jerusalem as joy and delight. The newness consists in an actual human city, not the remoteness of "heaven" or the vagueness of "earth" but rather a city of bricks and mortar, of law and government, of commerce and labor—real people living real lives together. But this is not just any city; this is *Jerusalem*, the place of divine habitation, the holy city that recently had become a wilderness and a desolation (64:10). What follows in the poem is a lyrical rendering of what the Holy City will be like when God works God's transformative newness. There will be no more weeping (see Psalm 30:5), no more sadness or loss or pain, no more impact from violence, exploitation, or predation. The new city will have transformed institutions and transformed policies and practices. We can identify four features of deep newness in the coming restored Jerusalem.

First, the new Jerusalem will be a place of *universal health for all*. On the one hand, there will be no more infant mortality (65:20) and no more babies whose end is calamity (v. 23). On the other hand, life expectancy will be greatly extended, so that a hundred years will be considered a normal lifespan, and any death before that will be unusual and abnormal.

> No more . . . an old person who does not live out a lifetime;
> for one who dies at a hundred years will be considered a youth,
> and one who falls short of a hundred will be considered accursed.
>
> v. 20

We may, moreover, imagine that the poet intends not only an extended quantity of life, but an enhanced quality as well.

This level of "health care," as it were, is a contradiction to our lived experience. We have come to believe that a struggle for adequate health care is a normal enterprise that pits "haves" against "have-nots" in a contest for limited resources reinforced by the endless assault of drug and medicine ads on TV, not to mention insurance companies with their inscrutable premiums and deductibles. The poet invites us to imagine otherwise. We know, moreover, that the basis for poor health in our society has to do with eating bad food and treating our bodies badly. And poor health in zones of poverty is even more widespread and scandalous. The poet would have us notice that such current health "norms" are both abnormal and unnecessary in the new regime. There is, in fact, no place for such "norms" as those widely accepted in our world.

Second, the poet anticipates a *revamped economy* that means an end to greedy predation. It is a pattern among us that acquisitive greed causes the eviction of vulnerable people from their houses, the confiscation of property, and the dislocation of people.[1] All of this is quite normal in our current economic arrangement, which is accepted by us, even if with resignation, as status quo. The prophetic tradition refuses such predatory practice. We need only consider the narrative of Naboth's vineyard in 1 Kings 21 and the way in which the royal sovereign preempted his inheritance. Or consider the stricture of Isaiah, wherein *hôy* ("woe" or "ah," as in the NRSV) once again means "big trouble coming":

> Ah [*hôy*], you who join house to house,
>   who add field to field,
> until there is room for no one but you,
>   and you are left to live alone
>   in the midst of the land!
>   Isaiah 5:8

The prophet anticipates manorial estates now abandoned.

> The LORD of hosts has sworn in my hearing:
> Surely many houses shall be desolate,
>   large and beautiful houses, without inhabitant.
>   5:9

Beyond that the poet seems to know that greedy, exploitative farming will cause the land to refuse to produce abundantly:

> For ten acres of vineyard shall yield but one bath,
> and a homer of seed shall yield a mere ephah.
>
> 5:10

But now in Isaiah's vision of newness, all of that can end. There will be no more big ones devouring little ones. Even the most vulnerable peasant will be able to keep her own home, her own orchard, and her own vineyard (see 2 Kings 8:1–6).

Third, the new city will feature a new religion of intimate dialogical communion:

> Before they call I will answer,
> while they are yet speaking I will hear.
>
> 65:24

In the old Jerusalem, religious practice seemed often overloaded with endless provisions for purity regulations that often functioned to exclude, along with an extensive inventory of sacrificial requirements that were easier for those with means. In our time, religious practice is heavily infused with ideological claims that aim at coercion. Religion has become a zone of manipulation and ideological advocacy.

But now, in Isaiah's vision of newness, there will be none of that—nothing of requirements, nothing of codes of qualification, nothing coercive, and nothing of ideological manipulation. There will only be *intimate, trustworthy communion*. This promise is perhaps an echo of Jeremiah's expectation:

> I will put my law within them, and I will write it on their hearts; and I will be their God, and they shall be my people. No longer shall they teach one another, or say to each other, "Know the Lord," for they shall all know me, from the least of them to the greatest, says the Lord. (Jeremiah 31:33–34)

The attentiveness of the covenant God will be intense. There will be no need for instruction because *all will know*. Indeed, the attentiveness of God in Isaiah 65:24 might evoke a maternal image of God, since it is characteristically "Mom" who knows and hears a child in the night before the child speaks or cries, who knows attentively and intuitively what is needed, and who responds in kind. It is no wonder, then, that Isaiah can finish with this maternal declaration:

> As a mother comforts her child,
>   so I will comfort you;
>   you shall be comforted in Jerusalem.
>
> 66:13

The psalmist puts it differently but with equal intimacy:

> But I have calmed and quieted my soul,
>   like a weaned child with its mother;
>   my soul is like the weaned child that is with me.
> O Israel, hope in the LORD from this time on and forevermore.
>
> Psalm 131:2–3

Fourth, the poet anticipates a *renovation of nature*, a reconciliation between competing elements of our environment:

> The wolf and the lamb shall feed together,
>   the lion shall eat straw like the ox;
>   but the serpent—its food shall be dust!
>
> Isaiah 65:25

It is normal to assume that predator and prey will be forever in agonistic relationship. The poet, against such an assumption, trusts that such estranged hostility is not necessary and is not a requirement for God's created order. Perhaps the poetry's movement entertains the prospect that when *health care, economic order*, and *religious practice* are healed and transformed, it follows that the nonhuman creation can (and will?) also be reconciled. This poem in Isaiah 65 echoes an earlier poem in the book:

> The wolf shall live with the lamb,
>   the leopard shall lie down with the kid,
> the calf and the lion and the fatling together,
>   and a little child shall lead them.
> The cow and the bear shall graze,
>   their young shall lie down together;
>   and the lion shall eat straw like the ox.

> The nursing child shall play over the hole of the asp,
>   and the weaned child shall put its hand on the adder's den.
>
>   11:6–8

The new Jerusalem will have *good health care, changed economic policy, revised religious practice*, and a *restoration of the natural world*. The sum of these renewed factors is the reimagining of the Holy City in exactly these terms: health, economy, religion, environment. All better, all intimate, all restored.

The final line of our poem in chapter 65 echoes an earlier Isaiah text. "They shall not hurt or destroy on all my holy mountain, says the LORD" (65:25c) appears also in Isaiah 11, though the earlier instance is more extended:

> They will not hurt or destroy
>   on all my holy mountain;
> for the earth will be full of the knowledge of the LORD
>   as the waters cover the sea.
>
>   11:9

The basis for the rehabilitation of the earth is that "knowledge of YHWH" will pervade the earth. This "knowledge of YHWH" is not abstract or propositional. It is rather covenantal engagement that knows, at long last, that the only way to prosper in God's new world is by a relationality that practices social solidarity, that generously shares resources, that attends gracefully to the vulnerable, that respects the requirements of the earth, and that knows itself to be a participant in a world governed by God. Such "knowledge," which blatantly contradicts our contemporary technological grasp of the world, is on offer in Isaiah's poetry. But it requires a radical revamping of how we think, perceive, and act in the world. This new knowledge begins with the glad recognition that we are not self-made but are creatures of the good creator. As Kent Dunnington has put it,

> The path to humility requires confronting our illusions of independence and self-sufficiency and coming to peace with our ultimate neediness. . . . Humility is the disposition to gladly accept our neediness and assume a posture of dependence.[2]

God's Newness (Isaiah 65:18–19)

All of this is anticipated about Jerusalem in Isaiah 65. From what we know generally of the old city of Jerusalem, that anticipation is a heavy lift. But the poet has done some of the hard work for us and before us. It is, to be sure, very hard work to imagine Jerusalem in its newness when all we can remember is the deep hostility that surges in the old city, where religious traditions clash, where exclusions are practiced, and where there is abiding and ready violence. And it is no different in any of the earth's cities. Our cities—our towns too!—abound in predatory greed, in poor health care, in posturing religion laden with political agendas, and with environmental conditions that are aggressively anticreation.

In the New Testament, we are told that Jesus "set his face to go to Jerusalem" (Luke 9:51). He had to go there to face the authorities. He had to go there to initiate his new governance. He knew the Isaiah tradition. He knew how the city had been devastated, how lady Jerusalem had become a tramp:

> This faithful town has become a prostitute!
> She was full of justice;
>   righteousness lived in her—
> but now murderers.
> Your silver has become impure,
>   your beer is diluted with water.
> Your princes are rebels,
>   companions of thieves.
> Everyone loves a bribe and pursues gifts.
>   They don't defend the orphan,
>   and the widow's cause never reaches them.
>   Isaiah 1:21–23, CEB

But just there, in the old city over which Jesus had wept, he laid his life down for new governance. And out of that act of self-giving the Christian tradition articulates a new Jerusalem:

> And I heard a loud voice from the throne saying,
>   "See, the home of God is among mortals.
> He will dwell with them;
> they will be his peoples,
> and God himself will be with them;

> he will wipe every tear from their eyes;
> Death will be no more;
> mourning and crying and pain will be no more,
> for the first things have passed away."
> Revelation 21:3–4

The coming promised city will be a fitting habitat for the holiness of God. It will be a place where Death and its nihilism do not govern or intimidate. It will be a place of ordered well-being.

The function and purpose of this astonishing poetry in Isaiah are to shake and shatter our conventional imaginations, to take us out of our feeble accommodationist assumptions. The poetry invites us to entertain as God's possibility an urban—nay, *full world*—renovation, which we commonly take to be impossible. The new city (world) is, to be sure, *a gift from God* that is still yet to come. But that new city—and the way to that new city—also reflects and requires *human work*. The human work is to mobilize resources and formulate policies that help live toward the vision. What we know, moreover, is that the circumstances in the city are not beyond transformation. What is missing in our current arrangement is *political will*. The poetry aims at changing imagination *and* evoking political will. We will not do what we cannot imagine. And we cannot imagine what is not given us in poetic rendering. But once imagined, it is doable! The thinkable is achievable—with God's help! Thus the covenantal-prophetic tradition of the Bible, commonly shared by Jews and Christians, knows this much:

- *Good health care* is possible with proper planning and funding.
- *Good neighborly economic practices* are achievable that contradict practices of predatory acquisitiveness.
- *Good religion* is on offer when we dwell in the power of the Holy God. None of our doctrinal, liturgical, or pietistic habits will save us, but only our readiness for resolved penultimacy before the Holy One.
- *Good environmental practice* awaits implementation; all it requires is an abandonment of our hubristic assumption that the world is our resource to be exploited.

It is all there in Isaiah's poem. That *divine* poetry serves to alter our all-too-stuck imaginations and to motivate our all-too-recalcitrant political will. The rest, what follows, is good human work . . . rejoicing in what the Lord has done.

Questions for Discussion

1. How could better health care now be a harbinger of God's newness to come?
2. What does it mean to be ready for "resolved penultimacy before the Holy One"?
3. How can human endeavors now connect with and help toward God's vision of newness for the future?
4. Is Isaiah's poetry, full of visions of the divine, strong enough to make a difference in the "real world"?

Notes

SERIES FOREWORD

1. See, among other publications, Walter Brueggemann, *A Commentary on Jeremiah: Exile and Homecoming* (Grand Rapids, MI: Eerdmans, 1998); *Like Fire in the Bones: Listening for the Prophetic Word in Jeremiah*, ed. Patrick D. Miller (Minneapolis: Fortress, 2006); *The Theology of the Book of Jeremiah*, Old Testament Theology (New York: Cambridge University Press, 2007); *Preaching Jeremiah: Announcing God's Restorative Passion* (Minneapolis: Fortress, 2020); and *Returning from the Abyss: Pivotal Moments in the Book of Jeremiah*, Pivotal Moments in the Old Testament, ed. Brent A. Strawn (Louisville, KY: Westminster John Knox, 2022).

2. On what follows, see Brueggemann, *Returning from the Abyss*, 91–96.

3. See Ellen F. Davis, "Exploding the Limits: Form and Function in Psalm 22," *Journal for the Study of the Old Testament* 17 (1992): 93–105.

4. Marilyn Chandler McEntyre, *What's in a Phrase? Pausing Where Scripture Gives You Pause* (Grand Rapids, MI: Eerdmans, 2014).

5. McEntyre, ix.

6. McEntyre, x.

7. McEntyre, x.

8. The word occurs no less than forty-one times in Mark: 1:10, 12, 18, 20, 21, 23, 28, 29, 30, 42, 43; 2:8, 12; 3:6; 4:5, 15, 16, 17, 29; 5:2, 29, 30, 42 (two times); 6:25, 27, 45, 50, 54; 7:25; 8:10; 9:15, 20, 24; 10:52; 11:2, 3; 14:43, 45, 72; 15:1.

9. See Walter Brueggemann, *Delivered out of Empire: Pivotal Moments in the Book of Exodus,* part 1, Pivotal Moments in the Old Testament, ed. Brent A. Strawn (Louisville, KY: Westminster John Knox, 2021); *Delivered into Covenant: Pivotal Moments in the Book of Exodus,* part 2, Pivotal Moments in the Old Testament, ed. Brent A. Strawn (Louisville, KY: Westminster John Knox, 2021); and *Returning from the Abyss.*

PREFACE

1. More information on these matters can be found in William L. Holladay, *Isaiah: Scroll of a Prophetic Heritage* (Cleveland: Pilgrim, 1978); Jacob Stromberg,

An Introduction to the Study of Isaiah (London: T & T Clark, 2011); Andrew Abernethy, *Discovering Isaiah: Content, Interpretation, Reception* (Grand Rapids, MI: Eerdmans, 2021), esp. pp. 25–37; C. L. Crouch and Christopher B. Hays, *Isaiah: A Paradigmatic Prophet and His Interpreters: An Introduction and Study Guide* (London: T & T Clark, 2022); and, in a slightly different vein, John Goldingay, *The Theology of the Book of Isaiah* (Downers Grove, IL: IVP Academic, 2014).

2. See, e.g., H. G. M. Williamson, *The Book Called Isaiah: Deutero-Isaiah's Role in Composition and Redaction* (Oxford: Oxford University Press, 2005).

3. Richard B. Hays, *Echoes of Scripture in the Gospels* (Waco, TX: Baylor University Press, 2018).

4. John F. A. Sawyer, *The Fifth Gospel: Isaiah in the History of Christianity* (Cambridge: Cambridge University Press, 1996), 1. See further there, as well as Robert Louis Wilken et al., eds., *Isaiah: Interpreted by Early Christian and Medieval Commentators* (Grand Rapids, MI: Eerdmans, 2007); Steven A. McKinion, ed., *Isaiah 1–39*, Ancient Christian Commentary on Scripture (Downers Grove, IL: InterVarsity, 2004); Mark W. Elliott, ed., *Isaiah 40–66*, Ancient Christian Commentary on Scripture (Downers Grove, IL: InterVarsity, 2007); and Brevard S. Childs, *The Struggle to Understand Isaiah as Christian Scripture* (Grand Rapids, MI: Eerdmans, 2004).

5. In addition to the volumes that are cited in notes 1, 2, and 4 above, major commentaries include the following (in alphabetical order), though others could easily be added: Klaus Baltzer, *Deutero-Isaiah: A Commentary on Isaiah 40–55* (Minneapolis: Fortress, 2001); Andrew H. Bartlelt, *Isaiah 1–12* (St. Louis: Concordia, 2024); Joseph Blenkinsopp, *Isaiah 1–66*, 3 vols. (New York: Doubleday; New Haven, CT: Yale University Press, 2000–2003); Walter Brueggemann, *Isaiah 1–39* (Louisville, KY: Westminster John Knox, 1998); Brueggemann, *Isaiah 40–66* (Louisville, KY: Westminster John Knox, 1998); Brevard S. Childs, *Isaiah: A Commentary* (Louisville, KY: Westminster John Knox, 2001); Paul D. Hanson, *Isaiah 40–66* (Louisville, KY: John Knox, 1995); J. Gordon McConville, *Isaiah* (Grand Rapids, MI: Baker Academic, 2023); Shalom M. Paul, *Isaiah 40–66: Translation and Commentary* (Grand Rapids, MI: Eerdmans, 2012); J. J. M. Roberts, *First Isaiah: A Commentary* (Minneapolis: Fortress, 2015); Christopher R. Seitz, *Isaiah 1–39* (Louisville, KY: John Knox, 1993); Seitz, "The Book of Isaiah 40–66: Introduction, Commentary, and Reflections," in *The New Interpreter's Bible*, vol. 6 (Nashville: Abingdon, 2001), 309–552; Gene M. Tucker, "The Book of Isaiah 1–39: Introduction, Commentary, and Reflections," in *The New Interpreter's Bible*, vol. 6 (Nashville: Abingdon, 2001), 27–305; Claus Westermann, *Isaiah 40–66: A Commentary* (Philadelphia: Westminster, 1969); Hans Wildberger, *Isaiah 1–39*, 3 vols. (Minneapolis: Fortress, 1991–2002).

6. As with any aspect within biblical studies, there are many books one could consult on reading the prophetic literature. We recommend the following, all of which are relatively short and accessible: Carolyn J. Sharp, *The Prophetic Literature* (Nashville: Abingdon, 2019); Sharp, *Old Testament Prophets for Today* (Louisville, KY: Westminster John Knox, 2009); James D. Nogalski, *Introduction to the Hebrew Prophets* (Nashville: Abingdon, 2017); Jack R. Lundbom, *The Hebrew*

Prophets: An Introduction (Minneapolis: Fortress, 2010); and David L. Petersen, *The Prophetic Literature: An Introduction* (Louisville, KY: Westminster John Knox, 2002).

7. See Walter Brueggemann, "That the World May Be Redescribed," *Interpretation* 56, no. 4 (2002): 362–363: "Indeed, I ask my students as they focus on a particular text to imagine that this is the only text we have. If *this* were the only text, what would we have disclosed of God, of world, of church, of self? The text needs to be entertained in its own starkness before rushing to more general claims that inevitably tone down its particularity. Only after such an exercise do I ask students to reposition the text in the larger scopes of canon and ongoing confessional traditions. The intention of such a strategy is to encourage the most radical non-foundational possibility, to engage the text without reference to protective universals." The same sentiment is found in Brueggemann, *A Pathway of Interpretation: The Old Testament for Pastors and Students* (Eugene, OR: Cascade, 2008), 39.

CHAPTER 4: FOUR CONTRADICTIONS VERSUS THE ONE LORD

1. For a contemporary rendering of such "false religion," see David Zahl, *Seculosity: How Career, Parenting, Technology, Food, Politics, and Romance Became Our New Religion and What to Do about It* (Minneapolis: Fortress, 2019), which catalogs the "secular" values that take on religious thickness through our devotion to them.

CHAPTER 6: ISAIAH'S SECOND VISION

1. "Ye Watchers and Ye Holy Ones," hymn by Athelston Riley (1909).
2. Rudolf Otto, *The Idea of the Holy*, 2nd ed., trans. John W. Harvey (London: Oxford University Press, 1958). See also Karl Barth, *The Epistle to the Romans*, trans. Edwyn C. Hoskyns (London: Oxford University Press, 1968), 10.
3. The temptation of Christians to take the three-times "holy" as an allusion to the full-blown doctrine of the Trinity would have made very little sense to eighth-century Isaiah.

CHAPTER 7: THE HOLY SEED-STUMP

1. The classic study is Norman Habel, "The Form and Significance of the Call Narratives," *Zeitschrift für die alttestamentliche Wissenschaft* 77 (1965): 297–323.
2. Walter Brueggemann, *Isaiah 1–39* (Louisville, KY: Westminster John Knox, 1998), 62.

CHAPTER 8: STANDING FIRM

1. Gerhard von Rad, *Old Testament Theology*, vol. 2, trans. D. M. G. Stalker (New York: Harper, 1965), 160, 162.
2. H. Richard Niebuhr, "The Grace of Doing Nothing," *Christian Century*, March 23, 1932.

3. Niebuhr was answered in the same issue of *Christian Century* by his brother, Reinhold Niebuhr: "Must We Do Nothing?" *Christian Century*, March 23, 1932.

CHAPTER 9: "GOD-WITH-US" AND THE "VIRGIN"

1. In fact, the Hebrew word *bĕṭûlāh*, not *'almāh*, appears to be one used for virginity in the technical sense.
2. Another main option is that the *'almāh* could be Ahaz's wife.

CHAPTER 10: A CHILD HAS BEEN BORN FOR US!

1. For more on these names, see Walter Brueggemann, *Names for the Messiah: An Advent Study* (Louisville, KY: Westminster John Knox, 2016).

CHAPTER 11: THE ROD OF GOD'S ANGER

1. Paul Kennedy, *The Rise and Fall of the Great Powers: Economic Change and Military Conflict from 1500 to 2000* (New York: Vintage, 1989).

CHAPTER 13: THE LORD'S PLAN

1. John Barton, *Understanding Old Testament Ethics: Approaches and Explorations* (Louisville, KY: Westminster John Knox, 2003), 138.

CHAPTER 15: APOCALYPTIC POLLUTION

1. A helpful work is Terence E. Fretheim, *Creation Untamed: The Bible, God, and Natural Disasters* (Grand Rapids, MI: Baker Academic, 2010).
2. See David Novak, *The Image of the Non-Jew in Judaism: The Idea of Noahide Law*, 2nd ed., ed. Matthew Lagrone (Liverpool: Littman Library of Jewish Civilization, 2011).

CHAPTER 16: YOUR DEAD SHALL LIVE

1. Jon D. Levenson, *The Death and Resurrection of the Beloved Son: The Transformation of Child Sacrifice in Judaism and Christianity* (New Haven, CT: Yale University Press, 1993); Levenson, *Resurrection and the Restoration of Israel: The Ultimate Victory of the God of Life* (New Haven, CT: Yale University Press, 2008); and Kevin J. Madigan and Jon D. Levenson, *Resurrection: The Power of God for Christians and Jews* (New Haven, CT: Yale University Press, 2009).
2. Levenson, *Resurrection and the Restoration of Israel*, 94.

CHAPTER 17: THE STRANGE WORK OF GOD

1. "Christ Is Made the Sure Foundation," hymn by John Mason Neale (1851).

2. D. W. Winnicott, *The Maturational Processes and the Facilitating Environment* (London: Routledge, 2018), 146.

CHAPTER 18: SALVATION BY RETURNING AND REST ALONE

1. Norman K. Gottwald, *All the Kingdoms of the Earth: Israelite Prophecy and International Relations in the Ancient Near East* (New York: Harper & Row, 1964), 206.

CHAPTER 19: EXODUS 2.0

1. See also 49:11. The theme continues into later Isaiah as well (see 57:14; 62:10–12) and is found as early as 11:16.

CHAPTER 20: THE LORD SAID TO ME: DESTROY

1. The Hebrew text switches here and there between second-person singular ("you") and second-person plural ("all of you") forms, indicating that the Rabshakeh's speech is addressed to the king but also to the people. This distinction is lost in English translation, and so we have not bothered representing it, but it is important to note its presence nevertheless.

CHAPTER 21: HOPE (IN/FOR) THE LORD!

1. "Wait for the Lord," song from the Taizé community, copyright © Ateliers et Presses de Taizé, 71250 Taizé, France, based on Psalm 27:14. Used by permission.

CHAPTER 23: CYRUS, GOD'S MESSIAH

1. The shepherd metaphor was commonly used for kings across the ancient Near East who were expected to show care for their people (flock). See, e.g., Ezekiel 34.
2. Bruce Lincoln, *Religion, Empire, and Torture: The Case of Achaemenian Persia with a Postscript on Abu Ghraib* (Chicago: University of Chicago Press, 2010), 95.
3. Lincoln, 96.

CHAPTER 25: A MAN OF SORROWS, ACQUAINTED WITH GRIEF

1. A collection of Jewish readings is found in Ad Neubauer and S. R. Driver, eds., *The Fifty-Third Chapter of Isaiah according to the Jewish Interpreters*, 2 vols. (New York: Ktav, 1969).
2. Tryggve N. D. Mettinger, *A Farewell to the Servant Songs: A Critical Examination of an Exegetical Axiom* (Lund: CWK Gleerup, 1983), 45.
3. David J. A. Clines, *I, He, We, and They: A Literary Approach to Isaiah 53* (Sheffield: JSOT Sheffield, 1976), 33.

4. See J. Gordon McConville, *Isaiah* (Grand Rapids, MI: Baker Academic, 2023), 585.
5. McConville, 584.
6. Shalom Paul, *Isaiah 40–66: Translation and Commentary* (Grand Rapids, MI: Eerdmans, 2012), 398; see also p. 18.
7. Clines, *I, He, We, and They*, 61.
8. See Donald H. Juel, "The Image of the Servant-Christ in the New Testament," *Southwestern Journal of Theology* 21 (1979): 7–22, esp. 19, whose conclusions are confirmed in Richard B. Hays, *Echoes of Scripture in the Gospels* (Waco, TX: Baylor University Press, 2018), 85–86, 160, 334–35.
9. Clines, *I, He, We, and They*, 64 (his emphasis).

CHAPTER 26: WRATH, FOR A SECOND—LOVE EVERLASTING

1. Jürgen Moltmann, *The Crucified God: The Cross of Christ as the Foundation and Criticism of Christian Theology* (Minneapolis, MN: Fortress, 1993), 243.
2. Unless the reference to God's "overflowing wrath" implies or involves also the cause of that wrath (thanks to Caleb Punt for this observation). Even if it does, Second Isaiah is candid about God's role in punishing Israel—there is no escaping the reality of that, and it is a crucial part of the prophetic strategy according to Katie M. Heffelinger, *I Am Large, I Contain Multitudes: Lyric Cohesion and Conflict in Second Isaiah* (Leiden: Brill, 2011).
3. "Our God, Our Help in Ages Past," hymn by Isaac Watts (1708).
4. See Heffelinger, *I Am Large, I Contain Multitudes*.

CHAPTER 27: A HOUSE OF PRAYER FOR ALL PEOPLE

1. The verb "to join" implies close connection and can be used of marriage (Genesis 29:34) and tribal relationships (Numbers 18:2, 4), as well as of political allies (Psalm 83:9; Esther 9:27) and those who join in worship of YHWH (Jeremiah 50:5; Zechariah 2:15).

CHAPTER 28: WEALTH BROUGHT AND TRANSFORMED

1. A fascinating study is Charles B. Strozier, *Apocalypse: On the Psychology of Fundamentalism in America* (Boston: Beacon, 1994).

CHAPTER 29: PARENT AND POTTER

1. "I Greet Thee, Who My Sure Redeemer Art," hymn attributed to John Calvin (1545).
2. Tod Linafelt, *Surviving Lamentations: Catastrophe, Lament, and Protest in the Afterlife of a Biblical Book* (Chicago: University of Chicago Press, 2000), 60.
3. Except for the final verse, which explicitly uses "father" and "him," the individual who gives bread or fish to a child could as well be mother as father. In

much of contemporary life, it is the mother (often the "single mom") who does the generative work that in patriarchal societies was typically assigned to father.

CHAPTER 30: GOD'S NEWNESS

1. See Matthew Desmond, *Evicted: Poverty and Profit in the American City* (New York: Crown, 2016); and Desmond, *Poverty, by America* (New York: Crown, 2023).

2. Kent Dunnington, "Living Humility: How to Be Humble," in *The Joy of Humility: The Beginning and End of the Virtues*, ed. Drew Collins, Ryan McAnnally, and Evan C. Rosa (Waco, TX: Baylor University Press, 2020), 252.

www.ingramcontent.com/pod-product-compliance
Lightning Source LLC
Chambersburg PA
CBHW032013161025
34115CB00001B/1